Time and Stress

Today's Silent Killers

ROBERTA CAVA

Copyright © 2013 by Roberta Cava

All rights reserved. No part of this work covered by the copyrights hereon may be reproduced or used in any form or by any means - graphic, electronic or mechanical, including photocopying, recording, taping or information storage and retrieval systems - without the prior written permission of the publisher.

Time and Stress

Today's Silent Killers

Roberta Cava

Published by Cava Consulting

105 / 3 Township Drive,

Burleigh Heads, 4220, Queensland, Australia

info@dealingwithdifficultpeople.info

Discover other titles by Roberta Cava at
www.dealingwithdifficultpeople.info

National Library of Australia

Cataloguing-in-publication data:

ISBN: 97809923579-2-4

BOOKS BY ROBERTA CAVA

Dealing with Difficult People
(22 publishers – in 16 languages)

Dealing with Difficult Situations – at Work and at Home

Dealing with Difficult Spouses and Children

Dealing with Difficult Relatives and In-Laws

Dealing with Domestic Violence and Child Abuse

Dealing with School Bullying

Dealing with Workplace Bullying

What am I going to do with the rest of my life?

Before tying the knot – Questions couples Must ask each other Before they marry!

How Women can advance in business

Survival Skills for Supervisors and Managers

Easy Come – Hard to go – The Art of Hiring, Disciplining and Firing Employees

Human Resources at its best!

Time and Stress – Today's silent killers

Take Command of your Future – Make things Happen

Human Resources Policies and Procedures

Employee Handbook

Belly laughs for All! - Volumes 1-4

Wisdom of the World! - The happy, sad and wise things in life!

That Something Special

DEDICATION

Dedicated to my support group of loyal friends and family who were always there when I needed them.

ACKNOWLEDGEMENTS

My thanks to Holmes and Richard Rahe for allowing me to use their Holmes-Rahe scale that determines a person's stress level.

TIME AND STRESS, TODAY'S SILENT KILLERS

Table of Contents

Introduction	*11*
CHAPTER 1 - *Where does the time go?*	*13*

How long can we expect to live?
What is normal aging?
A strong will is one way to live longer
How to live a longer fuller life
How do we age?
You know you're older when ...
Does having money make a difference?
Retirement
How much time do we have?
Time breakdown
Fear of failure
Fear of success
Self-sabotage

CHAPTER 2 - *Time management techniques*	*33*

The busy man
Principles of time management
Are you over-planning your day?
Keeping a time log
How to choose priorities
Daytimers and 'To Do' lists
Different kinds of tasks
Swiss cheese approach
How to start complex long-term tasks
Procrastination
Reward vs. punishment
Lateness
How to deal with professionals who keep you waiting
I can't say No
How to say No

CHAPTER 3 - *Time management at work*   45

Time 'leakage'
Bottlenecks
Helping your staff set priorities
Bring forward file
Is your in-basket out of control?
Working overtime
Delegation
Where are you now?
Interruptions and crisis
How to prevent interruptions
How to control crisis situations
Solutions to time-wasters

CHAPTER 4 - *Time management at home*   63

Introducing business to home management
How to organise yourself for work
Finding the right child-care
Obtaining help at home
In the middle
How to give your family 'loving time'
Are you a night or morning person?
The hurry-up epidemic
How to 'hang loose'

CHAPTER 5 - *The Importance of Goal Setting*   77

Where do you want to go?
The importance of goals
Types of goals
Framing my goals so they're attainable
Guidelines for personal goals
Guidelines for career goals
How to plan to attain my goals
Goal setting plan
Driving and restraining forces
Brainstorming
Using goal setting plan

CHAPTER 6 - *What is stress?*   **95**

Fight or flight syndrome
Flight or fight response
First signs of stress
Physical
Psychological
Interpersonal
Positive and negative stress
Can stress be good?
What is bad stress?
Are you always conscious of stress?
Stressor, stress and *dis*tress
When does stress become *dis*tress?
Traumatic and daily stressors
Tracking the chemistry of stress
Stress and your immune system
Does poverty make a difference?
Stress and mental health - men, women
Chronic stress

CHAPTER 7 - *How prone are you to stress?*   **119**

How vulnerable are you to stress?
Misery measure
Holmes-Rahe scale
Evaluate your stress level
Stressed by success
Stress in the workplace
Can companies help?
Lethargic, apathetic, unhappy?
Why Women feel the cold more than men
Activity level
Detecting Type A Behaviour
What to do about a high Type A behaviour
Detecting Type B Behaviour
What to do about a high Type B behaviour

CHAPTER 8 - *Results of too much stress* — *135*

Results of too much stress
Other stress-related results
Obesity plus stress = trouble
Heart attacks and stress
Early warnings of a heart attack
How to help a possible heart attack victim
What is a stroke?
Why do strokes occur?
What are the warning signs of a stroke?
Are some people more likely to have strokes?
How to fight strokes
Cancer, linked to stress?

CHAPTER 9 - *Dealing with anger and worry* — *151*

Control your anger
How do you deal with your anger?
Frustration and anger
Process of feedback
How to deal with whiners, bellyachers and complainers
Eliminating frustration and anger
Controlling your moods
Repression of anger
How to handle anger
Are you a worrier?
Schedule a worry-time into your day

CHAPTER 10 - *Sleep and fatigue* — *169*

The A to ZZZZZ of sleep
Daily rhythms
Why do we sleep? Why do we dream?
Insomnia
Women suffer more sleep problems than men
I am man - hear me roar
Sleep problems
When you just can't wake up
Sleep Apnoea

Narcolepsy
Having a mid-day nap may be natural
Good or bad tired
How to get a good night's sleep

CHAPTER 11 - *How to relieve stress*   ***187***

Have a strong personality
A disease-resistant personality
Positive vs. negative thinking
Negative stress relievers
Positive stress relievers
Learn to relax
Change the situation
Change your response
Controlling stress is power
Do you need psychotherapy?

CHAPTER 12 - *Handling stress at work*   ***207***

Reducing stress for co-workers
Reducing stress for your staff
How to improve working conditions
Employees who stand all day
Working behind a counter
Noisy working environment
Bright lighting
Working with a computer
Do colours make a difference?
When sitting
Choosing a chair
Reducing stress for your supervisor or manager
Job stress - how to cope during the tough times

CHAPTER 13 - *Stress exercises and relievers*   ***219***

Stress relievers
Deep breathing
Transcendental meditation
Biofeedback
Massage
Self-massage

CHAPTER 14 - *Workaholism and burnout* — 233

What is a workaholic?
Is the company at fault?
Are you a workaholic?
How do you break the workaholic habit?
How can we tell when we're under too much pressure?
What is burnout?
Watch for signs of burnout
Misconceptions about burnout
Job burnout
Burnout in the helping professions
How to relieve burnout

Conclusion — 251

Bibliography — 253

INTRODUCTION

Initially, my interest in time management occurred when I found myself financially and emotionally responsible for the welfare of not only myself, but my three children. There just didn't seem to be enough hours in the day to get everything done.

Later, my interest was stimulated when I started my own company. What I did with my time, would decide whether my training and development firm succeeded or failed. But my high energy level caused me to go around in ever-widening circles, starting many projects, but finishing few. I needed to learn how to focus my interest in one direction at a time without being distracted by future tasks and the constant interruptions that plagued my day.

Faced with many conflicting (and often urgent) demands on my time, I developed techniques that gave me maximum benefit from the minimum investment of time. I learned that cutting corners, was not cheating - but rather good management of my time. After I compared how I used my time to how I really wanted to spend my time, I began applying the practical principles of time management. I became energised and was able to accomplish much more than I had in the past.

My interest in stress management occurred when I discovered that every time my stress level rose, an old back injury reared its ugly head. With the responsibility of single motherhood, I couldn't take the chance of being incapacitated with the pain - too much was riding on my paycheque.

Later, I learned to cope with the constant stress of my job - the trials and tribulations of keeping my company going, the pressure of always being up-to-date with material for my seminars, arranging seminar bookings for myself and my twelve associate trainers, the travel and living out of a suitcase and being centre stage while conducting my seminars. So, I read everything I could about how to handle stress and found many techniques that helped me in my business and home life. I also learned that if you manage your time, you're more likely to be able to manage stress as well.

If you believe time and stress are controlling your life, read this book and start practising prevention.

CHAPTER ONE

Where does the time go?

Time is important in today's society. We make such statements as:

'I don't have time.'
'Time is money.'
'Where did the time go?'
'We save time and waste time.'

We know that referees call time, prisoners serve time, musicians mark time, historians record time and loafers kill time. As consumers, we often invest in labour-saving devices that are really time-saving devices. Union and management discussions often concentrate on: Shorter work week ... flexible hours ... overtime ... double-time ... full time ... part-time ... and permanent part-time.

We sense its importance, but talk about time as if it was something concrete that we could see, feel and hold. If a person from Mars were to hear us talking about time, I'm sure he'd think it was something physical that he could see and touch. In reality, time is our most valuable commodity. If you asked an average eighty-year-old what he cherished most in life, most would state: good health and having more time.

Unfortunately, most of us squander our time. Many spend it existing, rather than living, never realising that life is like a taxi - the meter is always running. When you think of it, the minute you just spent reading this book has gone and will never return. It can't return no matter what you do.

How we use the time we have - whether we waste it just existing or whether we live each minute - depends on each of us. Are you in a rut, just plodding along through life doing things by automatic rote? Then stop your slide into oblivion and ask yourself these questions:

1. Am I doing what I planned to do with my life or did I get off track somewhere along the way?
2. How can I put more 'oomph' into my life so I spend my time living instead of existing?

3. Are there things I want to do in my lifetime, but haven't taken the time to plan how I'll make them happen?
4. Do I have concrete, realistic, written-down goals that guide me in the right direction?

Think of life as a journey. If you wanted to take a road trip, you'd likely study the map carefully to determine which route would be the most suitable. You'd spend time planning it. Why is it then, that so few people sit down and plan their lifetime; where they're going and when and how they expect to get there? Instead, many leave it to chance, luck or whatever comes along to determine their life's path.

How are you spending your valuable time? Is it time to make some changes in your life?

How long can we expect to live?

For centuries, society believed that the maximum human lifespan was close to 70 years (the biblical three score and ten). The entire animal kingdom seemed proof that, whether dictated by God or by genes, whether measured in months or years, heartbeats or cell divisions, Earth's creatures seemed destined to live (and die) in highly consistent rhythms: Galapagos turtles within 150 years, elephants within 70, horses in 45, mice in two or three.

All human teenagers enter puberty at roughly the same time; their mothers reach menopause within a similarly small range of years. Such consistency means these basic biological changes must be under genetic control. For all creatures, the ultimate purpose of life is passing on one's genes. After that, there are few evolutionary reasons for sticking around. Pacific salmon for example, die immediately after laying and fertilising their eggs. In humans, similar, though more complex, inborn limits also may make it impossible to boost life expectancy beyond 100. Others believe there are no limits at all, especially if one can enhance the good genes that bestow health and longevity. The encouraging message emerging from new research is that most of what we view as signs of aging - the crippled hands, the laboured steps, the stooped shoulders, are not signs of aging at all, but because of inactivity or disease.

Presently a women's average lifespan is 84 years and rising and men's is 79 years and rising. The gap between men and women's life spans is decreasing because of two major reasons. Women are quitting smoking at a slower rate than men and are sharing the decision-making, which raises their stress level. Because women are sharing the decision-making, men's stress levels are declining.

Unfailingly, studies have shown that when seniors keep active, their lifespan increases. The person who has nothing to get up for is the one who will likely die young.

One radical new conclusion is emerging among some scientists. Rather than aging and dying at a certain point, humans could live to be 200, 300 or more! It may take more than a hundred years to achieve this, but some scientists believe it is possible. With new drugs and genetic tinkering, the odds are good that we could not merely live much longer, but do so in good health. Even if they're only partly right, the implications are staggering. For instance, what would marriage be like, if 'until death us do part' meant 100 years together? Could the workplace employ people for 80 to 100 years? How would our planet overloaded with people now, absorb masses of elders who did not feel a 'duty to die?'

Soon most people can look forward to being alive well into their 80s. Within the next thirty years, half the population in North America will be 65 years of age or older. This should convince you to take care of your body and keep your mind active. By correcting eating or drinking habits, reducing obesity, by exercising and quitting smoking you'll probably enjoy those extra years much more.

We can boost life expectancy with no fancy science at all. Already, with no special tricks, the number of centenarians (people over 100) has doubled since 1980. If we simply reduce deaths from cancer and heart disease, life expectancy could jump. Such a reduction in deaths would impact the baby boomers (our largest population group, born between 1946 and 1964).

The idea there might be no built-in limits to the lifespan is galvanising researchers. For instance, a chemical has reversed brain damage in aging gerbils and extended the lifespan of mice by 20 per cent. This is the equivalent of giving 15 more years to 75 year-old humans. Another drug has rejuvenated the failing immune systems of aged rats so quickly (within 24 hours) that AIDS patients are scrambling for street versions of it. Scientists have rolled back the physiological clock for older men by giving them injections of growth hormone.

Meanwhile, geneticists are searching for genes that could boost human lifespan. A geneticist has found four longevity assurances genes in yeast. When mutated, one gene shortens life; when enhanced, the same gene seems to cause cells to live 30 per cent longer. Pieces of this DNA or genetic material similar to these genes have been found in humans. This suggests that genetic manipulation might lengthen human life as well.

Culturally, it would be a disaster if people lived to age 150 or more. Many who are now in their 80's and 90's wouldn't want to live much longer. However, those attitudes would likely change if the extra decades were years of health and vigour. When baby boomers hit 65 and retire, our already strained health and pension plans could collapse. Some countries have changed the retirement age from 65 to 70, which has made many 64 year-olds very angry.

We worry that increasing life expectancy could add to the time we spend sick and disabled at the end of life suffering from non-fatal, but serious problems (such as severe arthritis, osteoporosis or dementia). Many feel this view is too gloomy; that the same measure that can expand life expectancy will extend the health span as well, compressing disability into an ever-smaller segment at the end of life. The real goal of research is not only to add years to life, but life to years. We wouldn't have a bunch of senior citizens in nursing homes at age 150. We'd probably have people making contributions to society for longer periods, not requiring health care until the late stages.

What is normal aging?

The rate of aging varies enormously among individuals and even among different organs in the same individual. Nevertheless, some changes predictably occur in most humans.

Although it's usually years before we notice, our immune system starts to decline while we're still in our teens. In our 20s, lungs become slightly less efficient and our nerves start sending messages a bit more slowly. By 35, bones stop growing and by the time we're in our 40s, there's no denying it: Time is catching up! Gravity takes hold and as one person put it, 'Everything starts drooping, including my face.'

At this point, kidneys shrink, muscles lose bulk and elasticity and blood vessels begin to narrow. Vision fades and many are forced to buy bifocals. We don't remember things like we used to. We all have physical and mental changes as we grow older:

Memory: Treatable:

Most key mental functions diminish only minimally with the years and researchers are working hard to slow or reverse these declines. Physical exercise improves mental function in some older people. Using one's intellect actively throughout life helps others.

Overall, the brain's ability to process information does slow as we age. However, when we give most healthy elderly people enough time and an environment that keeps anxiety at bay, they can score about as well as young or middle-aged adults on mental tests. The elderly may not learn or remember quite as rapidly, but they may learn and remember nearly as well. In most people, the capacity to focus on a task or follow an argument is also well-maintained throughout life. The chief decline in healthy older people is their ability to perform several tasks at the same time or switch back and forth rapidly between tasks. They can overcome this, by organising their work so they can focus on one task at a time.

Memory: Untreatable

For many people, the most dreaded aspect of aging is not the chance that the body may falter, but that the mind (the core of one's personality) may shrivel into nothingness. There are, sadly, many ways to lose one's mind. A few of these are; strokes, Parkinson's disease and severe depression. However, the sinister ailment that realistically terrifies many is the progressive, irreversible dementia called Alzheimer's disease. By age 85, a study showed that 47 per cent of people have enough symptoms to meet the definition of

Alzheimer's. Other researchers, using different criteria, put the figure closer to 20 per cent.

People suffering from Alzheimer's disease have difficulty in communicating with others. Some cannot make themselves understood or don't understand others. They may become angry or defensive if they can't find the words to answer questions. They forget information within seconds. Some can read words, but fail to understand those words. Others may understand face-to-face encounters, but fail to understand phone conversations.

Eventually, they lose their sense of direction and become lost. The route they took to the corner store is suddenly unfamiliar to them. They forget where their bedroom is in their homes. Others try to put cakes into the dishwasher to bake, put milk in the cupboard and sugar in the fridge. (We've all shown these signs from time to time, but only in isolated incidents.) Alzheimer's patients often live in the past. Some believe their sons (who may resemble their fathers) are their long-departed husbands and talk to them as if they were. Unfortunately many caregivers forget that the patient may understand more than they think and talk about them as if they weren't there.

There is encouraging news for those with severe cognitive losses. Scientists are finding that experimental new drugs (especially a compound called nerve growth factor) can trigger brain regeneration.

Personality: A person's personality does not have any radical changes after age 30 unless the person receives psychotherapy. This is particularly true in individuals who've lived in abused relationships, either during childhood or as young adults. Many continue to live in the past, locked into passive personalities or become aggressive themselves as a response to the violence they believe is normal in everyday interactions between people. Personality changes also occur if the person develops a dementing illness.

Sense of smell: This starts to decline slowly at age 45, but escalates at a faster rate after the person reaches 65.

Thymus: When a child enters puberty, her thymus begins shrinking and his/her immune response begins a slow decline.

Lungs: There is a 40% drop in maximum breathing capacity between ages 20 and 70.

Muscles: With lack of exercise, 20% to 40% of muscle mass is lost between age 20 and 90. Exercise prevents most of this loss.

Ovaries: After menopause, a woman's body dramatically slows production of estrogen.

Blood vessels: The diameter of vessels narrows and arterial walls stiffen and there is a 20 - 25% increase in systolic blood pressure.

Pituitary gland and hypothalamus: Secretion of growth hormone declines at age 50, causing muscles to shrink and fat to increase.

Sight: The ability to see nearby objects declines at age 40, but the ability to see fine detail does not deteriorate until age 70.

Hearing: This begins to decline around age 20, but decreases faster in men than women.

Bones: After the age of 40, bones begin to weaken and many suffer from osteoporosis. The decline is more prevalent in women.

Heart: There's little decline in resting output, but a 20% decline in maximum rate during exercise occurs after a person reaches 40. At this stage the heart becomes less responsive to stimulation from the nervous system.

Adrenal Glands: After age 30, secretion of DHEA (which slows cancer and boosts immunity) declines and after 70, production of the stress hormone cortisol soars.

Skin: There are changes in collagen (a connective tissue) which causes the person's skin to lose elasticity in later years.

Nerves: Between age 40 and 80, the speed of messages along nerves drops 10%.

Having a strong will is one key to living longer. People who live to healthy old ages have several characteristics in common: a good immune system, a balanced lifestyle and a strong personality.

Learning how to manage stress is important for a long healthy life. Bad stress leaves a person feeling angry and hostile. Chronic stress can compromise the immune system and lead to anxiety disorders or depression, all of which can reduce longevity.

Immune system: Whether you have a good immune system or not is mostly the luck of the draw. If your parents weren't susceptible to infections, if they were sufficiently healthy most of their lives, chances are good you'll enjoy the same robust health.

In the same way, we can inherit many diseases related to a defect in the immune system, such as certain types of diabetes. The immune system also changes as we age. Cells in people aged 75 and older take longer to produce the antibodies that fight infection. It takes about seven days for the cells in a young or middle-aged adult to produce the antibodies that fight infection. It takes the cells in elderly people between 14 and 21 days. This probably accounts for elderly people being more likely to suffer infections that require hospitalisation.

Strong personality: Several personality traits contribute to a strong will, but two important ones are self-esteem and a sense of purpose. Such people believe in their ability to make things happen for themselves. Obstacles don't stop them and they're more likely to keep going at it. But those with low self-esteem blame themselves when things go wrong and stop trying. Reminding themselves about what they could have done or should have done better gets them nowhere.

Some psychologists say self-esteem goes back to the kind of bond you formed with your parents as a child. Maybe it does, but studies show that you can improve how you feel about yourself. But that's another book.

How to live a longer, fuller life

Aging is far more under our control than we once thought. Chronological age is now considered a bad marker of biological age. Heredity may account for up to 30% of change to vision, hearing and reaction times. You can't do much about that. However longevity is due to one's lifestyle, chiefly exercise and diet.

Although that message is important for people already in their later years, it's particularly crucial for people in their midlife years (the baby boomers). The changes that are observed in the aged are clearly long-term processes that start in midlife. The baby boomers are the first generation to enter midlife with information they can use to guide their behaviour and control their own aging.

In addition to exercise and diet, statistically there are several tricks to longevity. The first is to choose good parents with a good set of genes. Skip those with genes that result in fatal childhood diseases or predispose you to cancer or heart disease. Instead, choose rich, well-educated parents, which will lessen your chance of dying in infancy.

After you pass your toddler stage, the trick is to dodge bullets, cars, high stress and AIDS for the next 44 years. Up to age 45, accidents, homicides and suicides are the biggest killers. AIDS is gaining. Car fatalities often involve alcohol or passengers who did not wear seat belts. So if you drink, don't drive - and wear your seat belt. If you ride a bicycle or motorcycle, wear a helmet.

Violence is still a big killer as you move from your 20s into your 30s. If you feel hopeless or depressed, get help. A fatal combination for himself and others is to allow a desperate person to have access to a gun. Angry people are three and a half times more likely to have a heart attack; four times more likely to get cancer.

If you've reached the ripe old age of 45, congratulate yourself on making it through the first big statistical minefield. There are many other dangers facing you now. If you're a smoker or overweight, change your ways. The future yawning before you is stocked with big chronic illnesses, chiefly cancer and heart disease. It's here that lifestyle begins to kill you or save you.

You've reached 65 - congratulations again. Once you make it this far, the odds for a long life get better and better. If you're a woman, the odds now are you'll make it to age 84. At birth, the odds were only 79. If you're a man, the odds now are that you'll likely reach 79. At birth your life expectancy was 72. Keep exercising or start exercising and eat a sensible diet. If you don't - keep praying. By age

85, you're a statistical marvel. The odds of making it to 91 are now 50-50. How far you've come! At birth, the chance of reaching 101.5 was only 1.5 per cent!

Why do we age?

People accept aging like they accept their car wearing out, but living organisms can repair themselves. So why do we age?

In the wild, aging is rare because predators often make long life impossible for many. However, for humans, who have learned to beat back predators (including viruses and bacteria) the question of why we age at all is keeping researchers busy.

One theory states that living to an old age results from human's delayed reproduction cycle. Animals that mature slowly and wait years to reproduce often live the longest after reproduction. Genes that foster late reproduction, automatically eliminate genes with early detrimental effects. Estrogen, for instance, is essential for reproduction in females. Unfortunately, after reproductive years end, estrogen can trigger breast cancer. Similarly, testosterone helps males build muscle for winning and defending turf, but can be the cause of late-life prostate cancer.

There's proof that being able to laugh at life helps increase longevity. Those who are jovial and happy live longer, more productive lives. The following might give you your chuckle for the day:

You know you're growing old when ...

- Everything hurts and what doesn't hurt doesn't work.
- The gleam in your eye is from the sun hitting your bifocals.
- You feel like the night before and you haven't been anywhere.
- Your little black book contains only names ending with M.D.
- You get winded playing cards.
- Your children begin to look middle-aged.
- You finally reach the top of the ladder and find it leaning against the wrong wall.
- You join a health club and don't go.
- You begin to outlive enthusiasm.
- You decide to procrastinate, but never get around to it.

- Your mind makes contracts your body can't meet.
- A dripping faucet causes uncontrollable bladder urge.
- You know all the answers, but nobody asks you the questions.
- You look forward to a dull evening.
- You need glasses to find your glasses.
- You walk with your head held high, trying to get used to your bifocals.
- You turn out the lights for economic, rather than romantic reasons.
- You sit in a rocking chair and can't get it going.
- Your knees buckle, but your belt won't.
- You regret all those temptations you resisted.
- You stop looking forward to your next birthday.
- After painting the town red, you have to take a long rest before applying a second coat.
- People start calling you a Senior Citizen.
- You remember today, that yesterday was your wedding anniversary.
- You can't stand people who are intolerant.
- The best part of your day is over when the alarm clock goes off.
- You burn the midnight oil after 9:00 pm.
- Your back goes out more than you do.
- A fortune teller offers to read your face.
- Your pacemaker makes the garage door go up when you watch a pretty girl walk by.
- The little old grey-haired man you help across the street is your husband.
- You have too much room in the house and not enough in the medicine chest.
- You sink your teeth in a steak and they stay there.
- You wonder why more people don't use this print size.

Does having money make a difference?

Despite a generation of Medicare, the gap in life expectancy between the richest and poorest has narrowed only slightly. It may not buy happiness, but money adds four more years to the lives of the 20 per cent of people who live in the richer neighbourhoods.

The poor face barriers even before they're born. Babies born into poor families are more likely to be premature, smaller and have lower birth weight than richer babies. Many are born to teenage mothers without the income, diet or support they need. Though today's babies are getting much better care than they did a generation ago, the gap between the rich and the poor persists. Wealth provides proper nutrition, secure social support, comfortable housing in neighbourhoods more free of pollution and violent crime, safer motor vehicles and other safety devices.

Richer people are more likely to have families, friends and supporters that are important to health. They're more likely to get a good education. They have challenging jobs free of accidents and toxic fumes and the time and resources to fight everyday stress. Their jobs offer more security and opportunities to develop skills, exercise control or manage their time.

Somehow, a lesser start in life seems to lead one to make poor decision-makers when it comes to smoking. Sixteen per cent of the poor are heavy smokers compared to eleven per cent of the general population. Interestingly, the poor were less likely, to drink alcohol than the rich and they are less likely to drink and drive. When they do drink, they're more likely to do so to overcome stress or depression. They're also twice as likely to use tranquilisers and sleeping pills as the rich. The poor are less likely to use seat belts or wear motorcycle or bicycle helmets. Low-income women are less likely to have Pap smears and perform breast self-examinations.

Retirement

To many people, the word 'retirement' makes them rub their hands with glee. Others become depressed, because to them, it means the end of their productive lives. Those in their middle-aged years (40 - 55) should be seriously thinking of what they'll do with their lives when they retire.

Statistics now prove that men can retire earlier and with fewer cares than women. Only 70 per cent of men and 51 per cent of women have a pension plan. Women traditionally enter the work force later than men and have built up less in their pension funds. Working women don't plan to retire or retire as early as men do, unless they marry and their husbands have a good income.

An emerging trend shows that when husbands retire, many of their wives decide to stay in the workforce. The women's reasons for doing so relate to money (or lack of it) medical and pension benefits, job satisfaction and a sense of identity. Their husbands may have been in the workforce for 45 years but many wives (five to fifteen years younger than their spouses) have worked for 25 or 30 years. They aren't ready to retire.

Women who marry older men or marry for a second time may still be in the middle of their career paths when their husbands retire. Many husbands object to the reversal of traditional roles where they're the homemaker and their wives are the breadwinners. Power struggles often occur, which can affect the man's ego. Couples who are approaching this milestone in their lives should look carefully at the upheaval this might cause in their relationship. They should take steps to lessen the perceived problems - ***before*** retirement.

Divorced women spend three more years in the work force than married or widowed women. This shows that women usually come out of a divorce worse off economically than a man. Widows can collect from their husband's pension fund as well as from their own. Unfortunately pension funds are not as kind to divorced women. They end up with only one pension fund to count on. Many are exempt from receiving benefits from their ex-spouse's pension fund. Canada corrected this inequity by providing for a fair division of pensions for women obtaining a divorce after the year 1977. Women who divorced before that date are not allowed this benefit.

How much time do we have?

Have you ever considered how much time you have to do all the things you'd like to do in your lifetime? In the following information, I've shown total hours and days for a lifespan of 75 years. At the beginning of the twentieth century, the average man's life expectancy was 46. This meant that if you were 23 years of age, you were middle-aged! Here are some facts that might interest you.

There are:

- 24 hours in a day
- 1440 minutes in a day
- 168 hours in a week
- 8,760 hours in a year
- 657,000 hours in 75 years
- 27,375 days in 75 years

Time breakdown

What does the average person do with his or her personal 168 hours in a week? One North American survey identified that the average person spent his or her time as follows:

Activity and hours:

- Sleep: 56
- Personal Hygiene: 7
- Eating: 7
- Travel: 5.25
- Work: 66.5
- Pleasure: 9
- Self Improvement: 1.75
- Illness: 1.5

TOTAL: 150
Hours left: 18

The above survey shows that the average person sleeps eight hours a night. How many hours do you sleep per night? Is this through choice or necessity? Do you feel you need more sleep to feel fully rested? Less?

If you said you needed more sleep, could it be because life is so boring that you regularly choose sleeping as a way of spending your time? If this is the case, get more challenge into your life. If you wake up before your alarm goes off in the morning, it's probably because you've had enough sleep. (Get more information on this topic in Chapter 10 on Sleep and Fatigue).

Personal Hygiene includes bathing, shaving, putting on makeup or combing your hair. Eating, counts only the hours you spend actually eating, not those spent preparing the meal, cleaning up after it or socialising during the meal.

Travel is all the travel you do during the week including driving to work, doing grocery shopping, running errands and driving yourself or your children to activities.

Work, includes paid and unpaid work. Women's total in this area is normally much higher than men's.

Pleasure, includes watching television, reading a book, participating or watching sports or going to a party. This is the area of your life where you let your 'little kid' out to have some fun. An important part of your life is having fun: don't neglect it. Plan these activities, so you don't cheat yourself in this area.

Self-improvement includes all the time you spent at regular school as well as any courses you've attended since then. This includes reading non-fiction books, receiving in-house training at your place of employment and other developmental activities.

Illness (self explanatory)

We've accounted for 150 hours of our week. What are we doing with the 18 hours we can't account for? We spend it waiting for something or someone or just goofing-off (which may be necessary under some conditions).

How do you spend your time? To determine what you really spend your time on, complete the following information for one week. You may find some surprises. Possibly you're spending more time watching TV than you thought you did. You might decide to spend that time more constructively towards reaching your goals.

Minutes per week and percentage:
1. Sleep
2. Personal Hygiene (washing, hair, makeup, shaving)
3. Eating
4. Travel (commuting)
5. Work (salaried) (home, shopping, cooking, cleaning)
6. Pleasure (TV, sports, reading)
7. Self Development (education study)
8. Illness

Decide the %age of time you spend at or with:

a) Working
b) Family
c) Social (community)
d) Goof-off time or illness

I often have couples that attend my time management sessions together and I encourage them to complete the above questionnaire. After they completed the questionnaire, one couple decided to make some drastic changes in their lives. They lived in an older home with eight rooms (they'd had a large family) on an acreage out of town. Both of them worked weekends in the summer growing a market garden. Most of their spare time disappeared in just maintaining their big house and land.

Each spent almost three hours a day getting to and from work. (On an average working day, most people spend ten hours a day, getting ready for, travelling to and working at a job). Their last daughter was just leaving home to attend university, so there was no further need for them to keep their large house.

What the couple really wanted to do was travel. But they couldn't leave their property unattended for long periods. They sold their rural property and moved into a high-rise condominium in the city. This meant that they spent only fifteen minutes travelling to work and were free to lock their door and travel when they wished. No longer did they have to cut grass, tend their market garden or shovel snow. An additional plus was that they had a smaller dwelling to care for, so could enjoy their time off after their work days.

Another man felt discouraged because he wanted to advance his career by taking courses in the evenings. He felt he didn't have time because of his busy lifestyle. After completing the questionnaire, he found that he spent 24 hours a week watching television! He decided he did have time to take the courses he required.

Fear of failure

People's attitude to life keeps many from making full use of the years they have. Many turn down excellent opportunities but can't explain why they've done so. If this happens to you, ask yourself,

'Why am I not taking this opportunity?' Is fear of failure holding you back? Or is it lack of money, connections, time or possible family problems? Learn to analyse why you're being your own worst enemy.

Offer some people promotions and they automatically assume they're incapable of handling them. They'll think of every situation where they can't possibly measure up. They'll often turn down a promotion because of their fears. Unfortunately, if they *do* accept the positions and still have these negative feelings, they're probably setting themselves up to fail.

I know people who have sat on the fence wailing about their problems for so long, they're afraid to get off and begin living. I call them Mugwumps. Mugwumps are those who have their mugs on one side of the fence and their wumps on the other. They've got to get off that fence! All you get from fence sitting; is slivers.

These people don't comprehend that they're putting themselves under more and more stress the longer they're on that fence. Not deciding becomes more stressful than deciding. Think back a bit. When you had a tough decision to make, wasn't it stressful? Do you remember the relief you felt when you finally took the step and made a decision? The tension goes somehow. Fence sitting is very draining as people mentally bounce from one solution to another, without deciding which decision is right.

Anyone can overcome the fear of failure by keeping in mind that they're capable of accomplishing far more than they believe they can. In a work situation, I recommend that no one should take a promotion if they know every aspect of the job. If they do this, they're already overqualified for the position. All promotional opportunities should leave room for the person to grow and learn while on the job or through additional training.

We need courage to take risks, but life without risk is very mundane and boring. Some fear not being able to pull it off - that they'll fail. They believe that failure is bad, so in taking risks, they're facing the chance of ending up with not one, but two bad feelings. These are their failure at what they tried to do, plus their lowered self-esteem. If you wait until 'you're in the mood,' you may wait an eternity before reaching your goals.

I always approach new challenges with an open mind. When approaching a new task, I rationalise, 'I've never tried this before - but I'll try my best.' I resist feelings of panic if I don't do something well (and know I've given my best try). Instead, I acknowledge that this is something I don't do very well. Then I try something else. If I *do* succeed at the task, the positive results usually spur me on to try other new challenges. The momentum of my success keeps me 'up.' With this positive approach, I find that three out of five things I try, I succeed at and the ratio is improving.

Fear of success

Everyone has their personal definition of what success means to them. I feel successful when I set goals and achieve them. What would it take to make you feel successful?

Do you feel that if you become a success you might lose the love and comfort of important people in your life? Do you feel you might outgrow your close friends? Do you feel that your success might force you to find new support groups and friends? If you choose to start climbing, you may feel an obligation to keep climbing. You may not be sure how high you can climb. You'd hate to fail along the way. Some feel this would be worse than not trying in the first place.

Men are far more comfortable with success than women, because they're expected to succeed. Some women have the definite fear that they *will* succeed. This is often a well-hidden fear and their actions to thwart their success are also well hidden. Successful females often appear more competitive than the average woman. You may feel uncomfortable in this role. Will people think you're less feminine if you succeed? Many men feel intimidated by successful women and give put-downs you might not be able to handle.

Married women may be afraid that they might make their spouse feel uncomfortable with their success. Or their fear may be that they'll lose their mate. Single woman may feel that the number of available men willing to accept a successful female is too low for their liking.

Other women may feel they may have to choose between being successful in a career and having a spouse or mate. Some feel that they can have one or the other, but can't have both. (The majority of women have both).

When I started climbing the corporate ladder, I made a conscious decision to stop holding myself back. No longer was I afraid of stepping on others' toes with my competency and no longer did I feel the necessity of acting like a 'dumb blond.' This was very threatening territory, but it wasn't worth the pain of holding myself back. I had spent years back-pedalling and trying not to offend people who were more senior than myself.

Self-sabotage

People often blame others when they don't get what they want. But the reason they fail is not as obvious - they sabotage their own efforts. There's a 'little twerp' inside us who asks maliciously 'Who do you think you are?' and questions our every action. When these ideas take over, they block the good feelings we have after a job well done. Instead, we concentrate on some little task we've done wrong.

Do you let yourself feel that you've failed at something, when you've given it your best attempt? Early in life, I learned to take the word 'failure' out of my vocabulary. Tell yourself that you just didn't succeed at it. Make it a learning experience, rather than expecting yourself to be perfect. You can't be good at everything! If you think you have to be, you're likely going to spend most of your life in misery.

If you're holding off doing something because you're afraid to take the risk, do the following:

a. Define as closely as possible, what you think the risk is.
b. Determine what you could gain emotionally and physically by trying it.
c. Determine what you could lose emotionally and physically by trying it.
d. Do you need more information before taking the risk? Where would you get this information? Who has this kind of information?
e. How could you lessen the risk?
f. Is it now worth taking the risk?

A more simplistic method is to ask yourself two questions before trying something that's possibly risky. These questions are:

What have I got to gain?

What have I got to lose?

If you have much to gain and little to lose, it's foolish not to try. To get yourself started, identify some of the things you do well. Do you excel at swimming? Try snorkelling or SCUBA diving. Any time you try something that is close to the activities at which you excel, your likelihood of success is increased. If you're a musician, try another similar instrument. This will boost your self-esteem level.

CHAPTER TWO

Time management techniques

The Busy Man: Author Unknown

> If you want to get a favour done by some obliging friend,
> And want a promise safe and sure on which you may depend,
> Don't go to him, who always had much leisure time to plan,
> But if you want your favour done, just ask the busy man.
>
> The man of leisure never has a moment he can spare;
> He's busy 'putting off' until his friends are in despair;
> But he whose every waking hour is crowded full of work,
> Forgets the art of wasting time - he cannot stop to shirk.
>
> So when you want a favour done and want it right away,
> Go to the man who constantly works 20 hours a day.
> He'll find a moment somewhere, that has no other use,
> And fix you while the idle man is framing an excuse.

Principles of time management

Time management works no matter what kind of situation you're in. Whether you work in an office, a warehouse, in the home or out in the field, use these in your management of time.

1. Plan effectively. Every hour spent in effective planning saves three to four in execution and achieves better results.
2. By failing to plan, you're planning to fail.
3. Plan early. Daily planning, formulated either the afternoon before or early the same day, is essential to effective use of personal time. (Do you spend some time planning your day?)
4. Budget or assign time to tasks in direct relationship to their priority.
5. Impose deadlines on tasks or decisions and exercise self-discipline in following them. This helps overcome indecision and procrastination.
6. Group similar tasks within divisions of the work day. (i.e.: making all your phone calls at one time).

7. Keep a daytimer or To Do list and use it faithfully.
8. Remember Murphy's Second Law, 'Everything takes longer than you think,' especially if you delegate the task, so make allowances for this.
9. Consider waiting as a 'gift of time' - use it, don't waste it. Be flexible in scheduling your time to consider forces beyond your control.
10. Avoid surprises by expecting the unexpected and plan for it. Assume that if anything can go wrong, it will. (Murphy's Third Law). Anticipatory action is usually more effective than remedial action. A stitch in time saves nine.
11. Don't over-estimate problems and treat all problems as if they are crises. Upon investigating crises you'll probably find they're mostly low priority items.
12. During the day, ask yourself *'What's the best use of my time, right now?'*

Are you over-planning your day?

Do you find that your problem is that you plan your day down to the last minute without considering that you might spend 30 - 40 per cent of your time just 'fighting fires' and helping others. Do you find there are always tasks still to do at the end of the day? Is your day nothing but interruptions and crisis? Don't schedule every minute of the day with appointments; save some uncommitted time.

Keeping a time log

This will identify your constant interrupters. In business this could be a simple entry such as: Bill Jones - talked about Miller Account, 5 minutes. Mary Smith - needed figures for the budget, 10 minutes. Apply the 80/20 rule. 80% of the calls will be coming from 20% of the callers. Consider setting a special time for calls or to have a personal assistant screen them. Or assign calls to someone else. If you repeatedly spend a lot of time on the phone with the same people, try to find a time to handle all the person's problems at once.

At home, do friends often telephone or drop in unexpectedly? If it's a telephone problem, keep the caller informed about your time constraints. If they drop in, ask them to call first.

How to choose priorities

Whether you plan your day the afternoon before or early in the morning, choose what is most important. Rank items from A to D. Do the A's (which are usually more difficult) first. Getting them done will increase your self-esteem. Don't let an easy C task get you off track.

- **Priority As** - Important and urgent, must be done right away.
- **Priority Bs** - Important but *not* urgent, can be done now or later.
- **Priority Cs** - Often urgent to others, but of low importance to you.
- **Priority Ds** - Garbage, throw away.

Now consider how you plan your time. Do you use:

1. Daytimers and 'To Do' lists, or
2. To keep track of appointments do you use:
   (a) A desk calendar?
   (b) A daytimer?
   (c) Use another (possibly more complex) system?
3. How effective do you find your personal system?
4. Do you make 'To Do' lists every day - even on weekends?

It's important that you consistently use whatever system works best for you. And I stress the word 'consistently.' Try a variety of methods to show which one works best for you and stick with it. My philosophy is, *'If it ain't broke - don't fix it,'* so if you're happy with your present system, keep it up.

I use both a daytimer and a 'To Do' list. When a company hires me to do a seminar, I write down everything I have to do for their seminar on a separate 'To Do' list. I then put dates next to the tasks and then put the information in my daytimer. Using this method, I seldom forget anything and have a back-up list that I can tick off when I complete the activities. For example, my daytimer would have entries on when I would send a training contract and when a signed copy should be returned; book airline tickets when contract was confirmed, etc.

You can imagine what would happen if I forgot anything such as:

Forgetting to tell a company that I required a PowerPoint projector so I could show my slides or forgetting to make travel arrangements until the last minute. For me the dual 'To Do' system works well. What alternate system might work for you? Once you decide, use it faithfully.

Different kinds of tasks:

Try to see which of these tasks cause you the most difficulty (possibly because there are so many of them):

1. Simple short-term tasks:
   These are routine activities found in any job. These tasks are simple and short-term in nature, which can occur frequently.
2. Complex short-term tasks:
   These are complex, but require only short-time effort for accomplishment. They require an intermediate level of planning and effort.
3. Simple long-term tasks:
   These are simple, but require long-term effort to complete. These tasks also may need an intermediate level of planning, due to the long-term effort required to complete them.
4. Complex long-term tasks:
   These take a high level of effort and planning and are often avoided in favour of a less complex task.

Did you identify either #1 or #3 as those that gave you the most problems? If you're a supervisor and these tasks are so simple - why aren't you delegating them downward? Could you pass some of those tasks on to your staff or family members? On the job, this would allow you to do the more important tasks you're paid to accomplish.

Swiss cheese approach

Large blocks of uninterrupted time are a comparative rarity. If again and again (a few minutes before lunch, etc.) you choose to work on an unimportant task rather than begin a difficult, important task, then you're procrastinating. You're avoiding what's really important.

One way to tackle complex long-term tasks is to use the 'Swiss cheese' approach (this is the cheese with holes in it). Take 'little bites' out of your long-term task (instant tasks).

Instant tasks can take from one minute to an hour to accomplish. Most are ten minutes or less. What might appear at first to be instant tasks, often turn out to be groups of tasks that you could divide into smaller 'bites.' After each instant task, you would identify the time it would take to complete it.

In your planning you might have several group tasks that can be broken down into instant tasks. For example: Your task is to hire three new employees. Two sample instant tasks could be:

1. Obtain the job description of the position - 2 minutes
2. Write an advertisement for the newspaper - 15 minutes

The following are group tasks that have been broken down into instant tasks:

1. Screen one resume or application form - 5 minutes (a group task would be reviewing all of them)
2. Set up one appointment - 5 minutes
3. Conduct one interview - 45 minutes
4. Evaluate one candidate - 7 minutes

Using this method, you could fit small instant tasks throughout your day as time permits. For instance, if you were waiting for a phone call or had to go to a meeting in five minutes, you could screen one resume or application form.

Try the Swiss cheese approach in family chores as well. For instance removing wallpaper from the wall and painting the room takes planning. You don't have to do this task all at once. Instead, do it in bits and pieces (instant tasks). Removing the furniture from the room is a group task. Removing one piece of furniture from the room could be an instant task. Covering the remaining (immobile) furniture with drop sheets is another. Sloshing hot water on the existing wallpaper is another. After wetting down the walls a few times (group task) it's time to strip off one strip of wallpaper (instant task). This is how you can fit tasks in at home as well.

How to start complex long-term tasks:

Suppose you're responsible for setting up your company's annual meeting (not their annual report) and can expect about 150 people to attend.

1. Choose several 'Instant Tasks.'
2. Set a time estimated to complete each task.
3. Determine obstacles you could run into while completing each task.

Here are some suggested instant tasks.

1. A group of tasks is to check all hotels for availability. An instant task is to contact one hotel to see if they have facilities available when you want them. Also ask what accommodations they have available for any out-of-town guests. The next instant task would be to call another hotel.
   Time: 15-20 minutes
   Obstacles: Person was not there, could not get information on first call. Facility was not available.
2. Arrange for audio-visual equipment.
   Time: 10 minutes
   Obstacles: Equipment was not available in-house. You now have to add a task to your list, 'Investigate equipment rentals.'

Saving time

What is the one major time saver you could use for the overall assignment that would save you about 50 per cent of your time? Should you:

a) Spend the necessary time planning the project?
b) Delegate most of the work to others?
c) Use a computer or word processor to record information?

These would all help. But there's something more important. What was the assignment? To set up your company's Annual Meeting. This means your company holds it every year. So find out who did it last year! Has the person left the company? There should be a company file identifying all the details of last year's project.

Consider too, those tasks completed by co-workers or friends. Don't start projects from 'scratch' unless it's absolutely necessary.

Before planning any long-term assignment, try to determine how you can be 'lazy.' Being 'lazy,' is really using effective time management. Take five minutes before tackling long-term assignments to identify how you can cut corners or use work done by yourself or others in the past as a pattern. Stop re-inventing the wheel.

Procrastination

Are you forever dragging your heels, putting things off, being late? Procrastination is a serious work-place problem. It's such a serious matter that it's second in line as to why companies fire employees. (First in line are personality clashes between supervisors or co-workers). It also ends friendships both at work and in private life.

How can you tell when procrastination has become a serious problem?

- When you have something important to do, not much time to do it in, but find yourself looking for other diversions instead.
- When *you* set deadlines and don't meet them.
- When you constantly delay making important decisions.
- When you work furiously at the last minute to complete crucial assignments.

There are five basic kinds of procrastinators:

1. Last-minute type - They wait until the last minute and work around the clock to meet deadlines.

2. I'll decide later - They postpone decisions until events resolve the situation or they're forced to decide.

3. Perfectionists - They must complete all tasks faultlessly, no matter how small or insignificant. They need to learn how to discriminate in the importance they place on assignments.

4. I'll show you! - They delay assignments as a way of retaining a sense of personal power and control. (Watch for this sign in your staff or your children. They may use it to 'get back' at you).

5. Muddler - They put off work because of bad habits, poor organisation, trying to do too much or there's a lack of set procedures. They are the people who go around in ever-widening circles getting nowhere. They start an assignment and before it's completed, go onto another one. They seldom complete assignments on time.

When facing a distasteful task, promise yourself you'll give fifteen minutes of hard effort on it. You'll probably find that the momentum you've started will keep you going until you finish the task.

Others don't get tasks done simply because of disorganisation. They start tasks, but don't finish them; they rush right in at the beginning of the day without thinking about what they should be doing and when; or neglect the important step of determining what has priority and what doesn't.

Think for a moment of someone you know who's well organised. I'll bet you'll agree that they're effective time managers. So learning how to manage your time will help you do the things you want to do in your life. Try increasing your work pace from time to time. On the other hand, don't be a clock-watcher - tense about filling every minute. Recognise the value of time spent relaxing.

I was fortunate to be born with a high energy level. This can be an asset or a detriment. Instead of gearing my energies at a specific target, I found that I was going around in 'every widening circles' accomplishing little and often getting in the way of others who were more organised. Before I learned time management techniques, I had a tendency to start more than one assignment or task and move onto another before finishing the first one. It was normal for me to have several assignments on the go at one time, with very few finished at the end of a day. Then I learned how to set priorities and how important it was to spend my time on issues that were of high priority to me. This took diligent effort on my behalf to tackle one task at a time, but the rewards were many.

After I listed my priorities and had chosen the most important one, I could push the other assignments out of my mind. I knew my 'To Do' list would prompt me when I was ready to tackle the next task.

No longer was I distracted with thoughts about my next assignment, while completing the first one. This way, I could focus my high energy on one task at a time. I learned that because other matters weren't distracting me, I could get much more done than I ever thought possible.

That's the secret - focusing your energy in one direction at a time, instead of letting it get scattered around. Consider time as money and invest it wisely. So focus, focus, focus.

Reward vs. punishment

If you have problems motivating yourself to get something done, try giving yourself a reward for completing the task. Behavioural science experts explain that: 'Any behaviour that's followed by something pleasant is inclined to be reinforced and is more likely to happen again. Punishing yourself for goofing-off is not nearly as effective as rewarding yourself for success.'

This reward could be as simple as giving yourself an extended break after completing a difficult assignment or as elaborate as arranging to go on your dream vacation.

Lateness:

There are three basic kinds of personalities relating to time management. Let's assume there was a meeting called for 10:00 am:

Type 1: This person arrives right at 10:00 am.
Type 2: This person arrives at 10:10 am and acts as if s/he's on time.
Type 3: This person arrives at 9:50 am and acts as if s/he's 'just made it!'

Those who arrive ten minutes late run into more problems than the early bird. What do you think runs through the minds of those who cared enough to be there on time? Those waiting probably felt that the latecomer thinks they aren't important. Otherwise, why would they act as if their time was more important than those waiting? This is a serious put-down that can cause repercussions for the latecomer.

The ones who worry unless they're early for everything; can waste valuable time. They should bring some short-term task they can complete in the ten minutes they're early for the appointment.

How to deal with professionals who keep you waiting

Have you ever seethed because a doctor, dentist, lawyer or other professional keeps you waiting for your appointment? Are patients becoming impatient or are professional people guilty of thinking their time is more valuable than everyone else's?

One man decided he'd had enough and billed his tardy doctor. When William Ennis sent his doctor a $90 bill for the hour he spent in the waiting room, he became a hero in North America. He received many calls from people - just thanking him for his courage.

What Ennis did was fight back. Although promptness was a recurring problem with his doctor, he'd done everything he thought possible to make sure he would see him promptly at 8:45 am. He'd also made it clear to the receptionist that he didn't want to wait. He even called ahead twice to confirm the time of his appointment.

After waiting an hour, Ennis vowed he wasn't going to take the doctor's lateness sitting down. So, he billed his doctor. When the doctor ignored the bill, he filed a lawsuit. The matter was settled out of court when the doctor agreed to donate the $90 to a community eye bank.

The Ennis' case was unusual. It was a visibly public battle, but it represents a quiet rebellion sweeping the country. Patients who have bucked the traditional waiting game say there are two reasons. They're more crunched for time and they've come to view doctors and other such professionals as simply business people and peers who should have the same time consideration for them. People have become less sheep-like and less in awe of professionals, so they're no longer accepting those inconveniences as a necessity of life. They're attacking the pocketbook of professionals. And it's working.

The bottom line is that a fifteen minute wait is okay - a half-hour or more wait that can't be blamed on an emergency, is unreasonable.

I can't say 'No!'

With your busy lifestyle, you probably have to manipulate your life to fit in all your responsibilities. Then something comes along that blows your plans. You find that people take advantage of you by coercing you into doing things you don't want to do. This can be a frustrating use of your time. Learn how to say *'No.'* Too many people feel guilty about saying *'No,'* but remember you're the master of yourself and have the freedom to choose how you spend your time and energies. Don't get involved in something you don't really want to do just because you couldn't say *'No.'*

Don't respond to requests or demands right away. Give yourself time to see if they really make sense. If you need to say *'No,'* don't feel guilty. Refuse additional requests or demands on your time by learning how to say *'No.'*

Do you find yourself saying *'Yes'* for any of the following reasons?

- You don't want to hurt someone's feelings.
- You don't want to explain why you want to say no.
- You don't want to say anything the other person might interpret as negative.
- You feel compelled to spend time with the person because you haven't seen him or her in months.
- The other person is particularly important to you.
- You would really like to oblige, but the timing is inappropriate.

Learning how to say 'no' when you want to, depends on increasing:

- Your self-respect.
- Your confidence about following your own standards and decisions.
- Your comfort about meeting your own personal needs.
- Your recognition that you aren't responsible for others' feelings.
- Your understanding that your worth does not depend on other people's judgements.
- Your comfort and confidence in pleasing yourself.
- Understanding that you can't please all the people, all the time.

How to say 'NO'

Try the following, should you have trouble saying *'no'* to any situation. Each step forward can help you learn when and how to say *'no'* comfortably.

Step 1: Pick one type of situation where you've said *'yes'* inappropriately several times during the past few months. Concentrate on this area first.

Step 2: Identify your reasons for saying *'Yes.'* Are you concerned that the answer *'no'* might injure the relationship? Are you worried about the other person's feelings?

Step 3: Put together a plan of action for preventing this next time. Mentally prepare yourself to say *'No.'*

Step 4: Practice your new response. Concentrate on how you sound and feel as you say *'No'* in a skilful and thoughtful way. Rehearse with an uninvolved person who has good judgement.

For example you've been willing to pick up a friend to take him to regularly planned meetings. You don't mind helping out, but are irked because he always keeps you waiting. The solution is to inform him of how frustrated you are by having to wait. Then explain that the next time you are to pick him up at 7:00 pm that you'll wait only until 7:05 pm and if he's not ready you'll leave without him. Be strong enough to follow-through with your plan.

Don't allow yourself to feel compelled to return a favour from a friend. Stop saying *'Yes'* to people because you believe *'No'* will hurt their feelings.

CHAPTER THREE

Time management at work

In the business world I've heard the following complaints about time:

1. I have too much to do in my job.
2. Everyone wants everything now!
3. I have no time to do the things I really want to do.
4. Everything is done half-way, not the way I'd like them done.
5. I make mistakes because I hurry and it frustrates me.
6. I wish for once I could finish everything.
7. I want to advance my career, but don't have time to learn the things I require to advance to the next promotional level.
8. I'm sure my boss can't be pleased with my work - because I'm not!

Time 'leakage'

How much time do you lose through these 12 common time 'leaks?'

1. Starting a job before thinking it through. (Prepare 'To Do' Lists.)
2. Doing unproductive things from sheer habit. (Set priorities).
3. Keeping too many unnecessary records. (Clean out files on a regular basis).
4. Paying too much attention to low return on investment items. (Weed out the non-productive use of your time).
5. Failing to anticipate crises. (Use the 'A stitch in time saves nine' of preventive maintenance).
6. Making unnecessary visits or phone calls. (A poor time waster which can be deadly to your career).
7. Socialising for too long time between tasks. (Same as above).
8. Failing to build good barriers against interruptions. (Hold your phone calls and close your office door).
9. Doing things that should be delegated. (Let go of tasks - delegate).
10. Doing things that aren't part of the job. (Make sure you have an up-to-date job description).

11. Failing to plan regularly with your boss. (Set up regular meetings.)
12. Engaging in personal work before starting business work. (Set priorities and stick to them).

Bottlenecks:

Bottlenecks occur whenever a person fails to take essential action, because of indecision, laziness, mistaken priorities, stubbornness, overwork or because they procrastinate.

Supervisors can be bottlenecks when they don't delegate properly so their employees are always busy.

Here's an example of how to deal with one kind of bottleneck. You need to submit month-end reports and require information from people in other departments to complete them. One of the people is always late sending the necessary material to you. You have two choices in dealing with her.

1. Talk to her to identify the problems she's causing you. Start by saying, *'I have a problem and I need your help in solving it.'* Then add: *'For the last three months, I've had to scramble to get my month end report ready. The problem is that I don't have the necessary information from you to complete my report. Is there anything you can do to make sure this doesn't happen in the future? I really need your co-operation on this.'*
2. If step one doesn't work, ask your supervisor to speak to the other person's supervisor so you can get the necessary information on time.
3. Or submit your report stating, 'Information from XYZ department was not available.'

Helping your staff set priorities

How much time does your staff spend determining what are priority As Bs etc.? Do they have to guess what you want done first? Try attaching coloured labels to the work you give them. For instance, you might use a red label for Urgent (require immediate attention), yellow (do today) and green (can wait until tomorrow). On the label, make sure you include date and time of day you need the task completed.

If you share an assistant, make sure you and the other supervisors keep in touch. Have an early morning meeting with them. Instruct your personal assistant to let you know if there is too much to do and help choose priorities by discussing work with the other supervisors.

Are you making the situation easier for your support staff or do you sabotage their success? Assistants suggest that you keep them informed by communicating with them regularly. Many supervisors keep their support staff 'in the dark' as a way of maintaining control. Not only do they maintain control but they isolate themselves from the people hired to help them do a good job.

- Tell your staff what you expect of them.
- Explain how they're doing and what's behind your e-mail.
- Why a particular e-mail is so important
- Where you're going and when you'll be back.

If a client makes a complaint about one of your staff, listen carefully. Then tell them, 'I'll get back to you when I've had an opportunity to investigate this matter.' Try to stay away from situations where you have to make a snap judgment without consulting your staff or giving them the chance to defend their actions.

Let your support staff do some decision-making, especially with routine matters when they know the answers. Have them answer routine e-mails for you. Give your personal assistant the authority to send routine letters on your behalf, leaving critical, sensitive or legal e-mails and letters for your attention. S/he'll gain confidence, feel more important and more a part of the team. Prepare before giving support staff instructions (consideration), don't change it all with an afterthought.

When you make appointments, keep them. Save your staff the embarrassment of having to make excuses for you. When clients or other senior people leave messages or request information, get back to them promptly, otherwise your staff are forced to make explanations for you.

Keep their work-flow consistent. Your assistant must see you early in the day so s/he can help you plan his/her day. Be sure you check your e-mails before sending them – you can't get them back if there are errors.

Make sure your assistants are aware of your deadlines and how much you need their help to reach them. Get their help with such tasks as; making sure files are ready and getting the necessary information for you - anything that will make for a smooth-running project.

Bring-forward file:

Rather than sift through paperwork three or four times, it's handy to have a Bring-forward file. This works for e-mails as well. A bring forward file is usually a pocket file with dates on each pocket or separate files with dates on them for follow-up. Use them to file information about tasks you want to do on specific days.

For instance, you called to speak to George and find he is out-of-town until Friday, the 6th. You would file the information in your BF file for Friday, with a note to remind you what you wanted to ask him. This way you won't forget to call him that particular day.

Is your in-basket out of control?

One of the few certainties of working life is a perpetually refilling in-basket whether it is on our desk or a raft of e-mails we face on our computer. As soon as you reach the bottom, it starts filling up again! Just when you think you've finally gained a grip on things, your control is shattered by catching a glimpse of your overflowing in-basket.

In part, we have progress to thank for this predicament. Technology promised us the paperless office and then promptly gave us faxes, photocopies, computer printouts and spreadsheets. Since we all have better assignments to do than look at every piece of paper the moment it crosses our path, we often wind up with teetering in-baskets. This can add to our personal stress and send a signal to higher-ups in the organisation that we're not on top of our work.

Is there nothing to do, then, but complain? The problem isn't too much paper or too little time. We don't use our in-baskets correctly in the first place. We substitute them for a daily paperwork system. Something lands on our desks and we put it in the in basket and leave it there until we get around to handling it. Eventually everything piles up. Instead, use the philosophy of - toss it, refer it to someone else, act on it or file it. Just don't leave it there.

Handle each paper only once after sorting. This means that if you can't deal with something until Friday, it goes into your bring-forward file for that date. Start a sorting system for your paperwork so, if you can't do something right away, you can keep it somewhere and take care of it later. (Not in your in-basket!) If you have to talk to someone about the information, put that item on your to do list or route the information directly to the individual with a note explaining what you want done with the material.

Keep in mind the 80/20 rule. Only 20% of what lands on your desk are 'A' priorities and at least 20% of it should be thrown away immediately. This is how you can set priorities with all the information from your in-basket and other sources:

1. Classify information into 4 piles - Priority As, Bs, Cs and Ds (I do the same with telephone messages and left over assignments from the day before).
   You should put your Ds in 'File 13' (your garbage can).
   Don't keep anything unless you really have a use for it. You could throw out 20% of your mail and not even miss it!
   Cancel unnecessary subscriptions.
   As the day progresses and new assignments come along, add them to your To Do list (slotting them between two other tasks)
   Update your list as new items come up during the day.
   I make my To Do list in pencil, so I can change a priority A5, to an A6 if necessary. Have one list - not scraps of paper. Remember, it's not crossing out items that counts, but making better use of your time.
   Remember to check your BF (bring forward) file for that day. If you're sorting your mail on Monday and find that there's something you can't do until Friday, put it in your bring forward file for that day. This way, you're only dealing with that piece of paper once after sorting (one crucial time management rule).
2. Now that you have three piles - As, Bs & Cs. Determine whether you have enough time to complete your As. Do you have time to do any Bs as well? If so, add them to your list. If not, put these Bs in your bring forward file for later completion.

3. Find an empty folder and put all your Cs into it and put the file out of sight. Now you can deal exclusively with only the important and urgent items.
4. Make a To Do list of what you wish to accomplish that day. Update 'To Do' list throughout the day (including the time you estimate tasks will take) as you add new assignments.
5. Clear your work area of all unnecessary items. This is the secret for those who always have a messy desk. When everything has its place and everything is in its place, time saving is an obvious asset.
6. Next determine which is your Priority A1, A2, A3, A4, etc. and try to identify the time each task will take to complete.
7. Remember to check your daytimer or calendar for appointments and deadlines.
8. Know your limitations. If you find that you can't do all your tasks that day, decide whether you can delegate any tasks to someone else. Keep your boss informed if you see that you can't finish something.
9. Don't start another project before you finish the first one.
10. Train yourself to focus all your attention on the task you're doing. If you're distracted by other assignment, the job you're doing will suffer. When the next job is on your To Do list, train yourself to forget about it until it's time to tackle that project.
11. Keep a red-coloured file that contains information relevant to phone calls you can expect to receive. If you leave a message for someone to call you, place a little reminder note on the information to remind you of the questions you want to ask them. Keep this file near your telephone for easy access.
12. When you know you're likely to procrastinate when completing certain tasks, make sure you slot those tasks into your high energy time. When they're next on the list, self-discipline can make you 'get it over with' instead of putting it off unnecessarily.
13. Are there days when you wonder what you've been doing all day? Here's when your To Do lists prove their value. Just look at what you've checked off. It also proves to those who monitor your work, that you have completed your tasks. Remember that 80% of the value comes from 20% of your time, so put your time where the value is.

14. Make proper use of filing cabinets. When you finish a project, immediately file it out of the way. Filing cabinets can be a problem too. They often have too much out-dated material in them. Try to determine a discard date when you can eliminate much of the material in each file - just keep the important information.

If you take a stab at desktop organisation and dutifully file everything away and can never find anything again - there's a good reason. You're probably a creative person. Creative people often function best with clutter around them. They need the sensory stimulation. If they try to conform to a system that deprives them of this, they can't do their best work. Still, there are ways for even the most clutter-driven types to keep notes, e-mails and other documents from getting out of control

One helicopter company employee uses humour to keep things in order. He keeps three baskets on his desk. One he labelled 'In.' One he labelled 'Out.' A third he labelled 'Hovering.'

Since creative people get bored with routines quicker, investing in a few gadgets might be the key. Try separating your piles and putting them in see-through plastic file boxes. They're still your piles, but now they'll appear more orderly. Multicoloured notepaper and oversize coloured paper clips can help turn tedious tasks into a game. As for the in-basket - give yourself permission to shuffle through it from time to time to pick out the important items. If you can find something in three minutes or less, you're fine. Files or piles, it doesn't matter, as long as you can find it.

If you're receiving work from more than one person, you might think, 'How can I keep multiple bosses happy when they say everything is a priority red?' The employee should take the stack of red labelled work to each boss and ask his or her co-operation in re-defining what is actually a red priority.

Working overtime

Do you find that overtime is a usual activity rather than the occasional occurrence that it should be? Do you find that you're so tired at the end of the day that it takes you twice the time to complete assignments? Try coming into work early (before the rest of the employees). That extra time at the beginning of the day will enable you to accomplish twice as much because of fewer interruptions. This is far better than trying to fit your work into the end of a stressful day (unless of course - you're not a morning person in the first place).

In most areas, when an employee works over a certain number of hours a week (most often 44 hours) overtime is paid. Their overtime is usually paid at time-and-a-half or even double time. Instead of making their staff work overtime when they're tired, employers would be wise to have someone else come in to do the overtime work. There are several reasons for this:

1. The part-time employee is 'fresh' and not tired after putting in a full-day's work.
3. It enables former employees who wish to work only part-time to keep their skills and knowledge of the company current. This enables former employees (often women with small children) to keep up-to-date on company practices and procedures.
4. A retired person can often provide the skills, wisdom and experience to fill-in for the shorter hours of work.
5. The company saves money on company benefits and by paying straight time rather than time-and-a-half. They'll also save money because they're paying the extra person only straight time instead of paying overtime to a tired employee.

Delegation

When delegating a task to anyone (whether it's to an employee, a child or a friend) you must give them both the responsibility to do the task and the authority necessary to get the job done. Here are some criteria you should know about delegation:

Responsibility: The actual tasks that require completion.

Authority: Having the authority necessary to make the decision and take the appropriate action. Consider these examples:

- An employee had the responsibility of ordering office supplies for his department, so he went to the supply depot to fill the

order. He learned that he couldn't take the supplies because he didn't have signing authority for his department.
- A supervisor asks a staff member to go to Human Resources Department to obtain a personnel file of an employee. They won't release the file because he doesn't have the authority to receive the confidential file.
- A staff member goes to a computer company to pick up a new computer monitor. They refuse to give it to him because he doesn't have a purchase order from the company.

These employees were delegated the responsibility to do the task, but lacked the authority to fulfil their obligations. What an unfortunate waste of the employees' time.

Accountability:

1. Delegated accountability:
   A task is delegated to an employee by the supervisor. The employee is accountable to supervisor for the task.
2. Final accountability:
   This stays with the supervisor (or parent) who delegated the task to the person. Employees must understand that they're accountable to their supervisor but that the supervisor is ultimately responsible for what they do.

Where are you now?

How are you handling your work-load right now? The following will help you determine areas where improvement will help:

1. From memory - try to recap the duties you fulfilled yesterday (or your last working day. Write these down.)
2. For each of your duties - ask yourself the following questions:
   (a) What would have happened if you hadn't done the task?
   (b) What could have happened if you'd left it until later?
   (c) Could someone else have done it? Who?
3. Did you attend to all 'Priority A' matters?
4. Did you feel comfortable that you had a productive day? Why?
5. Were there any bottlenecks that kept you from completing your tasks? What solutions would you suggest?
6. Are you subject to constant interruptions? How do you handle them? Is there a better way?

7. What do you feel you can do to follow-up on the above suggestions? (Start a To Do list to correct any of the above.)

Interruptions and crises

Do you get upset every time the phone rings? Do you find it difficult getting back to your original task? But phone calls can be as important (if not more important) than the task you were doing. Say to yourself, *'That's my job calling!'* Quickly get to the purpose of a telephone call and then recognise your need to return to other priority 'A' tasks. Productivity will increase. Frustration will decrease.

Get back on track after interruptions. Don't use interruptions as excuses to procrastinate. Don't complain or take a break. Ask staff interrupters to write their problems down including perceived solutions to their problems before approaching you for help.

Supervisors should keep an open-door policy so their staff feel confident coming to them when they need help. An employee's major function is to do a good job for the company and make their supervisor look good. Because a supervisor's main function is to help their employees do a good job, it's to the supervisor's advantage to be available when needed. However, this does not mean that they have to coddle their staff.

If supervisors have employees who are constantly interrupting them with trivial matters, they should answer their staff's questions with one of their own. Ask, *'What do you think you should do?'* Most employees know the best solution to their problem, but just want their supervisor's confirmation that they're right. Soon the employees' confidence in their own decision-making ability will make sure that they don't bother the senior official with trivial matters.

If interruptions are the norm for your day, you can start by separating the good interrupters from the bad ones. Good interrupters are those who convey information to you or want answers to important questions that only you can answer. Bad interrupters can be workers who refuse to accept responsibility and want to delegate upward. Others are those that are of low priority when you compare them with your existing priorities. Knowing the difference between the two and applying the systems on this page will help you regain control of interruptions.

Since interruptions have different purposes, you need to classify them and treat them differently. For instance:

How do you deal with idle chatting and non-productive complaining? Depending on your style and workplace atmosphere, you may want to inform others of your ground rules. One might be to have others think twice before interrupting you by asking themselves:

a) Have you stopped to think if you can answer this question without bothering me?
b) You may interrupt me if there is something you think I need to know right away or under one of the following conditions:
- You're genuinely stumped.
- You must make a decision that exceeds your authority.
- You have a personal problem that's affecting your work.
- You have an interpersonal problem with another worker that you've already tried at least twice to resolve.

Kinds of interruptions:

Quickly classify interruptions. It enables you to get the information you need and cuts time lost dealing with people who interrupt for no good purpose or at the wrong time. Using this system, you can group interruptions into four classes based on why and when they happen.

- The right question at the wrong time. A worker has an important question or problem - but arrives at your door when you're unable to devote enough time or attention to it.

Solution: Take a few moments to assure the worker that s/he has made you aware of a valuable piece of information - something you really needed to know. Let your attitude convey your eagerness for further discussion and agree to a time to discuss the problem later.

- The wrong question at the right time. Just because you have a quiet moment is no reason for you to take part in a decision that a worker could make for him or herself.

Solution: If you see that a worker is attempting upward delegation, don't be tempted, even if you do have time to devote to it.

- The wrong question at the wrong time. When a worker interrupts your busy day with an unnecessary question, it's time to let them know you're displeased. Don't, however, just get angry, since that's not instructive and won't cause the worker to improve.

Solution: Underscore your policy about interruptions.

- The right question at the right time. What about the staffer who asks the right question at the right time? That's an activity to reward. Your staffer has shown judgement and tact.

Solution: Encourage more of such activity with statements like, *'I'm glad you brought me up to speed on this at once,'* or, *'Good idea.'* Encouraging excellent judgement will have a greater benefit on departmental operations and will discourage the bad.

How to prevent interruptions

Be less accessible to drop-in visitors by re-organising your work area. Don't have too many chairs in the room or place them too close to your desk. Have a clock in a prominent place for easy referral. Also:

a) Keep a log to determine when, how long and who causes your interruptions.
b) If the person wants to chat, suggest they catch you at coffee break.
c) Set time limits - and stick to them.
d) Meet others in their office, so you can leave when you wish or
e) Meet visitors in a conference room, reception area or in the hall if you want the meeting to be short and there's no need for privacy.
f) If receptionists' desks are of average height, they might feel the need to chat with those waiting for appointments. Solve this problem by installing desks with a higher front. This allows them to continue working, without having the guilty feeling that they're being rude to office visitors. This still allows them to see

over the top of the barricade to check what visitors are doing and to watch the waiting room.

Handle interruptions by setting a time limit and sticking to it. Say, *'I don't have a minute; but I do have five.'* Then start timing. After five minutes, tell the person you have to get back to your original project. Set the stage in advance. Let them know you're really busy! Don't be rude, but keep them informed about your time crunch.

If you're writing a report, keep a pen in your hand or fingers on the keyboard. If a person drops into your office, stay standing. If they sit down on a chair in your office, sit on your desk.

Avoid small talk when you're busy. Small talk makes large interruptions out of what could be small ones. Try not to feel annoyed. Give interrupters undivided attention. Listen carefully. Don't interrupt and don't let your mind drift - it's time-consuming. Help them get to the point. You might ask, *'What do you wish to discuss?'* or *'What can I do for you today?'* Don't be afraid to say *'no'* if they ask for too much (even your boss). If the meeting drags on and you have accomplished what you need, tell them you have another appointment now. Stand up, hold out your hand and ease them towards the door.

Train customers or co-workers to leave detailed messages in your voice mail or send you e-mails. Then you can have the answers ready when you call back or return the e-mail.

If you can't help them now, don't let them go away empty handed. Learn to say *'no'* graciously. Recognise that it is better to say *'no'* at the start than disappoint people because you're over-committed. Or promise to do what they want later. Explain that you're working on other assignments or tell them who else they might ask to help out. Or you might ask, *'Could we continue this, when I'm not so busy?'*

When possible have someone else take your telephone calls. In urgent situations, remove yourself by going to a conference room or other neutral zone.

How to control crises situations

Anticipate known deadlines and potential crises. Don't put tasks off to the last minute. Make contingency plans. Cross-train your staff so if one is away, another can take over. Watch that you don't lose your cool. That just makes matters worse and can alienate others.

Concentrate on solving the problem instead of giving blame to why the problem or crisis occurred. Don't make matters worse, by forgetting good time management. Use your 'fight or flight' energy to find solutions instead of yelling and blaming others. Spend your energy on finding a plan of action that will work. Recognise that this is just part of a normal day - not a catastrophe. It's also an opportunity to use your creative juices to come up with innovative solutions to the problem.

Solutions to time wasters:

Improper use of time by yourself or others causes many problems. Here are some suggestions:

1. Telephone interruptions:

While telephones can be essential lifelines of business, they also can waste a lot of time. An interruption by telephone calls can be distracting and disrupt our flow of concentration when we're working on an important project. It's useful to keep a three-minute timer by the phone to lessen the social aspects of the call. Be careful you're not too abrupt. Other steps to take are:

a) Schedule all calls for a certain time of day.
b) Differentiate between business and personal calls.
c) Keep business calls to business matters.
d) Set a time limit to conversations.
e) List the issues you wish to discuss when making phone calls. Many people encourage chatting. How you respond to someone who's showing signs that they want to chat, will determine the outcome of the conversation.

For example: A regular client phones in and enquires, *'Hi Merle, did you have a nice long week-end?'* They can hook you with this kind of question and you'll probably spend the next fifteen minutes discussing your respective weekends. On the other hand, you could reply, *'It was great, Merle. What can I do for you today?'*

You've steered the conversation right back to the topic. If you feel this is being too abrupt, you might say, *'It was great, Merle. I wish I had time to tell you about it, but I'm swamped. What can I do for you today?'*

2. Drop-in visitors:

Sometimes, we have a need to socialise at the office, but we must be realistic when this becomes detrimental to our effectiveness. Try to encourage others to come to the point. Find a polite way of getting people who ramble, back on track. One way of doing this is to ask concise questions until you get the information. Other solutions are:

(a) Distinguish business and personal visitors and treat accordingly.
(b) Have receptionist screen visitors before they see you.
(c) Discourage socialising - continue with your work.
(d) Be honest with visitors and state for instance, *'I've only got a few minutes - how can I help you.'* - and stick to it!

3. Meetings:

Meetings are held for a variety of reasons - legitimate business, to issue information, to provide an audience for someone, to socialise or simply out of habit. Other meetings are held by people who wish to pass the buck and get others to do tasks they should be doing. Some meetings outlast their original intent and become time wasters.

When preparing for a meeting, be clear about the goals you wish to reach. Give the participants a written agenda ahead of time, so they know what issues you'll be covering and can come prepared. Set time limits and stick to both the agenda and the time limitations.

If you're a supervisor, have regular morning meetings with your assistant to go over your respective To Do lists. When attending meetings, ask yourself, 'Is this meeting really necessary?' Be sure your attendance serves a purpose. Learn the purpose and objectives for a meeting and come prepared with related information. If you call a meeting, prepare a written agenda and distribute it in advance to give attendees time to prepare for the meeting. Then, stick to the agenda.

4. Ineffective delegation:

If you're a supervisor, avoid the tendency to 'Do it yourself.' Instead, think before acting and delegate. Never put off for tomorrow, what you can get someone else to do today. Is there anyone else in the organisation who could perform the task, attend the meeting or travel to the convention? Improve your follow-up when you delegate tasks. Your job description as a supervisor includes consideration, confidence and communication with your staff. Spend more time training subordinates to do a better job. Select the best time of day to do the type of work. Improve your follow-up on delegated tasks.

If you're in a support position:

a) Talk with your manager to see if someone else can handle a duty that you feel doesn't fit your position.
b) Use paraphrasing to make sure you understand what your supervisor expects from you.
c) Ask for written instructions.
d) Have magazines and articles routed to others in the department. Have others circle any interesting article in the Table of Contents. When you receive the magazine back, you'll already know which articles are worth reading.

5. Lack of objectives/priorities and planning:

a) Ask for an up-to-date job description that includes standards of performance.
b) Define priority items.
c) Make 'To Do' lists and follow them.

6. Dealing with crisis situations:

a) Assess how often it happens.
b) Determine how you can stop future crisis (preventive maintenance).
c) Allow time for 'fighting fires' every day.
d) Don't put off or procrastinate (which can start a crisis situation).

7. Attempting too much at once:

a) Set objectives and priorities
b) Make daily To Do lists
c) Know when to say *'No'* to additional duties

8. Cluttered desk - personal disorganisation:

a) Allow time to organise. It will save time later
b) Reduce paperwork

c) Use verbal communication as often as possible
d) Put away anything you're not working on at present.
e) Return everything promptly to its place.

9. Inability to say *'No'*:

(See Chapter 2 for more information on this).

a) Take an assertiveness training course.
b) Realise that you can't please all the people all the time.
c) Recognise traps, manipulative games which can 'con' you into doing things you don't want to do.
d) Offer alternative solutions.
e) Decide the consequences should you say *'Yes.'*
f) Don't feel you have to explain your reasons for saying *'No.'*
g) Count to ten before saying *'Yes.'*
h) Realise that it's better to do *less* well, than *more*, poorly

10. Unclear communication - instruction:

a) Develop listening skills.
b) Practice paraphrasing and feedback.
c) Repeat instructions.

11. Confused responsibility and authority:

a) Have up-to-date job description.
b) Determine your level of responsibility and make sure you have the authority to carry out your responsibilities.
c) Determine your subordinates' level of responsibility and authority

12. Delayed, inaccurate information:

a) Check information source - don't listen to grapevine
b) Identify and deal with bottleneck employees
c) Practice listening skills
d) Use paraphrasing and feedback

13. Lack of self-discipline:

a) Keep a daily To Do list.
b) Set objectives and plan daily.
c) Set priorities and stick to them.
d) Schedule unpleasant tasks *first*.

14. Leaving tasks unfinished:

(a) Same as #13.

15. Untrained, inadequate staff:

a) Use 'old Timers' in your department to train new staff.
b) Ask for training for both you and your staff where required.
c) Know where to find company policy manuals; read and update them regularly.
d) Keep an information file of techniques you've learned for future use.
e) Spend more time training subordinates to do a better job.
f) Ask your assistant, *'How can we improve?'*

16. Socialising:

a) Control the urge.
b) Keep your socialising to coffee and lunch breaks.
c) Keep busy!

17. Indecision - procrastination:

a) Take an assertiveness training course.
b) Daily 'To Do' lists will keep you on track.
c) Ask others to help you determine when you're being indecisive or showing procrastination.
d) Have faith that you have the ability to do the job.

CHAPTER FOUR

Time management at home

Introducing business to home management

Life runs smoothly at the office - but why does it fall apart at home? Where's the gas bill? When is Sally's next dentist appointment? What groceries do I have to pick up on my way home from work?

When you have a dual lifestyle (balancing a career and home duties) it's usually the home front that does you in. Learn to use business techniques in the home as well.

Planning is essential in getting your homemaking chores under control. Use lists for everything; groceries, chores that need doing around the house and yard (and who is expected to do them!) Also learn to set priorities. Is it more important to have a spotless house or to spend an hour teaching Sally how to knit or Johnnie how to fix his bike? Know what's important to you and what you can let slide when more important priorities come along. Your lists should be divided into:

>Have to: (Priority As)
>Need to: (Priority Bs)
>Hope to: (Priority Cs)

Do you find that the daily pressures of work and home responsibilities leave you little time for you to spend just socialising or having private time? You need to find time for yourself. This area is usually low on the list of priorities, but in reality should be near the top. Unless you feel good about yourself and what you're doing, you'll be sacrificing your priorities for others, instead of putting your wishes first.

Wise parents learn that they must learn to be 'selfish' and do special things for themselves too. In turn, they'll be more effective when they're dealing with other parts of their lives. Putting yourself number one is not a sin - it's a necessity (providing you don't take it to excess).

Delegate jobs to your family and follow up. Follow-up to make sure that they've completed the task properly, give them training so they can improve the quality of their performance and give praise for a job well done. Decide what you'll do, if they don't complete their tasks. Be consistent with discipline and fair to all members of your family.

When you're cooking, make multiple batches. It doesn't take much longer to make meals for four days than one. Use your freezer as much as possible and freeze the extra three days' meals. Stop wasting your time picking up groceries every second day. Make fewer trips.

Some leave most of the family chores until the weekend, but find that their family doesn't have time to do activities together. To correct this, do your shopping Thursday evening instead of Saturday. Then, instead of waiting until Saturday to do your laundry (which ties you to your home unless you do all the batches at a Laundromat) pop a batch of dirty laundry into the washer as soon as you get home from work. While you're fixing dinner or mowing the lawn, the clothes are washed. Just before serving dinner, switch the clothes to your dryer. After your meal, fold the clothing. Do a batch of wash every day to keep on top of the chore.

For those jobs that pile up (like cutting the grass, painting the fence, shovelling the driveway, helping with spring cleaning) consider hiring a student to help you out.

How to organise yourself for work

One essential ingredient for men and woman who successfully juggle two demanding roles is Organisation. You must be organised; you just can't hope it will happen.

1. Plan your time: First decide what the important issues are. Some helpful tips are:

- If you find you're constantly late, set your watch 10 minutes ahead and pretend it's right.
- Prepare for the next day by choosing the outfit and accessories you'll be wearing in the morning. Pack your lunch the night before.

- If you tend to procrastinate and put things off - set yourself written deadlines.
- Try to have your family's appointments with dentists, physicians, music lessons etc. within walking distance of home, so older children can go without you.
- Use waiting time properly. Bring letters and reading material with you when you're on the bus or train or if you know you'll have to wait for others. While watching TV, sort out your tool box, do hand mending, sort the laundry, fix the cord on a kettle or do the ironing. Just don't waste that time.
- Get up an hour before everyone else. The bathroom is free and you can make a good start on housework, lunch packing, making a grocery list, polishing the car or watering the lawn.
- Let your fingers do the walking. Phone ahead to make sure the item you need is available.
- Do banking on-line or at an instant teller whenever possible. Pay bills there too.

2. Organise your home:

- Make sure each member of your family has written lists of chores you expect them to do and enforce this list. List chores they must complete on the weekend.
- Buy non-perishable foods in bulk. Try to shop only once a week.
- Keep lists; a grocery list on the fridge that everyone in the family adds to when something is running short.
- Keep paper and pencil by the phone for messages. Have a special place where you keep messages.
- When house cleaning, carry a bag with furniture polish, dust rag, garbage bag etc. with you to save steps.
- Keep non-productive phone calls to a minimum. Discourage drop-in visitors if you have a busy day; explain you're busy.
- Have them tag along while you work if necessary.
- Make full use of convenience foods and appliances (microwave ovens).

3. Clothing:

- Make a list of your existing clothing and note what's missing. Take a little swatch from a seam and carry it with you. You

- won't buy the wrong colour - it will match your existing wardrobe.
- Avoid purchasing hard-to-keep clothing - keep dry cleanable items to a minimum. Watch for dry cleaning specials for the remainder.
- In the summer, consider hiring a 'mother's helper' so they can take care of the babysitting and home care too. Screen applicants for this position carefully - choose the person who has a genuine liking for children and does a good job around the home. Ask questions about how they would deal with emergencies. Do your homework and have emergency phone numbers ready for your substitute parent. This arrangement will eliminate the need for alternative childcare if one of them catch a communicable disease and be refused at their usual day care centre.

Finding the right child care

A mother decides to go back to work, either because she wants to or because it's financially necessary. Though excited about the prospect of returning to work, she's anxious about the contradictory feelings of going back to work versus staying home with her children. How is she going to find time to look after all her home responsibilities?

Who will take care of the children while she's away? The thought of searching for someone else to care for her children gives her cold shivers. She recalls all the horror stories in the newspaper about abusive babysitters and child molesters. Others worry that many nannies and babysitters are from other cultures, which could complicate the upbringing of their children. What these women are really looking for, are replacements for themselves, so they're not likely to find the exact match for their needs. Some compromises must be made, but never at the risk of the children's safety and well-being.

She'll need to check references of child-care workers and listen to her initial instincts about the person. After all, children are a couples' most precious legacy to the future. Even if the feelings about the child care worker are good, she'll still need to check references. If anything is questionable, she should listen to her instincts and look elsewhere. Unfortunately, many parents don't listen to their instinctive responses and serious problems are the result.

Obtaining help at home

Call a family conference whenever there's an important issue that involves the entire family. This could be when Mom goes back to work or when Dad gets a promotion and the family needs to move to another city. Have a meeting when a relative is very ill and may die or any other important family issue.

Leave 'chore' lists for your children for tasks you expect them to do during the day while you're at work. Make them feel part of a team - that they're contributing something valuable to the family unit. Plan special treats to reward good performance.

You may have scoffed at the above suggestion - because your children do little, if anything, to help out around the home. If you're working at a job away from the home (mothers and fathers too) it's time for your children to pull their load and do their share of the chores around the home. Hold family conferences to discuss problems within the family and to delegate new responsibilities. You also can use these conferences to touch base with how family members are doing towards completing tasks and activities.

To prepare for a family conference on delegation of tasks, the parents write down all the chores they need completed around the home and yard (include everything). Make a copy for each member of the family who's old enough to read. At the family conference:

1. Discuss the chores with your family and explain that because you work all day, you need their help in completing all the chores on the list.
2. Have each member look over the list and ask them to volunteer (yes volunteer!) for certain chores. Have them make a commitment to you that they will do the chores they've chosen. Don't eliminate children 'because they're too young' - even a two-year-old can do the following chores:
   a. put his or her dirty clothes in the clothes hamper
   b. put his or her toys away when required
   c. help with the dusting
   d. make shelves neat (your plastic dishes, pots and pans)

e. arrange shoes in a closet
3. Delegate the leftover chores to the applicable person. Again, get their commitment that they'll complete the chores and you're depending on them to do their assigned chores.

Explain to your children that once they've made a commitment to you, that you won't nag them to do their chores, but will expect them to live up to their promises. Be sure to give positive feedback when you see they've done a job well. To make sure this process works, make sure you give rewards, signs of love and appreciation. Acknowledge jobs well done and arrange special family treats for exceptional work or anything above and beyond the call of duty.

Make sure they've received the necessary training to carry out their delegated duties. Pretend they're a subordinate at work and you're training them how to do a task. Set standards of performance, so they know exactly what you expect from them. Your idea of 'clean' might differ widely from their description. Confirm that your spouse does his or her equal share.

If you've received the excuse, *'I don't have time,'* help them plan their time. Try to avoid power struggles. If one teenager or child has the job of taking out the garbage, another cleans the bathroom (including the toilet) while another mows the lawn. Start job rotation to guarantee completion of distasteful chores. As a last resort, cut allowances and pay a neighbour's child to do the chores your children won't do.

One woman complained, *'My children have a lazy streak in them, but then, so does my husband. They keep putting off chores until I end up doing them myself.'*

Have a family conference, and then do what supervisors do in the workplace - find their hot button and push it. Some motivators that can encourage them to do their share are: money, extra benefits or privileges, better working conditions or the work itself (different chores). Giving them a sense of security is another motivator. Removal of security works well. This would involve removal of allowances or privileges. For instance, a mother who has to clean up her children's mess when she arrives home from work, could state that they're responsible for preparing their own dinner because she's busy cleaning up their mess.

In business, a good motivator is competition and challenge. The best motivator of all, however, are awards, praise and recognition of a job well done.

Start by explaining exactly what you expect of them (in writing, so they can refer to your instructions) then give them ample opportunity to improve their performance. If they refuse to conform, explain the consequences, if they fail again (you choose what happens - discipline or withdrawal of privileges).

In many families, a unique problem is surfacing. When grown children leave home, we assume that they'll stay away, eventually get married and carry on with their lives. With the economic downturn, however, many of these grown children have returned to the safety of their parents' homes. In addition to having extra mouths to feed and tend for, parents revert to old supervisory roles. Adult children expect all the privileges they had as children. A conscious effort and frank discussion are necessary if two generations of adults are to live together harmoniously.

All sorts of new situations will arise. For example: where it was not acceptable earlier for a parent to consider allowing children conjugal rights with a partner, now their grown children may want and expect this privilege.

In the middle

Often adults in their forties, who are still responsible for growing children, find they have the added responsibility for aging parents as well. These middle caregivers might feel pulled at both ends by the needs of their children, their work, their home responsibilities and their parents. They may wonder when they'll have time to spend on activities they want to do themselves. We're seeing three-generational family conferences becoming more prevalent.

In other families, by the time their children have grown, the parents can spend more time, energy and effort on not only their own needs, but those of their parents. The change in roles - children looking after parents and parents becoming dependent on children, is a transition for all involved. Suddenly the parental support the grown children had expected to last a lifetime and had counted on has disappeared. Some feel as if life has cheated them and they feel adrift in life for the first time.

Women do most of the looking-after of elderly parents regardless of whether they're their own parents or their spouses'. Most have full-time jobs and children of their own. As the demands increase, the part of their life that suffers most is their fun time with friends, their children and their spouses. It also can have a heavy financial toll if the woman has to give up her full- or part-time job to become a parent's caregiver. This continues, even when the burden of the 'hands-on-care' is over and the parent is in a nursing home. She continues to be the parents' watchdog, is defender of their rights and protector of their wellbeing. Men are encouraged to give more support with aging parents.

Grandparents too, have had to adjust to the shift in traditional roles. They now face family units made up of children, step-children, parents and step-parents and all the problems that go with those relationships. Because forty per cent of marriages end in divorce, the role of grandparents is changing. Some grandparents lose contact with their grandchildren when one parent moves away or an estranged in-law won't let grandparents have access to the children.

Other grandparents find the opposite and find themselves back in the parenting roll they felt was over when their children grew up. These grandparents find themselves in the middle of the dropping-off-and-picking-up routine when the custodial parent needs economical day care or after-school tending of their children. In many cultures, extended families are the norm and grandparents provide this care, whether the parents are divorced or together. However, in most of North American society, this just isn't an option, because of the distance between grandparents, their children and grandchildren. The need for effective time management is paramount in all the above family mixes.

How to give your family 'loving time'

Parents face common challenges: How to make the most of the time they have with their children, when time is a premium? And how can they make sure their children get the love and attention they need when parents are away from home eight hours plus a day?

These are questions most parents can't even ask their own parents, who probably never had to answer them. Both parents must find time for the following:

- Spend individual time with each child where they can have 'special' time with each parent. This can be 10 to 15 minutes each day and a set time on the weekend.
- Keep track of your children's 'other lives' - at the babysitter, the day care, kindergarten, school, sports and artistic activities. Learn about special events at school and take time to attend. Make it the responsibility of your children to keep you informed.
- Practice effective listening - try not to be judgmental. Don't make contact times with your children an inquisition. 'Hear' what your children are not saying - watch their body language.
- Drop unnecessary steps to complete tasks that will give you more time with your family. Prioritise activities, remembering that your children should hold a high priority for your home time.
- Enlist children's help or ask for their presence when you're doing chores, so you can 'chat.' Parents could converse with their children while changing the oil in their car and encourage the child to hand the necessary tools to them. Or other children could help bring items out of the refrigerator and help make a salad while they talk to their parent.
- Plan special outings that fit individual needs. At a family conference, have each member state the special activities they like to do as a family. Use this list when planning special outings.

At one time, I wanted to reward my children because of all the hard work they'd done to help me with chores. Many times (without being told) they pitched in and simply did the tasks. I wanted to reward them and tried to think of a reward they deserved.

They had never seen a theatre production with live actors before, so (even though the tickets were very expensive) I decided to buy tickets. Thank goodness, I consulted them before doing so. When asked what they'd like for a treat for all their hard work, they surprised me by suggesting that we go on a picnic to one of their favourite spots. I learned a lesson that day. What I thought was a reward for them, was not what they would have chosen for themselves. So ask them what they would prefer, rather than choosing the reward yourself.

- Learn to be aware of your stress level - don't over-react to minor incidences with your children. If you've had a bad day, explain this to your children and ask if you can talk to them later. Don't put them off too long - do follow-up on things they need to discuss with you.
- Don't feel guilty when you need 'private time.' Honour your children's need for privacy too. If you come home from work tired out, rather than brushing by your children without comment, admit to them that you've 'had a bad day.' Explain to them that you need a few minutes alone to, 'get your act together.' This is important, because children often assume that you're mad at them, rather than just tired from a hard day at work. You may find that they copy your actions when they've had a hard day too. Rather than snap at you they'll say, 'I need some time out Mom. I'll talk to you later about this.'

Are you a night or morning person?

Does it matter when your high-energy time is during the day? Yes it does. It affects everything you do. For instance, if you're the sort that needs three cups of coffee and it's 10:00 am before you really feel alive, then you're going to be in trouble at a 9:00 am meeting. However, at 7:00 pm, you're probably raring to go.

You probably already know where you fit, but the following questionnaire might enlighten you more:

1. What time do you feel best about getting up?
    (5) 5 to 6:30 am.
    (4) 6:30 to 7:45 am.
    (3) 7:45 to 9:45 am.
    (2) 9:45 to 11 am.
    (1) 11 am to noon

2. How easy is it for you to get up in the morning?
    (1) Not at all easy
    (2) Not very easy
    (3) Fairly easy
    (4) Very easy
3. How tired do you feel the first hour after waking up?
    (1) Very tired
    (2) Fairly tired
    (3) Fairly refreshed
    (4) Very refreshed
4. You have a meeting tomorrow. What time do you think you'll give your best performance?
    (6) From 8 to 10 am.
    (4) 10 am to 1 pm.
    (2) 1 to 5 pm.
    (0) 7 to 9 pm.
5. One night you must remain awake between midnight and 4 a.m. for a work assignment. You have no commitments the next day. Which alternative suits you best? (Choose only one).
    (1) You would not go to bed until after the watch is over
    (2) You would take a nap before and sleep after
    (3) You would sleep before and nap after
    (4) You would take all sleep before the watch
6. A friend invites you to jog with him. He jogs between 7 and 8 am. How do you think you would perform?
    (4) Well
    (3) Reasonably well
    (2) Would find it difficult
    (1) Would find it very difficult
7. If you have to wake up at a specific time every morning, how dependent are you on an alarm clock?
    (4) Not at all
    (3) Slightly
    (2) Fairly dependent
    (1) Very dependent
8. At what time in the evening do you feel tired and need sleep:
    (5) 8 to 9 pm.
    (4) 9 to 10:30 pm.
    (3) 10:30 to 12:00 am.

(2) 12:00 to 2 am.
(1) 2 to 3 am.

Add up the scores for each answer. The higher the score, the more likely you are to be a morning person. A score of 22 is halfway between morning and night lark.

The hurry-up epidemic

In the past 50 years, our culture has sped up at an accelerating rate. If someone was transplanted from the 60's to the present, they'd be amazed at how fast things go, from the speed of our cars, to the pace of our movies.

People used to operate on the yearly, monthly and daily cycles of the sun and the moon, tides and seasons. Increasingly, we're living in a new, artificial kind of time that clicks by at the lightening-fast pace of computers. While the most basic human time reference is 60 seconds, a computer operates in nanoseconds - and one-billionth of a second is a unit of time beyond our ability to experience. Snapping your fingers - once the symbol of instant response - takes 500 million nanoseconds!

All the high-tech devices that were to give us more free time have had the opposite effect. One need never be further out of touch with our offices than the nearest phone or computer. Many people find it impossible to escape, no matter where they are. In the past decade, the average person's work-week has skyrocketed from an average of 40 hours to 48 hours. We're actually getting back very little from our high-speed gadgets - and we're losing our humanity in the process.

How to 'hang loose'

Tired of feeling trapped in a race against time? Time sickness can be cured. Coping with it can be as simple as sitting back in your chair or as involved as biofeedback, hypnosis or meditation. These techniques will help you slow down as well as become more productive.

Reset your inner clock. Does 15 minutes sometimes feel like 15 seconds? Individuals on the fast-track often have an accelerated sense of time because of the pressure to get tasks done - that only adds to their stress level. However, you could change your perception of time.

Take a time out. The first time-technique many therapists recommend to a time-sick person is to sit quietly for 10 - 15 minutes, four times a week. If you're at home, turn off the television or radio, turn on the answering machine and dim the lights. If you're at the office, close the door and have your calls held. Day One will be the hardest. Those 15 minutes will feel like an hour, but the more you do it the easier it will become. I call these 'mental health breaks.'

Set your priorities. Family is, friends are and perhaps only some parts of your job are priorities. Decide what is possible to accomplish, then be ruthless with time bandits. Shorten endless calls or unimportant office visits, with a polite *'Thank you for calling,'* or *'I have to prepare for a meeting now.'*

Find small ways to get back in touch with the natural flow of time. Ditch the digital watch because all you have are numbers screaming, *'Do it now!'*

Adjust your schedule to fit your personality type. Not everyone would be happy dropping out or moving to Hawaii or the Mediterranean. Nevertheless, most of us are more efficient when we take time off occasionally to refuel. Learn to put everything into perspective.

CHAPTER FIVE

The importance of goal setting

Where do you want to go?

A goal is a dream with a time frame. It's an effective method of planning for the future and gives life direction and a destination. It's important to write down your goals, so you can refer to them and can tell when you've reached them. Start by setting realistic, written goals.

It's unusual how some people spend their goal-setting energies only on pleasurable activities. For instance, they'll save for years for a trip to the Mediterranean yet won't spend one minute finding out what job would be the best for them. This doesn't make much sense considering that they'll be spending about ten hours a day, five days a week either getting ready for, travelling to or working for most of their adult lives.

Unless you participate in personal goal setting, you'll be missing out on one of the great highs in life. Mainly, we set goals to better ourselves or to reach a higher station in life. Many people set goals too low or give themselves escape clauses and wonder why they accomplish so little.

We can change all this by setting concrete goals for ourselves and writing them down. Goals are statements of measurable results we want to achieve. They provide a means for translating wishes into reality. They help people know when they've achieved or won and provide a basis for determining where to concentrate their effort in the future.

How often should you set goals? As often as necessary. Goal setting, whether it is a career or lifetime goal is an ongoing activity. As we set one goal, it's necessary to have another simmering on the 'back burner' that we can sink our teeth into as soon as we reach our earlier goal. Otherwise, you're likely to have a 'downer' when you reach your original goal.

Think about the last time you made plans for a special holiday. Remember the plans you made and how it became a large part of your life until it happened? Do you remember too, that when you came back, you felt somehow empty? This empty feeling would not have occurred if you'd prepared by having something exciting to return to. You could have planned a party with your friends to share the photographs you took on your vacation. Or before you went on your trip, you started working towards other goals.

Should you only work on one goal at a time? No - you can work towards several at one time, possibly one in each quadrant of your life - personal, family and career.

Lifetime and career goals

To be completely successful, set your goals in several facets of your life. You'll want to make personal, family, social, financial, spiritual, community and career goals. Here are examples of lifetime and career goals.

Lifetime goal: By the time I reach 30 years of age, I'll marry, have two children and be employed as a professional engineer.

Career goal: Before December of this year I'll become Assistant Buyer for my firm (a short-term career goal). Within five years I'll become Merchandising Manager for a clothing firm (a long-term goal).

The importance of setting goals

As I mentioned earlier, it's important that you channel you life in the direction you wish it to go. If you simply put your head down and do your work, you'll often lose track of what is really important in life. With our busy lifestyles, it's easy to continue doing what we've been doing and 'go with the flow.' Some people float through life without setting goals and drift into situations almost by accident. Some find themselves in a rut, but don't know how to get out of it. Others waste their talents and abilities waiting for 'something to happen.' Don't wait for something to happen - make it happen! Accomplish this with serious goal setting.

It's amazing how many people never spend time determining what they want out of life, nor how they intend to reach their goals. If you're already a goal setter, you may be ready for a reminder that goal setting is a life-time activity.

Think about the successful people you know. Did they put a lot of time, energy, effort and dedication into getting where they wanted to go? You'll probably find that they did, because success doesn't come without all of those attributes. You have to be willing to put out that energy. We're only on this merry-go-round once, so why not ride your favourite coloured horse?

Types of goals

Positive/negative goals

It's important that your goals are positive rather than negative. It's easier to start doing something, than to stop doing something you don't want to do. For instance, a positive goal could be: *'I'll budget my income better so that I can use it to ...'* Rather than a negative goal: *'I'll stop wasting money on unnecessary expenses.'*

Short and long-term goals

Goals can be short or long term. A short-term goal can take one day, one week or possibly up to six months to complete. It's usually part of a long-term goal which can take from six months to ten years or more. Long term goals are harder to realise, so if possible break them down into shorter, more easily managed goals.

Tangible and intangible goals

Then there are tangible and intangible goals. Tangible goals are those that relate to something you can see and touch. Intangible goals relate to behaviour and attitudes and are harder to achieve than tangible goals.

Framing my goals so they're attainable

Just stating your goals is not enough. Your goals must be clear and attainable. Here are some examples of good and bad lifetime goals:

1. To improve my tennis game by June 1st, 20__, at a cost not to exceed $150.00.

For practical purposes this may be okay, since presumably the only one who needs to know, is the one affected. From a purely goal setting standpoint however, this is weak. What does 'improve' mean? Is it related to serve, backhand, volley, foot work or all of these? If not identified in the goal itself, the specific results should be part of the action plan. This could be as simple as meeting the approval of your instructor or your tennis partner. One of the expense factors to consider would be the amount of time you'll be committing.

So your re-written goal would be:

Suggested: To win the approval of my tennis partner for my court performance by June 1st, 20__, with an investment of five practice hours per week and an out of pocket expenses not to exceed $150.00.

2. To give up smoking.

Obviously, you will need a target date at the very least. That may be all you need to add if you plan to do it 'cold turkey.' Otherwise, if you plan to taper down or introduce some compensating activities, your action plan becomes critical. You won't require cost factors unless you plan to enrol in a group or incur some other directly-related expense. However, as a strong incentive to quit, you could use the savings you'll derive by not buying cigarettes to buy something special for yourself.

Suggested: To give up smoking by September 1st, 20__. Action plan: Reduce to one pack per day by July 2nd: half a pack per day by August 1st: five cigarettes per day by August 15th: and none by September 1st, 20__.

3. To read one novel a month for the next 12 months, five hours a week, at a cost not to exceed $100.00.

This goal statement is okay. Set up a simple chart where you can record the novels you've read and the date you finished them. You could drastically cut the cost factor by using your public library.

4. To spend more time with my family, starting immediately.

This is a nice statement of intent (like a New Year's resolution) that has little likelihood of producing meaningful results. It needs to be much more specific and would need agreement and commitment from the rest of the family. (In this case, time would not be a cost since time spent is the result you're looking for.)

Suggested: To spend a minimum of one weekend day per month with family planned activities, beginning immediately, at an average out of pocket cost not to exceed $35.00 per occasion.

5. To learn five different square dances by September 1st, 20__.

Since you've related this to a specific course of instruction, this goal statement would be all right simply by adding the cost factors.

Suggested: To learn five different square dances by September 1st, 20___, spending three hours per week for the next eight weeks, for a total cost of $50.00.

6. To get a better job.

This goal is too large and too general. Break it down into smaller, more specific components before tackling this goal.

Suggested: To obtain career counselling and decide which two careers I might pursue By May 1, 20___.

An additional goal could be:

Suggested: To speak to at least three mid-management people in marketing to find out what they like and dislike about their jobs and how they reached the level of position they're in now. I'll complete this by May 15th, 20___.

7. To get more education by the end of the year.

As there are no quantitative and qualitative measures, nor time deadlines - you're not likely to meet this goal.

Suggested: I'll complete and obtain an above 70 mark in three courses towards a certificate in Computer Programming at the Computer Institute before June 17, 20___.

Guidelines for setting personal goals

The first kind of goal setting you could try is personal goals. Here are some guidelines that will keep you on track:

1. Your goals must belong to you and be your individual goal.

You're more likely to accomplish personal goals that you set for yourself than if you strive to achieve goals others want you to accomplish. This doesn't mean you can't accept the goals of your spouse, a friend or boss as yours. Consciously think and talk through the advantages and disadvantages of working towards a goal before deciding to pursue it. Prior knowledge of who you are and what you want, is essential, so you can establish goals based on your own internalised values

2. Goals need to be clear, concrete and written.

The purpose of writing goals is to clarify and make them concrete for yourself. Writing and revising goals also forces you to make a commitment to yourself. Once you've written a goal, you'll have more invested in it than before. Writing keeps the goal in front of you and reduces the chance you'll forget about it, as new problems and challenges appear. It helps integrate your goals into projects and identifies conflicting goals. It also takes the emotion out of goal setting and forces you to stand back and be more objective.

3. Start with short range goals.

Learning involves making mistakes as well as achieving success. Start your goal-setting by working on some short range goals that are easily attainable. Short range goals are more likely to be within your control. As you accomplish these, you'll gain more confidence to tackle the more challenging long-range goals. Don't concern yourself if you have to revise your first statement of goals more than once. Life is not stable and situations do change.

4. Consider legality, morality and ethics in your goals.

Most peoples' value systems include some degree of concern with the legality, morality and ethics of their actions. You should consider these before you commit yourself to a goal. This would include such situations as cheating on an exam or misleading others in a harmful way.

5. Goals require realism and should be attainable.

Having a goal is the first step to action. However, if your goal is unrealistic or unattainable - it's not even a goal - but fantasy and daydreaming. The higher the goal; the stronger the motivation. However, if you don't believe accomplishment is possible, there's probably no motivation. If it feels right and makes sense to you and your respected friends, then your goal *is* possible.

6. Specific time deadlines aid in accomplishment of goals.

Assigning target dates for completing each step of a plan, provides constant reinforcement and a sense of accomplishment that can help maintain your motivation. You can and should adjust dates, but make sure your excuses are authentic. Put crucial dates such as deadlines into your daytimer. You might find it helpful to write yourself a contract - stating what you're going to do. Give it to a friend so you won't renege. Then, have a contract-burning ceremony or party when you achieve your goal. This kind of contract is especially helpful when you're trying to stop smoking or want to lose weight.

Guidelines for setting career goals

What is a career? The word 'career' has a negative connotation to many people. It conjures up the image of someone totally dedicated to work, someone who always has his or her nose to the grindstone. If this image has put you off the idea of setting career goals, consider the following definitions - and think again.

A job is a position with specific duties and responsibilities. For example, teaching Grade 3 at Hillside Elementary School is a job.

An occupation is a group of similar jobs in society. It's a broad category that may or may not be specific to a particular company, government department organisation, industry or profession (teacher, engineer, accountant, personal assistant, carpenter, plumber, etc.).

A career includes all your work-related experience, including both paid and unpaid labour. Work-related experience includes full and part-time work, parenting and homemaking, volunteer and community work, hobbies and other leisure activities that may influence a person's work now or in the future. People may change jobs or even occupations, but each person has only one career. A job is what you do with your days - a career is what you do with your life!

Career steps

There are five major steps in planning a career:

1. Obtain career counselling and identify your transferrable skills:

If you find that you have trouble motivating yourself or you have little or no incentive to do a good job, you owe it to yourself and your company to change jobs.

Many people stay in an unsatisfactory job because they simply don't know what else they'd like to do. You should find a career counsellor while you're still employed. You'll likely find these through your local government or at universities and colleges.

Qualified career counsellors can help you decide which careers will use, not only your existing skills, but your potential skills as well. They can help you identify your transferrable skills that can you can use in a myriad of occupations. Transferrable skills are those skills you can take from one occupational field into another. For example, supervisory skills, interpersonal skills, accounting knowledge, aptitude with figures and scheduling skills are all transferrable skills. This will allow new horizons to open up for you.

You might consider our career counselling service, found on: www.dealingwithdifficultpeople.info/unique-career-counselling-service

2. Choose your career:

After rating your strengths, weaknesses, your likes and dislikes and make many choices, you'll likely come up with several choices of occupations. Choose two or three occupations. Your next step is to determine if there is a market for those careers. Talk to at least two or three people in each of your chosen occupations. This is necessary because one may be in the wrong profession. Ask them:

- What do you like about your job?
- What do you dislike about your job?
- What is your normal day like? What tasks do you perform?
- How did you get to the position you're in.

- What education and experience were necessary?
- If you could to do it over, would you still choose that profession?

3. Return to learning:
Then, you'll want to plan where and when you'll receive the necessary training or education, what kind of company will provide the proper on-the-job training (if applicable) what knowledge you'll need before being ready for the next step up.

4. Find a vacant position:
This can be through word-of-mouth or through an advertisement in the newspaper or on-line. Some find a position through employment agencies. (In most countries, employment agencies don't charge the applicant - they charge the employer. So apply at several: it won't cost you anything for their help). If you're applying to an advertisement, circle the verbs or action words they use. Then use those action words in your resume and covering letter. This will give you an edge over other candidates. Answer all questions asked in the advertisement. Recruiters look for similarities between your qualifications and the job requirements (but don't lie!) Every new job applied for, should have a custom-built resume.

5. Apply for the job:
Many people don't use a resume. They fill in an application form and hope it will represent them well. Unfortunately, it doesn't - so use a resume - a good one that 'sells' your unique talents and abilities. This applies to blue- and pink-collar as well as white-collar workers!

6. Attend an interview:
Usually, the only thing representing you before an interview is your resume. If it isn't 'up to par,' you likely won't be asked to come for an interview. If they ask you to come for an interview, remember that you're there to 'sell' yourself - don't let shyness keep you from 'tooting your horn.' Know your strengths and weaknesses and be ready to discuss them with the interviewer. Have your facts clear in your mind, expect their questions and have information handy that they may need.

Know as much as you can about their company - its products and service. Make sure your physical appearance is neat and clean and that your apparel suits the position for which you're applying. Never, under any circumstances, wear old jeans or cords to an interview. Blue-collar workers may wear clean jeans and cords, but if you're an office worker wear apparel one step up from the vacant position. The interviewer knows that you'll be better dressed than you would be on the job. So if you come in wearing an outfit with stains on it or needs pressing, they know you'll be wearing something even worse when you're on the job.

Remember that you only have one chance to make a good first impression. Most employers decide whether they're going to hire you within the first four minutes of the interview. Your physical appearance plays a large role in that decision-making.

7. Send a thank-you note:
Follow-up with a thank you note to the interviewer. This will set you apart from other applicants.

8. Start your new job.

How can I start to plan my goals?

Life inventory
To find out where you want to go, you have to know where you are now and what your desires are. To help with this, complete the following on a piece of paper. List everything that comes to mind; don't censor anything. Consider asking a friend to help after you make an initial list.

1. Peak experiences I've had:

List the special moments in your life. They don't have to be the most exquisite moments you've ever had. There are or have been particular times when you felt you were really living and enjoying life to the fullest (self-actualisation).

2. Peak experiences I'd like to have:

These are situations you want to happen to you (a kind of 'bucket list'). Also list here peak experiences you'd like to have again.

3. Things I do well:

Quickly list your strengths. Notice that things you do well aren't always that fulfilling.

4. Things I do poorly:

Note these activities that you do not do well, but for some reason you want to or have to do them. However, don't list activities that you have no interest in doing or don't need to do.

5. Things I'd like to stop doing:

Do you have habits you consider bad? Are there things you have to do, but don't want to do?

6. Things I'd like to learn to do well:

What do you want to learn? What must you learn if you are to meet your goals?

7. Things I'd like to start doing now!

Be creative - dream a little!

Planning:

To start your planning, write down the following (be specific):

1. What are your lifetime goals? Make separate lists for personal, family, social, financial, spiritual and community goals. Give each portion of your goals time limits.
2. Then prioritise each list, 1, 2, 3, etc.
3. To help yourself define these goals, consider,
   a. If you could live anywhere in the world, where would that be?
   b. If you could have any kind of job or career you wanted, what would you want to do?
   c. What goals do you expect to reach within 2 years?
   d. How would you spend your life if you knew you had only 6 months left to live? (You have an inoperable aneurism, but will be healthy until the last).
   e. If you found out you had 24 hours to live, what would be the 5 most important things you'd want to do?

On question 3 (d), did you put down that you'd likely travel or spend more time with your family? That's what most people jot down here. Whatever you've identified in this question identifies what is truly important to you. If you said you'd spend more time with your family - why aren't you doing that now, instead of waiting until it's forced upon you? If you want to travel - why aren't you making plans now to make it happen?

Goal setting plan

When setting any life or career goals for myself, I use the following plan to keep myself on track and make my goals far more concrete. It's very simplistic, but it works. Steps 4, 5 and 6 will keep you heading in the right direction and help you reach your goal.

Step 1: Describe the situation as it is now (what you're doing now).

Step 2: Describe the ideal situation (what you'd like to be doing).

Step 3: Identify the gap between 1 and 2. (This is your goal, which should fill the gap.)

Step 4: List the driving and restraining forces. (Driving forces describe the benefits you'll derive when you reach your goal. Restraining forces are the obstacles that may be in your way that may keep you from reaching your goal. What problems might you face? What are the possible spin-off problems?)

Step 5: List ways you will overcome the restraining forces. (This is where you'll brainstorm.)

Step 6: Formulate a plan of action that includes these four headings:

Step:
Date or Time Limit:
People to Involve:
Resources Required.

Step 7: Implement your plan of action

Step 8: Evaluate the success of implementing your plan.

Driving & restraining forces

In Step 4, it's important to identify the driving and restraining forces. These lists give a clear picture of the benefits you'll have when your goal is achieved. For instance if your goal was to lose weight, you'd read your driving force list when you're tempted to take that piece of chocolate cake. By identifying the restraining forces, you'll be fully aware of the problems you might face. This enables you to come up with a plan of action that will help you go over, under, around or through obstacles that get in your way.

Here's an example of how you could identify driving and restraining forces. Let's say you've set your goal to lose ten pounds and want to do so by August 1st, 20___. Identify the driving forces that will keep you striving to obtain your goal and the restraining forces, so you will know what you're up against.

The following will give you an example of how you would do this if you were trying to lose weight:

Driving Forces:

I'll be healthier.
I can buy new clothes.
I'll feel better.
I'll live longer.
I'll be in better shape physically
I can do more.

Restraining Forces:

I like to eat!
My friends eat a lot too!
I'll have to buy new clothes.
Food and exercise plan may cost more.
I'll have to exercise!
I'll have to starve!

Rules for brainstorming

Step 5 is important because it enables you to find ways of overcoming your restraining forces. To do this, try brainstorming to come up with unique or creative ways to eliminate your restraining forces.

Brainstorming started in the workplace and normally involves groups of people. It's a way of coming up with very unique ways of solving problems. The advantage of using brainstorming is that not only do you come up with Plan A, but Plan B and C as well. Many job-finding groups find brainstorming an invaluable tool. Whether you're brainstorming alone or in a group, for business or home life, use these guidelines:

1. Concentrate on one restraining force at a time.
2. Encourage idea quantity. At this point, quality is not considered important. What you're seeking is as many ideas and suggestions as possible.
3. In group brainstorming, discourage critical judgment and evaluation. No one is allowed to say, *'That won't work because ...'* during a brainstorming session (not even you!) You're looking for ways of getting ideas, not trying to suppress them. Someone's idea (which really won't work) just might be the idea that triggers someone else to think of one that will work.
4. Encourage wild thinking and build on an idea. Offer any idea, no matter how questionable and encourage the group (or yourself) to build on ideas, altering, expanding and changing them. The purpose here is to get ideas, not to pass judgment on them.
5. During the actual brainstorming (which is of very short duration) there should be no side discussions. All members of the group are to concentrate their energies on coming up with additional ideas.
6. In group discussions, don't allow outside observers. Everyone in the room has to participate. Everyone should offer at least two suggestions during the session.
7. The brainstorming session itself should not last less than five minutes or more than fifteen. Shorter lengths of time don't allow enough good ideas to surface and after fifteen minutes, the greater portion of the ideas become clearly impractical.
8. One member of the group should take notes, recording the ideas as fast as they're offered. When working in groups it's a good idea to have the suggestions listed on a flip chart where everyone can see them. Previous ideas lead to further suggestions.
9. Have an idea or two in the back of your head to get the session started. This will provide a trigger to get the session moving. Once it begins, the ideas come fast and furiously.

In our example of losing weight, one of the restraining forces was that your friends and co-workers eat a lot too. Let's say you normally have coffee with your friends every morning and you've been in the habit of buying gooey cinnamon buns. If you want to lose weight, it's not going to be easy for you to resist if you have coffee break with them. You might have to grab an apple and walk around the block for coffee break to get through it. This way, you've removed one of the restraining forces that might have kept you from reaching your goal. In addition you'll have had some exercise and a healthy snack. You'll need to tackle each restraining force so you can remove all possible obstacles.

Using the goal setting plan

To describe how the process works, here is an example of a goal taken through the process:

Step 1: The situation as it is now

I have no supervisory experience or training.

Step 2: The ideal situation

I need supervisory training so I'll be prepared for a future supervisory promotion.

Step 3: The gap (or goal)

To obtain supervisory training (A general goal). I'll complete and obtain an above 70 mark in one course towards a Business Administration Certificate by March 15, 20__. (Specific goal).

Step 4: List the Driving and Restraining forces

Driving forces: (Benefits of reaching the goal)
- I'll be ready for a promotion.
- I want to learn, am ready to learn.
- I'll earn more money.
- I'll gain more status.
- I'll use my abilities better.
- I feel I can do it.
- My employer, co-workers and family have offered their help.

Restraining forces: (Obstacles to overcome)
a) I'm not sure what courses to take.
b) It will cost money.
c) I'll have less time for my family.
d) I've forgotten how to study and will have too many family distractions.
e) I could have problems with transportation and parking.
f) It's a long term goal; can I do it?
g) I won't have time to do everything I have to do.

Step 5: Determine ways to overcome restraining forces

The results of brainstorming in this example are:

a) I'll talk to the representatives at Smith College and Jasper University to determine what courses I should take and how much each of those choices will cost.
b) I'll talk to my employer to see if my company will help me with the cost of training.
c) I'll determine how I can eliminate all the extra activities that take me away from my family and from obtaining the training I need.
d) It will take time to re-learn the skill of studying - so I'll ask for my family's co-operation to give me uninterrupted study time.
e) I'll arrange to have the car and organise parking for the nights I'm attending classes.
f) I'll keep myself motivated by taking only one course at a time instead of worrying about all ten of them at once.
g) I'll resign from the condominium board so I'll have more time to spend with my family and to take courses.

Step 6: Formulate a plan of action that includes these four headings:

Step: Contact college re: courses and parking
Date or Time Limit: tomorrow
People to Involve: college rep.
Resources Required: phone / rep

Step: Contact university
Date or Time Limit: tomorrow

People to Involve: university rep
Resources Required: phone / rep

Step: Decide which course I'll take and costs
Date or Time Limit: within 2 days
People to Involve: boss
Resources Required: boss's time

Step: Talk to family – ask for help around the house
Date or Time Limit: within 3 days
People to Involve: family
Resources Required: family's time

Step: Talk to spouse re: use of car
Date or Time Limit: within 3 days
People to Involve: spouse
Resources Required: his/her time

Step: Sign up for selected courses
Date or Time Limit: within 4 days
People to Involve: college / university rep.
Resources Required: rep's time

Step: Talk to family re: help in obtaining uninterrupted study time
Date or Time Limit: within 3 days
People to Involve: family
Resources Required: family's time

Step 7: Implement your plan of action

Step 8: Evaluate the success of implementing your plan.

Goal setting won't get you that job or allow you to take that trip you've dreamed about. But putting your plan into action will. Don't allow yourself to get lazy. Keep your momentum going by realising that you're constantly moving closer to your 'dream job or dream vacation.' Learn to be flexible, bounce with the punches and keep your eyes open for unexpected opportunities that might surface.

Now it's time to put words into action. Write down several short-term goals you'd like to reach. Before using the Goal Setting Guide, ask yourself the following questions:

a) Is my goal specific? Can I tell when I've reached my goal?
b) Is it a tangible (something you can see) or intangible (relating to behaviour and feelings) goal?
c) Is it truly a short-term goal or will it take a long time to accomplish this goal?

The hardest goals to reach are those that are too general to gauge when you've achieved them or intangible goals. People often run out of steam when accomplishing long-term goals, so they must persevere by cutting their goal down to short-term ones. Then:

1. Go through the 8 steps of the goal setting process.
2. Follow the guidelines and reach your goals.
3. Don't forget to have a back-up goal ready to take over when you're close to reaching your first goal.

Goal setting - intensive goal setting - is hard work. It takes a lot of effort and time, but it's worth it. If it takes you two years to decide where you want to go, that's okay, as long as you're steadily working towards finding the right occupation and lifestyle for you. Good luck with your goal setting.

CHAPTER SIX

What is stress?

The reason I discussed time management in the first part of this book, is because a major cause of stress is trying to keep up with the time demands of modern society. A person becomes time-sick when their life becomes nothing but rush, rush, rush! My purpose is to help you understand stress better and turn its negative, energy-sapping side into a positive source of energy that works for you at home and on the job. Stress influences all facets of our lives and is a potential health hazard if not properly understood and handled. We're all exposed to stressful situations, but we can learn to cope with them through understanding and action.

A prime candidate for stress-induced mental or physical illness is an individual in a stressful job or home situation. This person feels powerless to cope with or adapt to their stress or to change the conditions causing the stress. Don't stay with negative situations!

I'm sure you'll agree with me, that in our modern society, stress is one of the most pressing problems (other than the economy of course - which in itself causes us stress).

It's well-known that people's lives would be a lot happier and longer if they identified and reacted to stress in more effective ways. A superficial understanding of stress is a good place to start, but a poor place to finish. Stress, especially in today's world, is a complex affair. The more we understand about the basic intricacies of stress, the better position we'll be in to survive the experience of stress and to use it as an instrument for growth.

Fight or flight syndrome

It's the dawn of human history and a man steps out from his cave to watch the rising sun. Suddenly, he hears a noise in the nearby woods. His muscles tense, his heart pounds, his breathing becomes rapid as he locks eyes with a sabre-toothed tiger. Should he fight - or run for his life (fight or flight reaction?) He reacts by reaching down and picking up a sharp rock which he hurls at the tiger. The animal snarls, but disappears into the trees. The man feels his body go limp, his breathing eases (release of the fight or flight reaction) and he returns to the safety of his den.

It's early morning and a man steps out of his home and begins his drive to work amidst the roar of rush-hour traffic. He picks his way through the traffic and finds himself behind a line of traffic that has to inch itself around a fender-bender accident. He drums his fingers on the steering wheel and clenches his teeth. He arrives late for work, opens his office door and is confronted by his pacing boss. He's told his report was due an hour ago and the client is furious. If he values his job, he'd better have a good explanation. And, by the way, he can forget about taking the weekend off as he had planned.

The man eyes a paperweight on his desk and wishes he could throw it at his boss. Instead, his blood pressure rises, his stomach churns and his back muscles begin to knot. He reaches for a Maalox and an aspirin and has a sudden yearning for a drink.

The sabre-toothed tiger and caveman days have gone, but the modern jungle is no less ferocious. The sense of panic over a deadline, a tight plane connection, a reckless tailgating driver, are the new threats make the heart race, put teeth on edge and initiate heart palpitations. These responses served our forefathers well; that extra burst of adrenaline primed their muscles, focused their attention and prepared their nerves for a sudden 'fight or flight.'

But what does a person do with this automatic response in today's traffic jams or boardrooms? The fight or flight emergency response is inappropriate to today's social stresses. It's also dangerous. When you get a modern person using the responses a cave man used to fight the elements, you've got a problem.

In the past 30 years, doctors and health officials realise how heavy a toll stress is taking on the nation's well-being. Two-thirds of office visits to family doctors are prompted by stress-related symptoms and people's inability to release their stored-up stress. For example, among tuberculosis patients, the onset of the disease had followed a cluster of disruptive events; a death in the family, a new job or marriage. Stress didn't cause the illness - that takes a germ -but tension did seem to promote the disease's process.

Companies have become alarmed by the tremendous cost of such symptoms in absenteeism, company medical expenses and lost productivity. Based on national samples, these costs are estimated at $50 billion to $75 billion in North America a year and Australia is showing a similar rate of escalation. Stress is a major contributor, either directly or indirectly, to coronary heart disease, cancer, lung ailments, accidental injuries, cirrhosis of the liver and suicide - six of the leading causes of death.

Stress also plays a role in aggravating such diverse conditions as multiple sclerosis, diabetes, genital herpes and even trench mouth. It's a sorry sign when the three best selling drugs in the country are an ulcer medication, a hypertension drug and a tranquilliser.

No one really knows if there is more stress now than in the past, but many experts believe it has become more extensive. The noise of air traffic for instance, takes its toll on people living close to airports. Blasted daily by noise, people living near major airports have higher rates of hypertension, heart disease and suicide than residents of quieter areas.

We live in a world of uncertainties - everything from lack of job security, high unemployment figures, to the dismal state of the economy. Today's pressures have developed a breed of thrill-seekers who, often to their own detriment, prefer excitement over tranquillity. Life in the fast lane becomes a dangerous habit for them. Skydivers get hooked on the jump (as do bungee jumpers). Others go white-water rafting and still others SCUBA dive.

A moot point may be whether or not daily stresses and hassles do more damage than life-change events. A single event can cause smaller changes that touch every aspect of existence. Divorce for example is not an isolated event. Accompanying divorce are often social isolation, a reduction in income and the problems of being a single parent. These become the chronic strains of life.

Joblessness has a similar ripple effect. The greatest source of stress is not the actual loss of the job, but the gradual domestic and psychological changes it imposes. These can be devastating. To be sure, not everyone falls to pieces because of the loss of a job or even a spouse. Research into stress and preventive medicine has focused on what psychologists call hardiness or coping behaviour. Certain population groups enjoy remarkable good health and longevity. This suggests that possibly their faith, pride of accomplishment or productivity play a role in lowering the ill effects of stress.

Fight or flight response

Stress acts upon five separate areas of the brain that govern five endocrine glands. These glands secrete hormones that prepare the body for action. So, the physical link between stress and metabolism is very real. When we're alarmed, our muscles tense, our heart speeds up, insulin and sugar pour into the blood stream and digestion turns off. But what if there's no outlet for this energy build-up? Scientists have discovered that metabolic problems persist when a person's body energy is triggered, but not released. This response was supposed to last only a few minutes. When stress remains for a long time, this response can lead to serious mental and physical problems. There are similarities in the physical response whether a lion is threatening us or whether we're taking a test.

Because stress factors thrive in modern society, we're not always aware of their existence. They may be as subtle as feelings of competition, income goals or lack of leisure time. Daily stressors - worries, annoyances and fears, accumulate and wear down the body's resistance. While some people deal easily with stress, others find themselves confused, accident-prone or physically ill. Think back to the last time you had a cold or the flu. Were you under an undue amount of stress?

In addition to stress research, scientists and medical practitioners are studying practical therapies that combat stress. Some rely on common sense, such as exercise, time management and diversions from workaday pressures. Others rely on more elaborate techniques where stress manifests itself as a disease; where lifestyle or heredity promotes vulnerability to stress; and where people seek to avoid stress by finding a simpler, calmer life.

In addition to the above-mentioned problems including congenital ailments, the following physical and mental symptoms are common in most people:

Physical symptoms:

- general fatigue
- rapid pulse
- increased perspiration
- pounding heart or palpitations
- tightness in the chest
- high blood pressure
- coronary disease
- rheumatoid arthritis can flare up
- tightened stomach muscles
- tensing of muscles of arms and legs
- shortness of breath (hyperventilate)
- bronchial asthma can flare up
- gritting of teeth
- clenching of the jaw
- in women, menstrual irregularities
- in men, impotence
- frequent colds or flu
- inability to sit still
- digestion slows down
- stomach aches
- constipation
- faster breathing, hyperventilate
- clammy feeling
- extremities cold
- body trembles
- tension and migraine headaches
- butterflies or nervous stomach
- eat more or less
- sleep more or less
- migraine or tension headaches
- voice rises
- stiff, achy joints
- sore back and neck
- muscles twitch in sleep
- rashes and hives
- enhancement of blood clotting mechanisms in case of injury. People who require surgery are often hospitalised or given full bed rest before they have their surgery. This is to give the

person's metabolism a chance to relax. The person is encouraged to keep their stress level as low as possible. This is necessary because, if their fight or flight reaction is triggered for too long, the person's blood clotting mechanism will not kick in after surgery when it's required for quick healing.
- swift elimination of waste products. (This is why we have to go to the bathroom when under duress. Ask most people to make a presentation in front of a group and most will want to go to the bathroom before doing so.)
- digestion is shut down (which causes the queasy stomach, gastritis and digestive disturbances such as diarrhoea). Note: Don't eat a big meal before you're heading into what you know will be a stressful situation - eat later.
- blood supply shifts away from the skin which makes the person feel cold and appears pale
- pupils dilate (which can cause difficulty if a person is working under bright fluorescent lights when they're under stress).
- hearing is more acute (which can be unbearable for the person under stress when in crowded environments).

Psychological symptoms:
- raging thoughts
- excessively gripping emotions
- person becomes 'jumpy'
- lethargic or hyperactive
- nightmares
- emotional
- feelings of incompetence
- the feeling that *'I just can't do it all!'*
- anxious
- short attention span
- difficulty in concentrating
- depression
- desire to run away from it all

Interpersonal symptoms
- short-tempered with mate, children, co-workers, friends

- increased conflict with colleagues
- inability to relax and have fun with others
- loss of patience
- angry, cranky, short fuse, lose temper
- complaining
- irritable
- withdrawn, quiet
- pout or sulk
- angry or resentful towards spouse, children
- working harder with less effectiveness
- missing appointments
- forgetting things

First signs of stress

What is the first thing that happens to you that tells you that you're under stress? Do you lose your temper? Lose your appetite, eat too much and get an upset stomach? Do you get cranky or lose your concentration level?

Write down the clues that tell you're that you're under too much stress. Now, back-track your symptoms. What happened *before* you noticed the stress? For instance, the first sign of stress you notice might be a knot between your shoulder blades. You could have acted sooner if you'd been watching for early warning signs. If you're prone to this kind of stress sign, you should have been checking your shoulder muscles (and those of your neck) regularly to check for tension there. If your first sign is a headache, again a quick check of the tension in your neck muscles would likely inform you that you're going to have a headache. If your first sign is indigestion, check to identify knotted stomach muscles, which show that indigestion is on its way. Act on this knowledge. Cut stress-related illness at the pass by listening to the signs your body is giving you *before* serious trouble occurs. Do spot checks throughout your day to head off trouble.

Learn how to read your body's red flags - and deal with them. Doctors still can't explain why one person's stomach-ache is another's migraine and there's more agreement than ever before that stress is the culprit. Knowing how your body reacts to anxiety can help you to anticipate and relieve the painful side effects of tension.

Positive/negative stress

Just as the body doesn't distinguish between the effects of consuming too much alcohol at either a wedding (happy occasion) or a funeral (sad situation) neither does the body distinguish between happy and unhappy stress. An employee who gets married and promoted (happy) in the same week, for example, could experience as much stress as a co-worker who gets divorced and fails to get a promotion (unhappy) at the same time.

Both negative stressors (getting a divorce) and positive stressors (getting married) can create stress. If we don't handle negative stressors properly, they can strain and damage an individual. Other events that should be happy events (such as pregnancy, the birth of a child, getting a promotion or retiring) can still be significant stressors.

Can stress be good?

It's helpful to understand that stress is not inherently destructive, but necessary for both physical and psychological growth. If individuals lived in a completely stress-free environment, they'd become a mass of inertia. Therefore, we should not avoid stress. In fact, we should judiciously seek it. Humans need both physical and psychological workouts to continue to grow and remain in good shape. So, while too little stress in an individual's life is stunting, too much stress can be damaging. The ideal combination is a moderate amount of stress and good stress skills so growth continues and stagnation and strain are avoided.

On the positive side, a student often does his or her best work under the stress of a deadline. We also know that too much stress can hurt. After a break-up with his girlfriend for instance, the same student could fail his exam. Equally, too little stress can be disastrous. Sudden inactivity following retirement from a demanding job can be critical unless retirees can find new interests.

Stress can help you write that article to meet your deadline, make you review your presentation one more time until you've got it down pat or make sure that your report is the best it can be. And that's good. That's good stress. That's when a situation motivates you to think clearly, act decisively and feel challenged. Stress increases strength, energy, alertness and concentration.

What is bad stress?

A certain amount of stress is healthy and beneficial; it stimulates some to perform, makes them excited and enthusiastic. Unfortunately, unless we quickly defuse stress, it brings a long list of trouble. These can include distraction, irritability, listlessness, fatigue, childishness, depression, insomnia and worry - especially worry.

When stress is inordinate, it adversely affects the body in three ways;

1. It decreases energy and the individual wears out.
2. It weakens the immune system, which makes the body more prone to contracting illnesses caused by viruses.
3. Dormant weak spots in the nervous system are activated (asthma, bronchitis, heart problems).

Many experts believe that stress-related illnesses and accidents account for three quarters of all time lost from work. Despite widespread media attention, stress-related problems still take most people by surprise. So be warned: If you don't learn how to handle stress, you may be unnecessarily courting ill health or even an early death.

How you respond to a difficult situation at work determines whether it will propel you forward or drag you down. The choice is yours. For better or worse, stress is a part of everyday life - and it's not all bad. However, when a situation induces chronic anxiety or hostility, when you feel threatened rather than challenged or when you become obsessed - that's bad stress. The way you respond to any potentially stressful situation, is influenced by two factors; your general approach to life and how many stressors rain down on you at once. Regardless of how resilient you are and what your outlook on life is, the research shows that you can learn to change your approach and thus convert bad stressors into good ones.

It's well known that people's lives would be a lot happier and longer if they identified and reacted to stress in more effective ways. A superficial understanding of stress is a good place to start, but a poor place to finish. Stress, especially in today's world, is a complex affair. The more you understand about the basic intricacies of stress, the better position you'll be in to survive the experience of stress and to use it as an instrument for growth.

Are you always conscious of stress?

When stressors become too threatening, the stress they generate is likely to be pushed back into the person's subconscious.

For example, Dan's new boss says; *'Dan, I have a little different philosophy of management than your former boss. To prevent any difficulties from arising between us, you need to know that I expect a full eight-hour work day and that you'll meet all your deadlines.'*

Because this message floods Dan with anxiety, he immediately represses and intellectualises it: *'My new boss is giving everyone a pep talk, but it doesn't really mean anything.'*

The problem is that Dan ignores the seriousness of the message. He doesn't allow the comments to change his behaviour and derails the anxieties into his subconscious. The result is that, during the weeks and months that follow, Dan is still being casual about his hours and deadlines. He's distant or passive-aggressive with his boss and complains about his boss to anyone who'll listen. In short, he's digging a deep hole for himself at work and he's the last one to realise it.

The point is that people can be under little conscious stress, but under a good deal of unconscious stress. They are not able to deal effectively with the stressors. As far as s/they are concerned, they don't have any stressors.

Stressor, stress and distress

To understand stress, it's important to distinguish between some basic concepts, such as stressor, stress and distress. A **stressor** is an external event (for example, failing to get a promotion) or an internal event (such as thinking and feeling about the prospect of failing to get a promotion) that create a state of imbalance in an individual. Stressors cause stress - feelings of frustration, fear, conflict, pressure, hurt, anger, sadness, inadequacy, guilt, loneliness or confusion. **Distress** occurs when stress reaches a point where the organism (the body and psyche) begin to show signs of damage.

The situation improves, once a person develops a plan of action to overcome the side effects of stress. One person (literally itching to change jobs) developed hives each evening at quitting time. After a week or so, he correctly identified what was causing the problem and decided to leave his job. The hives became less severe and when he actually changed jobs, they disappeared altogether.

Stress has become the career buzzword of today. So many things to do, not enough time to do them all really well and who's that new employee covetously eyeing the office you moved into just six months ago? What about that key presentation to the board next week? Will your staff have everything ready? Will you look sharp, talk smart - and get the budget you want?

Of course the pressure is more than the stress of juggling multiple demands; add to it your inner voice that says; if something's worth doing well, it's worth doing perfectly. A single flaw or failure is total disaster because I'll be revealed as worthless.

That internal monologue is the classic stress-plus-anxiety tape of the high-achiever. Stress doesn't have to be a time-waster and energy-drainer. It doesn't have to make you leave the office feeling drained every day or make you feel burned out after a year or two. Channelled properly, stress can be the edge that gets you through career crunches. It makes you rise to the occasion and helps you move on to the next level in your career. You can have the ambition without the anxiety.

When does stress become distress?

The only time stress causes problems to a person's metabolism is when it becomes *dist*ress. The stress that causes distress to one person may not bother another. A car trip to one person may be a distinct pleasure - the open air, the opportunity to meet new people, new surroundings and having a chance to think. To another, it causes distress because of possible physical discomfort - feelings that they're wasting their time (they could have flown).

Another example is planning a party. This may be very pleasurable for you, but for another, it's nothing but a bothersome chore.

Stressors are also highly subjective. Consider for example the situation where four employees did not receive an expected promotion. One individual had planned to leave the company soon for a much better job and therefore, did not perceive the experience as a stressor. This employee experiences virtually no stress. A second worker sees the event as a minor set-back and so, experiences mild (first degree) stress. The third individual looks at the event as a blatant personal insult and, as a result, experiences moderate (second degree) stress. The fourth person perceives the event as a personal, professional and financial catastrophe and therefore, suffers severe (third degree) stress.

Although these individuals experienced the same event, their physical, psychological and social reactions were dramatically different. The level of stress each person suffered depended upon the individual's expectations and his or her stress-prevention and stress-reduction skills.

Traumatic and daily stressors

When people speak of stress, they often are referring to a single traumatic event, such as the loss of a job. Obviously, such events can cause stress, but it's rare for a single stressor to cause lasting damage to the person. Even serious wounds can heal with time with the support of family and friends.

Although daily stressors are not as dramatic as a traumatic event, they can be more dangerous for two reasons. First, because daily stressors are less dramatic than traumatic stressors, they're far less noticeable. Comparably, daily stressors are similar to eating minuscule traces of poison in one's daily diet. The second reason is that by definition, they occur daily, which means they're relentless. Therefore, nickel and dime daily stressors can gradually, but relentlessly deteriorate the person's ability to handle larger, more traumatic stressors.

When you know there is going to be a stressful event in one part of your life - strive to eliminate as much stress as you can in the others. For example, you need to meet a difficult deadline at work and know that you'll have to work flat-out for about two weeks. Make sure that your family and social life are as stress free as possible (at least try).

Kinds of stress

There are three main areas of our lives where stress can be felt:

Social: This could be a person running for an elected office (political or a community club) or interaction with family, friends and co-workers.

Family: A mother in childbirth and her infant, a child on its first day of school and the student writing an exam could all be under stress.

Business or work: A person applying for a job or unhappy in his or her present position; too heavy a workload; too many deadlines; or being under- or overqualified for the duties of their position.

There are also three basic kinds of stress that can have an effect on us:

Mental: This could be too heavy a work-load, not enough to do, you're in a job you hate or because you have to meet a deadline.

Emotional: This normally occurs when there are problems between people (deals with feelings and behaviour).

Physical: This could be too much or too little physical exertion such as working long hours or having to maintain an uncomfortable body position for too long. Too much competitiveness in physical activity such as racquetball or other competitive sports. If the body has too little physical stress, the muscles waste away. Then, when the person over-uses them, sore achy muscles can be the result.

During one three-day seminar I was presenting, there were problems with the air conditioning system in the room. The fan vibrated very loudly, so I needed to use a microphone so my audience could hear me over the noise. No other room was available, so I had to make do. Unfortunately, the microphone was secured to the podium, so I had to stand at a podium for three days while I presented my seminar. After the second day's session, I noticed that my legs were shaking and rubbery - not because of the stress, but because of ordinary physical fatigue. My muscles were not accustomed to standing in one place for long periods of time. I normally move around while presenting my seminars. What did cause me stress was straining to hear every word spoken by my participants.

Tracking the chemistry of stress

Stress triggers chemical changes in the brain. Particularly sensitive to emotional strains are the concentrations of potent chemicals called neurotransmitters that act as messengers between nerve cells. Because stress alters the body's chemical balance, it influences the development of many diseases including psychiatric disorders. Depression is associated with low levels of two neurotransmitters - serotonin and norepinephrine. Similarly, schizophrenia is related to an excess of dopamine.

Adrenaline floods the bloodstream, causing the heart to pound. Breathing becomes shallow. Blood flows from skin and viscera to muscles and brain. The adrenal glands secrete substances call corticoids, which carry alarm messages to various tissues throughout the body. Muscles tense, particularly in the lower back, neck and shoulders. The spleen releases red blood cells into the bloodstream to increase oxygen supply and the liver sends out stored vitamins and nutrients in the form of glucose.

Blood pressure goes up significantly when people talk. If they're talking to strangers who argue or criticise, their blood pressure may rise as much as 40 to 50 per cent above resting levels. These changes in the cardiovascular system show how important human communication is to the body's health.

Under ordinary circumstances, the increase in blood pressure is a natural reaction (not harmful itself). In cases of chronic hypertension (where there's no known organic cause) the problem may stem from faulty communications and stressful relationships.

Stress and your immune system

Not all stress is bad. To be alive is to be under a certain amount of stress. The body functions well - even excels - under the right kind and right amount of stress. However, health suffers when the body is constantly drawing on inner reserves to respond to negative stressors.

Research is finding more and more proof that negative stress suppresses the body's immune system, leaving the body more vulnerable to illness. While some scientists don't believe in a direct link between emotion and disease, studies show that the mind has much to do with the body's health. People who feel in control of their lives can withstand an enormous amount of change and strive on it. People who feel helpless can hardly cope at all.

Research has repeatedly shown that extreme stress and depression can weaken the body's ability to fight off potential invaders. Now, it appears that even daily ups and downs can toughen the task of the immune system. The body cannot tell the difference between events that are actual threats to survival and events that are present in thought alone. The mind spins out endless fantasies of possible disasters past and future. This tendency to escalate a situation into its worst possible conclusion can be a key factor in tipping the balance towards illness or health.

The reserve energy (from the adrenal gland) can be lifesaving if one is running away from a lion or crossing a busy highway. Instead of relaxing, a person sitting in the security of his own home allows his mind to think of burglars or of the man who is out to destroy his business. His emotional centres will send out alarm messages to the glands, heart and blood-pressure centres - just as if an individual was actually attacking him. Although the body needs an excess of hormones for genuine emergency situations, an excessive and frequent production of hormones over weeks and months results in harmful effects.

A primary function of the brain (perhaps as important as rational thought or language) is health maintenance. The many connections between the nervous system and the immune system allow the mind to influence resistance to diseases.

To offset any negative stress and gain peace of mind, the individual must get in control of his own mind and emotions. That control gives hope for a brighter future. The value of peace-of-mind is priceless, not only mentally, but even in physical health. How can one establish and maintain peace of mind? In ordinary circumstances you - not anyone else - decide what to think about what happens around you and how you will respond. So control your thoughts, emotions and actions.

Studies of those who watch a spouse succumb after long battles with illness showed that bereavement caused definite psychological effects. The grieving people showed marked changes in their lymphocytes that help guard against disease. Only as the mourners adjusted to their loss did their immune systems return to full strength. Those who stay healthy - actively grieved. They cried, went into mourning, thought about what was happening to them and worked through their grief. Those who locked their feelings away caused their bodies to mourn by getting sick.

An Australian study of bereavement has shown that eight weeks after the death of their spouses, widows and widowers have diminished immune responses. This leaves them more vulnerable to infection and cancer. The most significant observation is that widows die at rates three to 13 times as high as married women from every known major cause of death.

Does poverty make a difference?

The relentless stresses of poverty and ghetto life have also been associated with higher health risks. Studies of poor Black neighbourhoods have correlated hypertension, twice as common among American Blacks as among whites, with overcrowded housing and high levels of unemployment and crime.

Many men live in an environment where poverty is the norm and violence is a way of life. They're kept on constant alert for the chance that they might be attacked and have to defend themselves or their families. They're on constant alert for disaster that wears them out with the effort. Some have fantasies about being on a desert island where they can just put their feet up and have someone serve them and meet their every whim.

Although a direct connection between poverty and mental health has not been firmly established, by every measure, women are consistently more likely than men to experience poverty and economic insecurity. The stress of constantly striving to make sure they maintain the material needs of life - food, clothing and shelter for themselves and their children - constitutes a serious threat to many women's mental health.

Stress and mental health

A report put forth by Health and Welfare Canada, in their book called Mental Health for Canadians: Striking a Balance states, *'Mental health is the capacity of the individual, the group and the environment to interact with one another in ways that promote subjective well-being, the optimal development and use of mental abilities (cognitive, affective and relational) the achievement of individual and collective goals consistent with justice and the attainment of preservation of conditions of basic equality.'*

Our current understanding of mental health shows that people's inherent capacities, abilities and characteristics are merely one set of factors that influence mental health. Experiences in childhood and throughout life, as well as social, cultural, economic and political influences, also play a profound role in determining mental health. Interactions with circumstances and events in their environment, affect how people perceive and value themselves. It affects how they view their position in relation to others and how they assess their personal potential and possibilities. Positive mental health requires many things:

- An environment that provides a sense of security,
- Trusting relationships with significant others,
- Opportunities for self-actualisation and growth,
- The power to direct their own lives and
- Opportunities to develop self-esteem, confidence and independence.

Mental health of men

Men are consistently more likely to experience anxiety over their ability to live up to society's expectation that they be good breadwinners. They're constantly faced with challenges and competition in the workplace. As soon as they feel comfortable that they've reached and can maintain their existing condition, along comes a better educated university graduate who threatens them for their positions. Many are exposed to dangerous environments, have stressful, unrewarding, repetitious and depersonalised work. Others are forced to keep up with the rapid changes in technology, which keep them on the razer's edge. Many have stated, *'If only someone else could take over for a while and give me a respite.'*

Men are expected to defend not only themselves, but their women and children and at the same time society tells them that it's not proper to use physical violence to defend them. The cultural stressors stem from society's changing expectations of the role of men and women. Men are forced to walk a fine line between being the protectors and the equals of women.

While women will openly discuss their problems with a spouse or good friend, men keep everything locked up inside. Compare this inner turmoil to a glass bottle full of water subjected to below zero temperatures. As it freezes, it expands and multiplies the space it originally took, until it bursts the glass. Men who keep all their stress inside, eventually 'burst.' They show this by: becoming physically ill (ulcers, back and neck pains, heart attacks or strokes); emotionally unstable where symptoms include violent outbursts, physical release by throwing or breaking things, deep sadness, depression and private crying episodes: and displaying signs of burnout or nervous breakdown.

Many men, after years of marriage, find themselves facing the excruciating loneliness of living alone with little access to their children. Many resort to alcohol and drugs as coping methods. They're more likely than women to use illicit drugs. 28.9 per cent of men used marijuana or hashish. Cocaine or crack use was 4.5 per cent; 5.1 per cent of male respondents had used speed and/or heroin.

Men successfully commit suicide about three times more than women. A study of the prevalence of suicide attempts found that 1.8 per cent of men had attempted suicide. To provide a comprehensive network of suicide prevention, we must address unemployment, poverty, violence and their feelings of alienation from others.

We expect young boys to be tough and unemotional. Media images portray males as strong and invincible. We expect boys to be experimental, try dangerous activities like climbing trees, crossing trestle bridges and railroad tracks. Adolescence is a time of tremendous physical and psychological change. There's an increased awareness of social, institutional and family power imbalances and injustice. It's an important stage for the development of their self-esteem. Body image is a crucial concern for all adolescents. During puberty, males watch as girls their own age suddenly are taller and more mature than they are. We encourage boys to lift weights and become 'hunks.'

As they mature, the elements of danger increase. It's 'cool' to have a powerful motorcycle, but 'not cool' to wear a helmet. They're expected to become drunk and smoke cigarettes at least once before they're twelve. They're expected to display their manhood by deflowering a female as early in their teens as possible. A male virgin is looked upon with disdain.

He's expected to continue sexual experimentation though he knows he might expose himself to sexual diseases that could eventually kill him. Wearing protection is the sissy way - and besides it's not as much fun to do things the safe way. He may suddenly hear the comments 'I'm pregnant,' from the female of the moment and have to pay the consequences of either having an abortion, a hurried marriage or supporting the child until s/he is eighteen years of age.

When dating, he receives mixed messages from females. He expects to go as far as he can go, but isn't sure where the line is. By the time he realises that he's crossed the line, he may find himself too physically charged to stop. His raging hormones seem to control him, not him controlling his hormones. Many teens are ashamed to be around any attractive women because their hormones kick in and it becomes obvious by their physical reactions. Many also suffer excessively oily skin, from acne and increased body odour.

Impotence terrifies men. Occasionally when more self-conscious men try to make love to a self-assured, assertive woman, they suddenly find themselves incapable of having intercourse. This is especially true if the woman takes the initiative in love-making. During marriage, many men are mortified to learn that they have episodes of impotence with their loving wives. When they examine the reasons behind their impotence, many find it's caused by stress or overwork. If they have empathetic understanding partners, they soon overcome this problem. If the woman in their lives is not sympathetic or belittles them, this can be a crushing blow to their feelings of manliness.

Because of the strong value attached to having children carry on their name, men who are sterile experience feelings of failure and shame. They may feel personally responsible for their infertility. It hits at their image of what constitutes manhood. In later years, a large percentage of men suffer from problems with enlarged prostate gland that can require surgery to correct. One side effect can be impotence.

Other men learn that they're homosexual and face all the problems that face gay men and women. Surveys show that some homosexuals face intense hatred, harassment and violence. Coping with this level of discrimination creates considerable psychological stress. Although homosexuality is no longer considered a psychiatric disorder, many gay men and women strive to keep their sexual orientation secret. Our societal ideal of the nuclear family and overt homosexual discrimination in the workplace are factors that add to mental health problems amongst this group.

Mental health of women

Women face cultural stressors that stem from society's sexism and its mixed messages. Women are expected to be sexy but not sexual; to have a child, but remain childlike; to be assertive but never aggressive; to hold a job but not neglect their home. Although revealing emotions is a healthy physiological release, women learn this must not happen in the workplace.

Violence and fear of violence are common experiences for many women. The perpetual sense of vulnerability - childhood sexual abuse and incest, assault in a parking lot, acquaintance rape and wife battering, - threatens women's basic need for personal safety and security. The physical, emotional and psychological results of violence can include bruises, broken bones, disfigurement (and even death). For abused women, feelings of terror, depression, loss of self-esteem, hopelessness, shame, guilt, isolation and severe anxiety are common. Their children who witness the abusive behaviour are also severely affected.

Early in their lives, girls are told to be dependent, responsive to the needs of others and emotionally expressive. Boys, on the other hand, are taught to be independent, competent, responsible and detached. These stereotypes are obvious in classrooms, in the media and cultural ways. Females are treated differently. Many women's problems have often been regarded as signs of mental illness, whereas in a man, he's over-stressed.

Women are also faced with the extra stressors of menstruation, pregnancy and menopause. For years, women were prescribed tranquilisers for misdiagnosed emotional problems that were simply the effects of pre-menstrual tension (PMS). PMS symptoms include irritability, fatigue, sadness and lack of concentration. In 5% of these women their symptoms were severe. This added dimension of being considered emotionally unstable was added to the already overwhelming monthly problem they faced. When women are correctly diagnosed as having pre-menstrual tension, they learn to live with the knowledge that their ailment is a passing hormonal deficiency - not an emotional or mental illness.

About 1 in 5 pregnancies ends in miscarriage and 16 in every 1,000 births result in peri-natal death. Often women are unprepared for these experiences and many can't find the information and support they need to help them manage. Feelings of guilt and confusion often accompany the experiences of miscarriage and stillbirth. Reactions such as fear, decreased self-image, powerlessness and depression are common. Women who find themselves unexpectedly pregnant face the difficult decision of whether to continue or end the pregnancy. She must decide in a society that may consider her decision to end a pregnancy unacceptable. At the same time, society may not provide adequate emotional or financial support for her, if she chooses to keep her child.

Although some women experience menopause positively, for others, negative social myths and preoccupation with youth make that difficult. At this time, women may also experience additional major relationship and life changes. They now have freedom from conception and child-care responsibilities and they may look forward to the joys of becoming a grandparent. Some may start a new career or make marital changes. They may face the death of their parents or spouses. Their adult children may come back home. A new concern may be whether they'll have enough financial backing for a comfortable retirement. Women who experience menopause artificially (through surgery) may become depressed, partly due to sudden hormonal changes.

Anxiety disorders are the second most common problem that prompts women to seek mental health services. Many have eating disorders, but often keep anorexia nervosa and bulimia hidden until their failing health alerts concerned family members or friends. 80 to 90 per cent of women dislike the size or shape of their bodies. Often, a woman's personal perception of her appearance and weight differs dramatically from how others perceive her. Many engage in cyclical starvation, binging, fasting and various diet programs to lose weight.

A few resort to jaw wiring, gastric and intestinal bypass surgery, liposuction and amphetamine use for weight reduction. Main contributors to women's eating disorders include low self-esteem and a lack of control over their lives. This accounts for the prevalence of eating disorders in adolescent females. Adolescence is when girls often feel out of control and confused about messages related to growing up. They feel that weight loss is the one area they can control.

Recent research suggests there's a relationship between acute eating disorders and childhood sexual abuse. A study of women with bulimia found that 60 per cent had been sexually abused or had negative sexual experiences. Treatment, to a large extent focuses on individual and family factors, with little emphasis on the real reasons behind the eating disorders.

Women continue to bear the primary responsibility for child rearing, housework, meal preparation and the emotional health of their family. They also may have to care for aging parents and relatives with disabilities. Maintaining these multi-faceted and demanding roles, along with paid employment, constitutes a double workday. From a mental health point of view, the double workday usually means that these women have little time or energy left to spend on themselves.

Chronic stress

Creative stress management requires preventing short-term stress from becoming chronic and long-term. When would that be most likely to happen? When we've have no time to recover between bouts of stress. When there's no respite, our psychological symptoms may give way to serious and very real physical ailments.

Although we can put many of the stressors in our lives to good use, it doesn't always happen that way. Sometimes stress has a way of hanging on. To determine whether stress has become chronic, look for the four 'Ds':

- Dependency: The needs have increased, but are denied;
- Decision-making: Is difficult;
- Depression: Dominates the emotions; and
- Disorganisation: Even panic - sets in.

Another symptom, perhaps connected with denial of dependency is a desire for isolation. All the symptoms are normal, unless they don't subside in time. That's when we need to shift priorities, delegate work, change management techniques and identify faulty thought patterns. A therapist often can help.

More women seek professional help than men. Many men don't want to admit to a problem in case they look weak. Women undergoing stress in corporations rely on social support systems as a way to off-load stress. It's particularly effective against acute, short-term frustrations and stressors. They benefit from their tendency to be open with others by relating an irritating incident to their friend, neighbour or spouse. Men tend to internalise problems and try to solve them with outside support or help.

We can talk ourselves into stress and we can talk ourselves out of it. We can talk so much, that we can avoid the real issues or we can talk enough to off-load tension and gather ideas for problem-solving. Stressors can test us to our limits and make us meet the challenges of our lives in creative ways we otherwise would not have stumbled across.

CHAPTER SEVEN

How prone are you to stress?

You may be more or less vulnerable to stress than you believe. Here are several stress tests that will help you determine where you are relating to stress:

How vulnerable are you to stress?

Complete the following as honestly as you can. Score each one:

    1 - Always
    2 - Almost always
    3 - Sometimes
    4 - Almost never
    5 - Never

Positives

1. I am within ten pounds of being the right weight for my height and body type.
2. Every day, I eat at least one hot, well-balanced meal.
3. I drink less than five alcoholic drinks per week.
4. I get enough sleep for my metabolism.
5. I have loving friends and family to meet my affection needs.
6. I drink less than three cups of coffee or cola drinks per day.
7. I have at least two friends or relatives nearby I can rely on to help me through my bad days and help me celebrate my good ones.
8. Instead of holding my feelings in, I talk out my problems with the people involved.
9. I enjoy good health - seldom have colds or flu.
10. I exercise an average of 15 - 30 minutes per day.
11. I get strength from my spiritual beliefs.
12. I smoke less than half a package of cigarettes per day.
13. I attend organisation or club activities regularly.
14. I have a network of trustworthy friends and acquaintances and see them often.

15. I let my 'little kid' out to have fun at least once a week.
16. I indulge my need for private time when necessary.
17. I organise my time in both my work and home lives.
18. My income is adequate to meet my needs.
19. I'm watchful of my physical and emotional reactions to situations and take steps when I realise that I'm under stress.

Score each one:

    1 – Never
    2 - Almost never
    3 - Sometimes
    4 - Almost always
    5 - Always

Negatives

20. I feel down or depressed.
21. I feel tired or fatigued.
22. I have trouble eating properly.
23. I have problems with insomnia.
24. I find I'm angry and complain a lot.
25. I withdraw from society.
26. I feel upset and frustrated.
27. My job pressures are overwhelming.
28. I keep my anger inside.
29. I have temper tantrums.
30. I take my bad moods out on my friends, relatives or co-workers.

Total (all 30 questions)

To get your score, add up the figures. Any number over 50 (for both tests) shows a vulnerability to stress. You're seriously vulnerable if your score is between 50 and 100 and extremely vulnerable if it's over 100.

Misery measure

What's the worst situation that could happen to you? According to a National Opinion Research Centre survey in which more than 1,700 respondents ranked 58 events from the most to the least miserable - the death of a child or spouse headed the list.

Near the top of the list were: Being able to purchase needed food; Death of a parent; Having a home destroyed by fire, flood, other disaster; Having a child with a drug or alcohol problem; or getting arrested.

Troubles that cause moderate levels of misery include; robbery, losing a job and having a car repossessed.

Although none of the events were particularly desirable, those rated the least troublesome include being unable to have a child, not receiving a promotion, breaking up with a fiancé and serious difficulties with a boss.

Health-related difficulties were the most common problems. Law and criminal problems were the least. The average adult surveyed said s/he had experienced four of the 58 troubles in the past year.

People who are poor, young or divorced and people who live in central cities are especially prone to troubles.

If you have excessive problems in even a couple of these areas, you might be suffering from stress overload. Being aware of what is causing you emotional trouble is the first step to dealing with it.

Holmes-Rahe scale

Holmes and Richard Rahe developed one of the most popular devices used to determine a person's stress level. They worked together to rate the amount of social readjustment required for various events. To measure the impact of life-changing events, the following list was compiled:

Some experts don't agree that the Holmes-Rahe scale is the best measure of personal stress. Some are convinced that the everyday annoyances of life or everyday hassles, contribute more to illness and depression than major life changes. Learning how to deal with the little hassles, can leave us with little energy required to deal with the really big ones.

      100: Death of a spouse
      73: Divorce

65: Marital separation
63: Imprisonment
63: Death of a close family member
53: Personal injury or illness
50: Marriage
47: Loss of job
45: Marital reconciliation
44: Change in health of family member
40: Pregnancy
39: Sexual difficulties
39: Gain of new family member
38: Change in financial status
37: Death of a close friend
36: Change to different kind of work
35: Increase or decrease in arguments with spouse
31: Buying a house (big mortgage)
30: Foreclosure of mortgage or loan
30: Change in work responsibilities
29: Son or daughter leaving home
29: Trouble with in-laws
28: Outstanding personal achievement
24: Revision of personal habits
24: Change in number of family get-togethers
23: Trouble with business superior
20: Change in work hours or conditions
20: Change in residence
20: Change in schools
19: Change in recreation
18: Change in social activities
17: Small mortgage on home
15: Change in sleeping habits
13: Vacation
12: Christmas
11: Minor violations of law

Evaluate your stress level

Take as long as you need, but write down your all your stressors. Be specific.

1. On a sheet of paper, write down anything that you believe causes you stress. (Leave space between each stressor). Try to give at least five stressors.
2. On a scale of 1 to 5 (5 being the highest) determine the stress level of each stressor.
3. Determine if the stressor is positive (weddings, promotions, new baby, moving, new job) or negative (rudeness of others, problems involving friends, family or associates, driving to work, etc.)
4. Next to each stressor, put down the feelings you have when in the stressful situation (anger, frustration, happiness, fear).
5. What part of your life did each stressor affect (family, social, work).
6. How many of the above stressors could you lessen if you tried?
7. What are you prepared to do about the stressors that remain?

Stressed by success

Here's a test you can give yourself. While someone observes you with a stop-watch, sit quietly and (without counting) decide when a minute has passed. Most stressed out people call 'time's up' at between 15 and 30 seconds.

Experts warn that constantly being in high gear causes the body's fight or flight mechanism to kick into action more frequently. This increases the blood levels of adrenaline, noradrenaline and other stress hormones and causes damage to the arteries.

Stress-related diseases - everything from headaches to heart attacks - are the most serious warning signs of time sickness. Other tip-offs include anxiety, depression, insomnia, fatigue, appetite changes and bizarre eating habits. In extreme cases, individuals may abuse amphetamines or barbiturates to speed up or slow their metabolisms. As the syndrome progresses, it can jeopardise family relationships - and even damage careers.

One engineer became increasingly impatient with his children because they didn't respond as fast as his computer could. Another fast-track executive was so anxious that she began perspiring at board meetings because she felt she was wasting time. She became embarrassed and started avoiding meetings altogether.

Humans are hitting their biological speed limit and predictions are that this new decade will prove to be a more easy-going era. The signs are already here. We're discovering that spending extra time at work doesn't always translate into productivity. Allowing ourselves to relax doesn't have to mean we cut down on what gets done. In fact studies show that when people have time to relax, they actually can achieve more. What's more, pushing to produce without limits can be destructive from an economic point of view. In Japan, for instance, the government plans to cut about 300 hours out of the average corporate employee's work year, because it fears over-production will cripple the economy.

Despite the obvious benefits of slowing down, the 'stress for success' concept has become so ingrained that even mildly time-sick people may have trouble letting go.

Stress in the workplace

Illness is the body's response to ignored stress. For generations, men have had physical ailments that were the direct result of stress in the workplace. No one thought any less of them. Dying of a heart attack proved how hard they worked. Short of dying, the valiant breadwinner in the grey flannel suit could have ulcers.

Today's prevalent ailment is back pain. Whatever they had, men didn't complain about feelings or psychological problems. They'd only feel comfortable complaining about their physical pain. Men reared in this sort of 'hold it in' behaviour, take the option of going out with the guys for a drink after work. It's no wonder, then, that expensive drug and alcohol rehabilitation clinics are filled to capacity.

Female executives, who would traditionally share their feelings, usually can't do so during the workaday. Women have learned the hard way that it's more appropriate to hide emotional problems. Showing psychological weakness is the kiss of death in today's hard-driving business. More and more, career women report the same kind of problems men do - gastrointestinal disorders and muscle tension. Physical problems are bottom-line quantifiable results - not moodiness.

Patients who seek help for physical symptoms often don't understand that the underlying cause is stress. They treat the symptom, but as soon as they bring it under control, another one pops up.

Men and women who juggle the multiple demands of home and business life are particularly prone to time sickness. Not only are the women propelled by the revved-up technology but they're more likely to try to prove that they can do it all.

Beware of bad employment.

It's not necessarily true about stress at the top. Studies show that those at the bottom of the workplace totem pole have a greater chance of developing heart disease. The very rich and well-educated and the very poor and badly educated, are most likely to report significant levels of stress because of the extreme pressure to get tasks done. However, people in senior, well-paying jobs are more likely to experience positive stress that gives focus to their work. They can control their work more effectively. They leave it behind by escaping to pleasant homes and leisure activities.

Women often have stressful, unrewarding and depersonalised work. Most lack the necessities and amenities of life, aren't part of the mainstream of society and receive little information and support. Many women in the workplace are under-employed, have insecure staff positions (who are the first to go when financial times are tough). They work in sectors that have low pay, poor benefits, little autonomy and few opportunities for paid further training or job advancement. Lack of convenient, affordable and high-quality child care, places an additional stress on many working parents, particularly mothers.

The small percentage of professional women with post-secondary degrees or advanced training, often report the experience of hitting a glass ceiling. This keeps them from reaching upper-level management positions regardless of their talents and accomplishments. Many are breaking out of this pink-collar ghetto, by becoming entrepreneurs themselves and starting their own business where they can make the rules of corporate gamesmanship fit a more female model of management.

Low ranking employees are more likely to feel frustration at a boring (but demanding) job that leaves little sense of accomplishment. They're more likely to worry about inadequate income and job security and are more likely to take their frustration home with them. Studies of both monkeys and people have revealed an unexplained link between hierarchy and cardiovascular illness.

A long-term study of 10,000 civil servants found workers at the bottom were three times as likely to develop heart disease as those at the top. Even when factors such as age, smoking, cholesterol levels and high blood pressure, the incidence of heart disease was 20-50 per cent higher for low-ranking workers.

Stress tests and interviews conducted in the private-sector showed again that it wasn't the management group who recorded the most stress on the job. The study showed that staff and operations people complained the most. What appeared to determine the incidence of stress was the individual's own notion of his or her own power to change frustrating situations. They had little power themselves. Management types, on the other hand, could tolerate more uncertainty, felt themselves important to others and were most satisfied with their jobs.

Little stressors can cause as much stress as the truly big ones. Police officers grouse about paper pushing more than physical danger. Teachers often rank administrative details second only to inadequate salary. Air traffic controllers, who have high rate of hypertension and ulcers attributed to job pressure, complained more about such mundane matters as management, shift schedules and irrelevant chores than the strain of guiding heavy air traffic.

Here's what to look for in a job that won't take years off your life.

a) Avoid no-brain jobs. Studies show that assembly workers are three to four times more likely to suffer heart disease. Similarly, telephone operators, data-input workers, waiters and freight handlers face serious stress. Males who suffered heart attacks before the age of 45, found that a lack of variety in their work was as big a factor, as a family history of heart attacks and excessive smoking.

The design of work can be a major factor in life expectancy. Workers who can use and develop new skills, exercise decision-making power and get feedback and support from bosses and other workers are more likely to live longer.

b) Watch out for shift work. If your work schedule constantly changes your working time or you work shifts, you could face health problems. It can seriously disrupt sleeping time, eating and social relationships.

When shift workers become isolated from family and friends, they can lose their social moorings and support system. Studies suggest that shift workers are more likely to suffer digestive disorders, heart disease and emotional problems.

c) Develop work skills. Middle-aged unskilled workers have a death rate four times higher than top managers and professionals. Cancer, cirrhosis of the liver and accidents topped the list. Unskilled workers are 50 per cent more likely than all other workers to die in middle age. Accidents and heart disease were the biggest culprits.

d) Get control over your own work. Workers who face demanding pressure in their work but have little control over their jobs face serious health consequences. Workers in monotonous jobs that provide no opportunity to learn and develop skills are especially vulnerable. These are people employed as cooks, garment stitchers, assembly-line workers, telephone operators, waiters and cashiers. Their work makes substantial psychological demands on them, but offer little opportunity for independent decision-making. This combination of high demands and low control raises their risk of heart disease by about the same magnitude as smoking or having a high cholesterol level.

Can companies help?

Many companies now offer employee-assistance programs, usually given to lower management. They deal with problems such as substance abuse after stress already has done its damage. Seldom are such programs integrated within the corporation and are only for individuals who admit they have a problem. Getting the green light to start a stress-management program is only a beginning. The true test of a corporation's commitment is what reforms come about as a result of a program's findings. Unless those at the very top take a continuous interest and maintain open communication with the stress-management consultant, the company climate will not change. Doing something as small as altering a dress code for example can do wonders for morale and makes employees feel that someone's listening. Or having a masseuse do neck massage to those who work long hours at their computers.

Many companies expect their executives to endure the extensive pressures hurled at them in the workplace such as mergers, hostile takeovers, constant restructuring and change in strategic direction. In the home, workers often juggle two-career families and face the problems of inadequate child-care and inflation.

The Japanese have an effective method of letting off steam. Some boardrooms have a soundproof closet to which an individual may retire during a meeting. He (in Japan, it's normally 'men only' at such meetings) can yell, weep, whatever - and no one finds it unusual. Although it's hard for Western societies to fathom getting up in the middle of a meeting and going into a closet, the Japanese accepts the practice. And it works. It's when you hold in stress, that it leads to emotional and physical problems. There should be no shame in admitting that work-related stress is as common as the cold. Unfortunately that's not always the case.

Lethargic? Apathetic? Unhappy?

One of the cures may be to increase the level of stress in your life. Students often study most efficiently just before a big exam; tennis players perform better when they're playing for points instead of just whacking the ball around. People with the most sedate work lives will surprise you by revealing that they're sky-divers, white-water rafters, mountain climbers or SCUBA divers. The challenge is stress, but a positive one that, if well-managed, can help you lead a fuller, more contented life.

This means that you don't sit in front of the television set all weekend or stare out the window mulling over the week's problems. Weekends should be exciting and full, so you can go back to your work Monday with your batteries recharged. All you need to do is change the stress and do something different from what you normally do all week. Stop worrying about situations you can't change and do something constructive about those that you can. Learn to pamper yourself. Give yourself mini-holidays. Do something special just for yourself (without feeling guilty).

People should look at themselves realistically. For instance, overweight people often use the excuse, *'Fat runs in my family'* as the cause for their extra pounds when the fact is that, *'Nobody runs in his or her family.'* Their exercise normally involves walking to the fridge to get something to eat while they watch television.

Why women feel cold more than men

Women feel the cold more than males, but their bodies are better at conserving heat when the weather turns colder. They are able to do this by shutting off the blood flow to the skin and extremities to maintain their core temperature of 37 degrees. If it drops below 35 degrees, it can result in hypothermia. However a woman's core body temperature is about .4 degrees higher than men's meaning literally that they have cold hands, but a warm heart. A man tends not to have such a big temperature change as a female, because he doesn't have the same distribution of fat.

We feel cold if our extremities are cold, even if our core organs are warm. The average woman has approximately 20 to 25 percent body fat compared to men who have about 15 percent. Therefore, women often feel cold before men do. Women's hands and feet are about 2.8 degrees lower than men's.

Constantly feeling cold could be caused by: hypothyroidism, diabetes, Raynaud's or anaemia, so see a doctor if you have persistent problems with body heat.

Activity level

Some people love to be busy; others like a slower, less busy pace. Evaluate yourself. See if the following might be a major cause of stress for you.

If you put busy people into routine, low-key jobs, they'll be suffering from stress before long. Are you this kind of person? Or:

If you place a low-key person into a demanding, deadline-prone kind of position you'll have a frazzled and distressed employee. Are you this kind of person?

If your metabolism doesn't fit the job you're in, think seriously about changing positions.

Types of behaviour

Type A: Extreme Type A people are like racehorses and have their own set of needs. They're doers, usually display assertive or aggressive behaviour, are often leaders and have high energy levels. This high energy level can be their worst enemy, because they might mis-channel their energy into hyperactive behaviour, going nowhere. Re-channelling their energy is necessary.

This group is constantly in motion. They're restless people, have louder voices, lack patience with procrastinators, despise lateness in others and could throttle people who are bottlenecks to progress.

Type B: Extreme Type B people are like turtles. They're usually followers, with low energy levels. Many expect others to look after them, are prone to depression, may feel anxious, are usually quiet and shy. They enjoy routine and have infinite patience. Changes disturb them. They're the ones who procrastinate, come late and generally slow up the progress of others.

The ideal situation is to be a good mixture of both. Which are you - a Type A or a Type B person? Now, complete the following questionnaire to see whether you guessed right.

Detecting Type A behaviour

Answer the following questions with a *'Yes'* or a *'No.'*

Vocal explosiveness: Do you overemphasise key words in ordinary speech and speed up the last few words of a sentence?

Constant motion: Do you move, walk and eat rapidly?

Impatience: Do you find yourself hurrying the speech of others or finishing their sentences for them? Is it anguish to wait in line? Do you always rush your reading? Do slow drivers in your lane make you boil?

Thinking or doing two or more things at once: Do you read a book and watch TV or read while you eat?

Dominating conversation: Do you always change the topic to subjects that interest you? Is it difficult to restrain from cutting in? When you can't interrupt, do you pretend to listen while thinking of something else?

Feeling guilty when relaxing: Do you begin to lose respect for yourself when you do nothing for a few hours? Do you have few hobbies or diversions outside work? Do you consider non-competitive physical activities a waste of time?

Preoccupation with having - not being: Do you have problems finding time to improve yourself or explore new and interesting activities? Have you neglected the aesthetic side of life for the sake of collecting achievements?

Scheduling more and more in less and less time: Do you fail to make allowances for unforeseen contingencies? Do you always feel pressured by time? Do you create deadlines if none exist?

Feeling compelled to challenge others: Do you find yourself competing even when the situation doesn't warrant it?

Nervous tics or gestures: Do you frequently clench your fist, bang your hand on the table or pound your fist into your palm to drive home a point? Do you habitually clench your jaw or grind your teeth? Do you have nervous ticks when under pressure?

Fear of slowing down: Do you feel that your success is due to your ability to complete tasks faster than others?

Attachment to the numbers game: Do you find yourself committed to translating achievement in terms of quantity instead of quality?

What to do about Type 'A' behaviour

Are you spending your time doing what's important to you in the three important areas of your life - career, family, social? Are you doing more and more and accomplishing less and less? If so, the following may help you:

1. Identify and set career and life goals.
2. Learn time management - set priorities.
3. Know that you shouldn't feel guilty if you're 'not busy'.
4. Spend time on activities of importance to you.
5. Take regular coffee and lunch breaks.
6. Spend some time alone - possibly in a nature setting and 'get away from it all.'

Take a moment now to determine which of your friends and acquaintances are Type A people. Will the above knowledge help you deal with them better?

Detecting Type 'B' behaviour

Answer the following questions with a *'Yes'* or a *'No.'*

Vocal quietness: Do you speak so softly that others ask you to repeat yourself?

Slow motion: Do you normally have to keep reminding yourself to 'get going,' which makes you late for appointments?

Patience: Do you find that waiting in line never bothers you. Do you drive below the speed limit and get beeped at by other drivers because you're not keeping up with traffic?

Thinking or doing two or more things at once: Do you find you become confused if you attempt to do more than one activity at a time? Do you prefer a routine, repetitive job? Do changes unnerve you?

Lacking in conversational skills: Do you find you spend most of your time listening rather than speaking when in a group?

Your own ability to relax: Do you enjoy loafing around and have difficulty 'getting your act in gear?'

Scheduling less and less in more and more time: Do you fail to meet deadlines or run out of energy long before the day is over? Do you seem to accomplish less now than you did before?

Feelings when challenged by others: Do others intimidate you or do you feel threatened by their successes?

Nervous tics or gestures: Do you display nervous habits when you feel rushed or intimidated?

Fear of slowing down: Do you believe that it's natural that you should be slowing down - you're older than you were when you were at top speed?

Anxiety: Do you feel that you have little control over your life? Do you feel inadequate, uneasy, unfulfilled, not satisfied with where you are or what you're doing but haven't tried to change?

What to do about Type 'B' behaviour

1. Are you in a dead-ended job? Do you have a low energy level or are you lethargic? If so, change jobs.
2. Are you using your potential - or are you floating through life - existing rather than living?
3. Identify and set life and career goals.
4. Set priorities. Don't waste time on trivial items and quit being a perfectionist.
5. Don't remain a follower; become a leader - participate fully - don't just become another body in a group.
6. Give yourself rewards for getting things done.
7. Stop procrastinating - do it today!
8. Build your self-image - take an assertiveness course.
9. Cultivate friends who encourage you to do your best - become a positive thinker.

Take a moment now to determine which of your friends and acquaintances are Type B people. Will the above knowledge help you deal with them better?

CHAPTER EIGHT

Results of too much stress

Stress causes fifty to eighty per cent of diseases. People react by having heart problems, ulcers, some cancers, mental illness, migraine and tension headaches. Chronic conditions such as asthma, arthritis, bronchitis and diabetes often flare up under stress.

These illnesses take up to half the hospital beds in the country.

Stress reduces the body's ability to fight off flu, colds, communicable diseases and simple superficial infections. If you know you're suffering from stress, be aware that you're more prone accidents. If you must decide whether you should or should not make that left turn with your car, opt to wait until you're absolutely sure you can make it safely. This is not the time to go skiing or indulging in any other dangerous activity, because your reaction time and reflexes may be out of sync.

Here are some common results of stress and the most up-to-date medical advice on how to vanquish them:

Insomnia or fitful sleep

People who feel anxious during their waking hours may have trouble falling asleep or sleeping through the night. Waking up super-early is also a sign of stress. (See more information on this topic in Chapter 10.)

Migraines and headaches

Seventy per cent of migraine patients are women, probably because fluxes in estrogen levels contribute to the nerve-cell disturbance. About a quarter of the migraines are stress-related. For the run-of-the-mill headache pain, over-the-counter drugs will normally keep discomfort in check. Migraines are trickier; it's important to learn to spot one coming and have the right doctor-prescribed medication on hand. New forms of meditation, including biofeedback and self-hypnosis, as well as relaxation exercises, are mind-over-body ways to try to outsmart migraines.

As any migraine sufferer knows, an attack can bring a pain so intense that it obliterates work, family and thought. Yet for all the suffering it causes, the migraine is a mundane and commonplace ailment, afflicting about 12 per cent of the population. It's a trait passed along from parent to offspring. 75 per cent of sufferers are thought to have an inherited predisposition to the disorder. These people are warned of a pending migraine attach by hallucinatory auras, a pulsating (often one-sided headache) waves of nausea and the unbearable sensitivity to light, sound and smell. Whether episodes occur once a year or once a week, they usually last for the better part of a day, if not longer.

Scientists are beginning to test a chelated form of magnesium supplements as a possible migraine preventive. Unlike currently available magnesium pills (which can cause severe diarrhoea when taken in therapeutic doses) the new supplements are absorbed without being broken down and don't seem to have side effects.

Headaches also can result from a person's reaction to certain foods, climatic changes or strenuous physical exertion. Muscle tension (which constricts blood vessels) causes non-debilitating but intrusive headaches. Even when it's time to relax, some people are unlucky enough to get out of bed with a so-called weekend headache.

Teeth grinding

Teeth grinding (a stress symptom itself) can make you wake up feeling like you've been on a construction site overnight. You can easily stop teeth grinding by wearing a thin plastic mouthguard at night. Any dentist can provide you with one.

Digestive troubles

Although anxiety is blamed for causing ulcers, doctors now believe that stress makes them worse, but doesn't cause them directly. Upset stomachs and emotional distress go hand in hand. Eating patterns often change during stressful times. Some people eat more - others lose their appetites.

Learning to relax is the key to avoiding this type of stomach trouble. Many people who have stomach upsets suffer from lactose intolerance. There are many medications on the market that allow them to enjoy dairy products without stomach upset. Those who suffer from motion sickness normally do so either because they have balance problems in their ears or because they tighten up their stomach muscles when they feel motion. This causes the muscles to contract causing retching in many.

Far more severe are gastric, peptic and duodenal ulcers that require prompt medical attention. Many people pop antacids thinking that their stomach problems stem from too much acid. We need stomach acid and often antacids rob us of our ability to handle our food. We can't absorb nutrients that are essential to health if we don't have enough acid in our stomachs. Too little stomach acid causes indigestion, mal-absorption and sometimes bloating, a burning feeling, gas and belching. This is because of *too little* acid - not because of too much. Antacids deplete bones of calcium every time they are consumed and contain aluminium that can contribute to Alzheimer's Disease.

Other stressed-out people suffer from lower-tract problems of constipation or diarrhoea. Constipation can be relieved by a high fibre diet. Many people who have bowel movements only once in three or four days, believe they suffer from constipation, when in fact, that's their normal cycle. Another problem is diarrhoea that can be treated with kaolin/pectin mixtures (kaopectate for instance). More serious problems are; irritable colon syndrome, Crohn's disease and ulcerative colitis.

Neck aches and backaches

Some people feel tightness in their shoulders and necks; others complain about stiff lower backs and shooting pains in their legs and buttocks. About 80 per cent of the population have back pain at some point. Hours of sitting at a desk causes the muscle-coiling, blood vessel-tightening response to tension. Weak stomach muscles (key for back support) spell trouble. Even a hard sneeze can send the vulnerable person running to a specialist.

Doctors rarely send back pain sufferers to bed any more - even during a serious bout with pain. Now, hot baths, muscle relaxants and appropriate exercise are more common treatments. Many rely on the manipulations of chiropractors to keep their spines in line.

Surgery is rarely the answer, but vigilance is the golden rule. Daily stretching exercises and a conditioning plan are keys to recovery. Also important are a decent desk chair, proper lifting, bending from the knees and careful carrying. Try intermittently standing during an extended meeting, meal or even a long movie. Frequent breaks on road trips and strolling down the aisle during transcontinental flights help too. Stretching after you've sat for a while is a good idea too.

Decreased sex drive or change in menstrual cycle

A decrease in female-hormone levels (estrogen and progesterone) can occur when a woman suffers from stress. Lowered hormone production is a stress by-product that can delay or completely interrupt a menstrual cycle. Pre menstrual tension (PMS) is also common among stress suffering women.

As with other stress problems, regular health rules apply. Exercise regularly, especially to relieve PMS symptoms. Avoid or cut down on alcohol, caffeine, sugar, fat and salt. If menstrual changes persist, see a doctor. For many women, eating right and getting regular exercise is the best medicine. While the woman battles these hormonal deficiencies, encouragement, support and acceptance from family members are a must.

Impotency

Is there a male menopause? The evidence hints that a similar phenomenon begins in many men's lives during their 40's, 50's or 60's. Physically, men notice a gradual decrease in muscle mass and strength. Common psychological symptoms are lethargy, depression, irritability, mood swings and a loss of well-being (similar to women going through menopause). They also may notice a slackening of sexual desire. If female menopause is a silent passage, the loss of potency that can accompany male menopause, is the unspeakable passage. It strikes at the core of what it is to be a man.

Men's reproductive glands don't shut down the way women's do and their changes are more gradual. It has nothing to do with fertility; men can still sire children well into old age. The major problem is impotency. Once it begins, the decline of potency can create the performance anxiety that triggers real problems. Men feel relief once they recognise that this is not a sign that they're inadequate as males, but is mainly a physical problem. The most common factor is impairment of the blood supply due to vascular problems. Even at age 40, nearly two thirds of those reporting a diagnosis of heart disease exhibit at least moderate impotency.

Prescription drugs for hypertension, for example, can be another enemy. Alcohol is also treacherous for middle-aged men. The steady drinkers of today are the lousy lovers of tomorrow. Smoking is devastating because it affects the vascular supply required to create an erection and is probably the major contributing cause of male sexual dysfunction.

A decrease in male-hormone levels (testosterone) can occur when a man is under extreme stress. This inability to perform can become a 'catch-22' situation. The more the man tries to perform, the more frustrated and stressful he becomes. Encouragement and support from wives and significant others and their willingness to accept hugs and cuddles are required until the cycle passes.

Depression

Depression is an illness caused by measurable changes in brain chemistry. It's more common in younger people, but the elderly also suffer. Normally, some important loss triggers depression. Younger people feel despondent when they lose items of value, friends, health, promotions, income and value as a human being. As people age, they lose many items of value - jobs, income, prestige, friends and health. For most people, recovery follows a period of grief or serious loss, but for others depression follows.

In the elderly, the most common signs of depression are insomnia, loss of interest in usual activities and loss of energy. Often there is weight loss as well as difficulty concentrating, feelings of worthlessness and thoughts of suicide. The person may sit around all day or become unusually active, although this latter response is uncommon.

There are three important reasons to recognise and treat depression. First, suicide is extremely common. Depression can be anger they're turning against themselves because they feel so helpless about the situation. The resulting depression can become so severe that they think of suicide. Some even carry out the thought. In most cases it's preventable, but we need to look hard for its warning signs.

Second, people with depression suffer. Quality of life is poor and they're unable to be enthusiastic or enjoy activities. Depressed people might say they 'don't feel right.' or 'don't feel at all like themselves.' Prompt treatment makes most people feel better.

Third, identifying depression often can clarify what's wrong for an elderly person who complains about an unending series of physical complaints. This can be of big relief to the physician and can save the patient the expense and risk of diagnostic tests.

Entire books are written about the drugs used to treat depression. The most important points though, are that these drugs can be extremely helpful and effective. Unfortunately, they also may have some dangerous side-effects. There's solid evidence that the very best treatment for depression is a combination of carefully used anti-depressant medication and counselling.

Other stress-related results

When stress builds up, it attacks us in other ways as well:

Renewal: Experiences that once renewed us, now cause stress instead. At this time we don't always enjoy having a weekend off, going to a movie or sporting event or visiting friends.

Concentration: Inner and outer stimuli easily distract us. It's difficult for us to sit still and attend to detailed tasks.

Memory: We forget where we've put objects. We forget details, deadlines and promises we easily remembered in the past.

Appetite: We over-eat or drink or can have a loss of appetite.

Patience: Our frustration tolerance is low, causing impatience and outbursts of anger.

Motivation: We lack the drive, energy and desire to attend to ordinary tasks and responsibilities.

Mood: We feel sad, depressed, helpless and hopeless or hyperactive. We display an inappropriate amount of energy, excitement, opportunism and happiness.

Relating: We experience a fight-or-flight reaction when dealing with others. We withdraw from or attack others with irritability, rudeness, sarcasm or hostility.

Stress leads to colds/flu

A study by a group of British and American researchers confirms what many people have long suspected - stress can make you more susceptible to colds. Researchers gauged how much stress 394 volunteers were feeling from family- and job-related sources and then exposed all of them to one of five cold viruses. Of those under the most stress, 47 per cent caught colds, compared to 27 per cent of those with the least stress. The researchers believe that stress affects the immune system and lowers resistance to viruses.

When is the last time you had a cold or the flu? Were you under more stress and strain than usual?

Obesity plus stress = trouble

Men with beer bellies and women with apple-shaped bodies have a high chance of having diabetes. Many may not even know that they have it, because there often are no symptoms. Doctors addressing a symposium on diabetes drove home the point that fat and diabetes often go together. One doctor stated, *'If you're a diabetic and especially one who's overweight, you can pretty well sign your death certificate today, but you just can't put a date on it.'*

While there are generally no symptoms, a diabetic who develops hyperglycemia (too high a level of glucose in the blood) may have great thirst and hunger, a dry mouth and a need to urinate often. The cause isn't completely understood, but anyone with at least one close relative with diabetes inherits the tendency to get it.

Eighty per cent of diabetics will die of cardiovascular disease. A greater number stand the risk of going blind (accounts for half of blindness under age 65 and one-quarter of visual impairment). Forty per cent of amputations (because of poor circulation) are due to diabetes. Diabetes is a lifelong disorder in which the body can't properly store and provide fuel to cells. Either the pancreas doesn't produce enough insulin, so the body can use glucose (or sugar) for energy or it's unable to use the insulin it does produce.

Doctors noted that some obese diabetics have been known to cure themselves by losing weight, maintaining a low-fat diet, exercising, quitting smoking and reducing alcohol consumption.

Heart Attacks

Heart attacks and stress

A workaholic lifestyle in itself does not necessarily predispose a person to one of the most serious effects of stress - heart attacks. Research confirms that a person's personality may play a contributing role. Control anger as much as you can. Direct your efforts towards being assertive with those who harass you or it will affect you physically. Those who are always in a hurry, talk rapidly, interrupt and exhibit the time-urgency of Type A behaviour were not in the high-risk category for heart attacks. But there is a relationship between hostility and severity of blockages.

Physical symptoms of stress are becoming so common that many individuals can tune into the underlying cause, be it an allergic reaction or tense shoulders. Instead of simply reaching for an antihistamine or calling a masseuse, (both of which can help with the immediate problem).the smarter response is to examine the stress and then do something about it. If you can't get rid of the problem, then at least you can learn how to change your response to it.

Early warnings of a heart attack

Pain, in one form or another, usually accompanies a heart attack. This pain ranges from a mild ache, to one of unbearable severity. Severe chest pain is often constricting or vise-like pain. Pain often includes the burning and bloated sensations that usually accompany indigestion. Pain may be continuous and then might subside, but don't ignore it if it does. It could be in any one or a combination of the following:

- Localised (just under the breastbone, in larger area of mid-chest or the entire upper chest.)
- A common combination is pain in the mid-chest, neck and jaw.
- Mid-chest and inside arms, (left arm and shoulder more frequently than right).

- Upper abdomen - where it's often mistaken for indigestion.
- Large area of chest, neck, jaw and inside arms.
- Lower centre of neck, to both sides of the upper neck; and jaw from ear to ear.
- Inside the right arm from armpit to below the elbow or inside left arm to the waist. (Occurs in the left arm and shoulder more frequently than right).
- In back area between shoulder blades.

Checklist of other heart attack early warnings:

None of the symptoms below is conclusive proof of a heart attack. However, the more of them present, the more likely it is that the patient is undergoing a heart attack.

- Difficulty breathing
- Heart palpitations
- Nausea
- Cold sweat
- Paleness
- Weakness
- Anxiety

Female heart attacks

Women who have heart attacks (myocardial infarction) rarely have the same dramatic symptoms that men have like the sudden stabbing pain in the chest, the cold sweat, grabbing the chest and dropping to the floor that we see in the movies. It is said that many more women than men die of their first (and last) MI because they didn't know they were having one and commonly mistake it as indigestion. Instead, they take some Maalox or other anti-heartburn preparation and go to bed, hoping they'll feel better in the morning when they wake up ... which doesn't happen. Pain in the jaw can wake you from a sound sleep, so the more women know, the better chance they have of surviving.

Here is the story of one woman's experience with a heart attack.

'I had a heart attack at about 10:30 pm with NO prior exertion; NO prior emotional trauma that one would suspect might've brought it

on. I was sitting all snugly and warm on a cold evening, with my purring cat in my lap, reading an interesting story my friend had sent me and actually thinking, 'Ah, this is the life, all cosy and warm in my soft, cushy Lazy Boy with my feet propped up.' A moment later, I felt the awful sensation of indigestion, such as when you've been in a hurry and grabbed a bite of sandwich and washed it down with a dash of water and that hurried bite seems to feel like you've swallowed a golf ball going down the esophagus in slow motion that is most uncomfortable. You realise you shouldn't have gulped it down so fast and needed to chew it more thoroughly and this time drink a glass of water to hasten its progress down to the stomach.

This was my initial sensation - the only trouble was that I hadn't taken a bite of anything since about 5:00 pm. After it seemed to subside, the next sensation was like little squeezing motions that seemed to be racing up my SPINE (hind-sight, it was probably my aorta in spasm), gaining speed as they continued racing up and under my sternum (breast bone, where one presses rhythmically when administering CPR).

This fascinating process continued on into my throat and branched out into both jaws. 'AHA!! NOW I stopped puzzling about what was happening. We all have read and/or heard about pain in the jaws being one of the signals of an MI happening, haven't we? I said aloud to myself and the cat, 'Dear God, I think I'm having a heart attack!'

I lowered the footrest dumping the cat from my lap, started to take a step and fell on the floor instead. I thought to myself, 'If this is a heart attack, I shouldn't be walking into the next room where the phone is or anywhere else ... but, on the other hand, if I don't, nobody will know that I need help and if I wait any longer I may not be able to get up.'

I pulled myself up with the arms of the chair, walked slowly into the next room and called the Paramedics. I told them I thought I was having a heart attack due to the pressure building under the sternum and radiating into my jaws. I didn't feel hysterical or afraid, just stating the facts. She said she was sending the Paramedics over immediately, asked if the front door was near to me and if so, to unbolt the door and then lie down on the floor where they could see me when they came in. If I could easily do so, I was to take an Aspirin.

I unlocked the door and lay down on the floor as instructed. I must have lost consciousness, because I don't remember the medics coming in, their examination, lifting me onto a gurney or getting me into an ambulance, but I did briefly awaken when we arrived and saw that the Cardiologist was already there in his surgical blues and cap, as he helped the medics pull my stretcher out of the ambulance.

The Cardiologist installed two side by side stents to hold open my right coronary artery.

'I know it sounds like all my thinking and actions at home must have taken at least 20-30 minutes before calling the Paramedics, but actually it took perhaps 4-5 minutes before the call and both the fire station and St. Jude are only minutes away from my home. Thankfully, my Cardiologist was ready to go to the OR.'

How to help a possible heart attack victim:

You can best help and possibly save a life, if you know in advance:

1. The nearest hospital equipped to handle heart attack emergencies
2. How to do cardiopulmonary Resuscitation (CPR)
3. How to quickly call a doctor, hospital or ambulance
4. The quickest route to the hospital.

Knowing these things, you should:

1. Place victim in the least painful position - usually sitting, with legs up and knees bent. Loosen clothing around neck and midriff. Be calm and reassuring.
2. Quickly call ambulance to get victim to hospital via your local rescue squad, police, fire or other available service. Once the ambulance is on its way, notify the patient's family physician (if known).
3. Comfort victim while waiting for ambulance. Otherwise, help the victim to a vehicle, trying to keep victim's exertion to a minimum. If possible, take another CPR-trained person with you. Victim should sit up while being transported.

4. Drive cautiously to hospital. Watch victim closely (or have other passenger do so). If victim loses consciousness, check for breathing and feel for neck pulse under side angle of lower jaw to check for circulation. If no pulse is found, start CPR and call for help. Continue CPR until trained help arrives to take over.
5. If the patient retains consciousness to hospital, make sure s/he is carried, not walked, into the emergency room.

How to survive a heart attack when you are alone

Suddenly you start experiencing severe pain in your chest that starts to radiate out into your arm and up into your jaw. You are only about five km from the hospital nearest to your home. Unfortunately you don't know if you'll be able to make it that far. What do you do? You're trained in CPR, but you weren't taught how to handle a case where it was *you* having the attack.

Without help you know that if your heart isn't beating properly, you'll begin to feel faint and have only about ten seconds left before you lose consciousness. There IS something you can do.

Cough repeatedly and very vigorously. Take a deep breath before each cough and the cough must be deep and prolonged as when producing sputum from deep inside the chest. A breath and a cough must be repeated about every two seconds without let up until help arrives or until the heart is felt to be beating normally again.

Deep breaths get oxygen into the lungs and coughing movements squeeze the heart and keep the blood circulating. The squeezing pressure on the heart also helps it regain normal rhythm. In this way you can get to a hospital even though you may be alone.

Strokes

What is a stroke?

A stroke results from an interruption in the blood supply to part of the brain. Without a continuous, adequate supply of oxygen-rich blood, nerve cells in that area cannot function properly. The nerve cells of the brain control the way we receive, interpret and respond to sensations and information and most of our movements as well. If some nerve cells are unable to function, then the part of the body controlled by those nerves cannot function either. For example, a stroke may produce difficulty in speaking, inability to walk or loss of memory.

Why do strokes occur?

A frequent cause is the blocking of one of the arteries that supplies blood to a section of the brain by a clot (cerebral thrombus). Often the clot occurs in one of the neck arteries.

Another cause occurs when a wandering clot (embolus) carried in the bloodstream, becomes lodged in one of the arteries of the brain. This cerebral embolism interferes with blood flow. Most often the clot comes from the heart.

A stroke also occurs when a diseased artery in the brain bursts, flooding the surrounding tissue with blood. This is a cerebral haemorrhage. A head injury can cause an aneurysm. An aneurysm is a blood-filled pouch that balloons out from a weak spot in the wall of a cerebral artery.

What are the warning signs of a stroke?

The primary one is a sudden, dramatic weakness or numbness of the face, arm or leg on one side of the body, which usually lasts for only a few minutes.

Others include:

- Temporary loss of speech or trouble in speaking or understanding speech.
- Temporary dimness or loss of vision, particularly in one eye.
- Sudden, severe, unusual headaches or a change in the pattern of headaches.

If you experience any of these problems, see your doctor immediately. You may well head off a stroke. Also remember the important three letters ... S.T.R. Doctors say a bystander can recognise a stroke by asking three simple questions:

- S.: Ask the individual to smile.

- T.: Ask the person to talk and speak a simple sentence coherently. (i.e. It is sunny out today.)
- R.: Ask him/her to raise both arms.
- Ask the person to 'stick' out his/her tongue. Check to see if the tongue is 'crooked,' if it goes to one side or the other.

If s/he has trouble with *any one* of these tasks, call emergency number immediately and describe the symptoms to the dispatcher.

Are some people more likely than others to have a stroke?

Yes. Your risk of having a stroke increases significantly if you have high blood pressure (hypertension) atherosclerosis (hardening of the arteries) heart disease of any kind or diabetes. Others are those with high cholesterol levels, are smokers, excessive use of alcohol, a family history of cardiovascular problems or are obese. A person with any of these conditions should see a doctor regularly and follow his other treatment to the letter.

How to fight strokes

- Have your blood pressure checked once a year.
- Don't smoke.
- Eat a well-balanced diet low in saturated animal) fats. Watch your weight.
- Exercise regularly and sensibly.
- Learn the warning signs of stroke and see your doctor if they occur.

Cancer linked with stress?

New research with psychiatric patients suggests a biological link between stress and the body's ability to fight cancer. They found a correlation between distress and the body's ability to repair damaged DNA in lymphocytes (cells that help defend the body against cancer). The study didn't prove that stress causes cancer, but identifies how stress could participate in its formation.

The researchers first measured the level of depression among 28 newly admitted psychiatric patients. They exposed lymphocytes from patient's blood samples to radiation so they could damage the

DNA. They then examined the samples to determine their ability to repair themselves. They compared these results with a control group of 28 blood donors of the same age and sex as the subjects. The results showed that the non-depressed subjects showed a marked ability to repair their immune system. If people are depressed, hostile or alienated at an early age, they're more likely to develop cancer than those who don't have those attributes.

A new study suggests that stressful life events (especially job-related problems) can increase the risk of colorectal cancer. The finding adds weight to the idea that stress can affect the body in a way that may lead to cancer - and that those who cope best may also avoid it. The event itself is only a catalyst. Researchers compared medical histories and questionnaires about life events over 10 years from more than 1,000 Swedes. Their findings were:

- Serious work-related problems made a person five times more likely to develop colorectal cancer.
- Unemployment of more than six months doubled the cancer risk.
- Those who moved more than 120 miles had nearly three times the risk.
- Divorce or a spouse's death increased cancer risk by 50%.

Researchers theorised that work problems may result in long-term stress, while emotionally traumatic events like the death of a loved one could be resolved more quickly. It may not be the event that causes stress, but our way of thinking about and handling it.

CHAPTER NINE

Dealing with anger and worry

Anger is a choice as well as a habit. It's a learned reaction to frustration. Severe anger is a form of insanity (you're insane when you're not in control of your behaviour). Therefore, when you're angry and out of control, you're temporarily insane. Certainly, give vent to your anger, but in non-destructive ways. Use your energy towards solving the reason for the anger, rather than on the person or situation that caused the anger in the first place.

Anger is an energy drainer and can cause many illnesses: hypertension, ulcers, migraine headaches, rashes, hives, heart palpitations, insomnia and physical fatigue to name a few. Anger breaks down love relationships, interferes with communication, leads to guilt and depression and just gets in the way.

It's healthier to express anger than to suppress it, but it's better not to have the anger in the first place. Anger doesn't simply happen to you. It's begun by thinking. You actually give up power when you become very angry, especially if the target of your anger responds with calmness.

Anger is a very real part of everyone. The time has come for us to learn about anger, accept that we have a right to it and learn how to express it.

Control your anger

If you have frequent quarrels or if you're usually defiant; learn to give a little. It's important that you hold your ground where principles and moral values are involved, but refusing to budge on a nonessential issue is absurd and serves to increase your stress level. Learn to compromise a little and don't view giving in slightly, as a sign of weakness or failure.

Choose something that's been bothering you for a long time. Now, instead of building up a pressure cooker of guilt and shame, turn the experience around and decide what positive ideas you can learn from it. When situations don't go as you would wish them to, it's not the end of the world - a major crisis. Sit down and figure out a different way of accomplishing your goal or dream.

If you're forced to interact regularly with someone you don't like, approach the person calmly and let him or her know what it is that upsets you. Practice your listening skills so you'll have a better chance of understanding their side.

Children of parents who have trouble making them behave often think, *'See what it takes to set mommy off? All I have to do is say this or do that and I get Mommy to go into one of her fits. Of course, I may have to stay in my room for a while, but look at the benefits. I have emotional control over her. Since I have little power overall, I think I'll do this some more and watch her go bananas again!'*

Don't let your children mismanage their anger. Help them find constructive, non-threatening ways of dealing with their emotions.

How do you deal with your anger?

- Do you find yourself expressing anger daily?
- Do you often find that people around you appear defensive, always ready to defend themselves?
- Do you have trouble keeping friends because of your way of expressing anger or a rather gruff communication style?
- Do you pick on service people to vent your anger knowing they're not likely to fight back?
- Do you occasionally resort to giving people the 'silent treatment,' instead of expressing your anger?
- Do you find it too stressful to let your anger out at all?
- Do others constantly take advantage of you because you're afraid to express your feelings to them?

Did you answer yes to any of the above? If so, you'll be able to identify some of the areas where anger is a problem to you, by completing the following questionnaire:

1 = yes   2 = no   3 = sometimes

1. Do I usually walk away from the other person when I'm angry?
2. Do I usually keep quiet when I'm angry? (Give the silent treatment?)

3. Do I simmer for days and then vent my anger in a big blow up?
4. Do I appear to feel hurt when I'm actually angry? (Want sympathy?)
5. Do I take out my anger on someone other than to the person making me angry?
6. Do I express my anger by labelling the other person, rather than dealing with their behaviour?
7. When someone else is angry with me, do I have problems keeping my composure without blustering?
8. Do I have trouble 'keeping my cool' when accused of something I didn't do?
9. Do I feel hurt and withdraw when someone's angry with me, rather than facing the issue openly with that person?

Rate yourself:

> Answers 1 = yes: You must work on these.
> Answers 2 = no: No problems here.
> Answers 3 = sometimes:

Judge for yourself whether these are causing you problems. If so, work on solving the problems.

Here's another way to identify how you deal with your own and others' anger. Check or circle the most applicable suggestion:

1. When I'm angry, I usually feel:
   a) Afraid to say anything directly, because I don't want to hurt others' feelings.
   b) Afraid that if I do say something, it will sound aggressive and others won't like me
   c) That it's okay to express what is on my mind.
   d) Anxious and confused about what I want to say.
2. When I'm angry with someone, I usually:
   (a) Drop hints about my feelings, hoping s/he will get the message.
   (b) Tell the person in a direct way, what I want and feel okay about it.
   (c) Avoid the person for a while, while I calm down and the anger wears off.
   (d) Blow up and tell him or her off.

(e) Express my anger sarcastically - getting my point across with humour or a dig.

Dealing with others' anger:

3. When others get angry with me, I usually:
    (a) Think they don't like me.
    (b) Feel too scared to ask why they're angry at me.
    (c) Feel confused and upset.
    (d) Think I have a right to understand why they're angry and to respond to it.
    (e) Feel wronged.
    (f) Feel guilty.
4. When others get angry with me, what I usually do is:
    (a) End up blustering.
    (b) Back off.
    (c) Ask them to explain their anger further or else I respond to it in some other equally straightforward manner.
    (d) Get angry in return.
    (e) Apologise if I don't understand why they're angry.
    (f) Try to smooth it over.
    (g) Make a joke out of it and try to get them to forget the flare-up.

Rate yourself:

The following answers indicate assertive beliefs and behaviours:

1. (c)
2. (b) & (c)
3. (d)
4. (c)

Frustration and anger

Seldom do people go from mere frustration to anger. Usually, it takes a person many negative instances or a long time of putting up with a negative situation, to become angry. When people become frustrated or angry, it's usually because they want something and for some reason they can't have it. Most people who go through the frustration and anger cycle have a need that's not being met. They run into what I call a 'block.' This concept is identified as follows:

A person has a Need
They encounter a Block
They want satisfaction of that need

It's important when you're dealing with someone who's angry, to determine what their 'block' is that's caused them to be angry. Then do your best to remove their block. Here are some frustrations (which can lead to anger) in clients and customers. You've probably felt some of them yourselves.

- Nobody's listening to me!
- Something went wrong.
- I'm being ignored
- The product doesn't work!
- I'm not getting your help

If clients verbally attack you for something you didn't do or have no control over, try the following steps to maintain control of the situation:

1. If you feel that your defence mechanism has kicked in, turn it off and concentrate instead on solving the person's problems.
2. Listen carefully to what they say. If it's a telephone conversation, jot down their general comments about their problem.
3. Paraphrase what they've said. *'I want to make sure I'm clear about your problem Mrs. Jones. This happened ... and this happened ...(etc.)'*
4. Ask questions. *'And then what happened?'*
5. Do your best to solve their problem.

Frustration and anger may occur in your everyday interaction with family, friends and co-workers. Some of the things that might cause your blocks are others who display the following behaviours:

- Aggressive or bossy
- Persistent

- Ramblers
- Pick fights
- Compulsive behaviour
- Rude or discourteous
- Indecisive
- Bored
- Negative thinkers
- Whiners, complainers and bellyachers

The criticism you give needs to be helpful. If there's little chance that they can change their behaviour - learn to live with it. For example, if a thirty-year-old woman bites her fingernails, it's not likely that she can stop biting them, just because it annoys you.

Use the skill of feedback to alter or stop negative behaviour in others. It's especially useful when you're upset or aggravated by something someone has done or is doing. Constant, repetitive behaviour can be highly annoying to some people. This could be a person saying the same phrase repeatedly during their conversation, *'You know ...'* or *'Like ah ...'* Identify what they're doing that bothers you and give them the opportunity of changing the situation.

Use feedback to express both positive and negative feelings other's provoke in you. An example of positive feedback is when you give praise, compliments and recognition to others. Negative feedback occurs when you let the person know that what they're doing is bothering you. This gives them a chance to change their behaviour. Feedback works as follows:

Process of feedback

A. Describe their behaviour
B. Explain what happens to you when they behave the way they do
C. Ask them for a solution or suggest one yourself

If they don't change their behaviour the first time you ask them to, then consider the following steps. (You can eliminate any of the stages if the situation warrants it.)

Feedback steps

1. Follow A, B and C steps from Process of Feedback.
2. The second time they display the unwanted behaviour, repeat step 1.
3. The third occasion:
   Ask person to explain why s/he's still doing something that s/he ***knows*** annoys you.
   Explain the consequences if the behaviour or situation happens again. (With children removing privileges has been found to be the best consequence.)
4. And the fourth occasion: Follow-through with the consequences.

How to deal with whiners, complainers and bellyachers:

We complain for all kinds of reasons. We complain about the weather, a child's messy room, our team's loss of a game, our age or our weight. Some do it for fun, some do it for attention and others gripe because they're not happy with, well, themselves. Complaining also can be healthy. Fear and anger are two of our emotions and it's good when we vent your frustration. However, when complaining is a significant component of a person's lifestyle, it could become a problem and damage their mental health.

The way they talk to others becomes part of their personality. If people complain all day, they're telling people how bad things are, but they're also hearing the complaints themselves. They're hearing negative comments all day and start looking for bad things to happen.

Many chronic complainers start this negative habit when they're children. Initially, they may start by complaining for attention. If that works and they get things done through complaining, the behaviour will continue. Because children's behaviour mimics the actions of their role models (usually their parents) complaining can start at an early age. If dad's a complainer, then the children will likely be complainers. What's even more damaging to their mental health is that they start believing that everyone's out to get dad and they can grow up prejudiced and suspicious.

Chronic complainers usually aren't very sure of themselves. They're the people who love to give bad news to others. Somehow this increases their self-esteem. This is an unconscious act - they don't intentionally set out to bring people down.

Chronic complainers are stifled by others who concentrate on the positives in situations. A person listening to a chronic complainer can ignore the person's complaints, by concentrating on the positives in the situation. The complainer will eventually notice that the listener isn't listening when s/he complains.

Here are the steps to take if when faced with someone who's constant whining and complaining. When this starts to irritate you:

1. Ask if they'd like you to help them solve their problem. If they don't want you to help them with their problem, go directly to number 7. Say, *'If you won't let me help you with this problem, I don't want to hear any more about it.'* Then stick to it.
2. If they do accept your help, have them write down their **specific** problem. You might have to interview them for some time to help them pinpoint the specific problem. This is usually necessary for chronic complainers, because they have trouble identifying the real problem or seeing the specific problem.
3. Ask them to write down all the possible solutions they can find that will lessen their problem. At this point, you can suggest other alternatives they might have missed.
4. Then, under each solution, have them identify the benefits and disadvantages (pros and cons) of each solution.
5. Have **them** choose the best solution. When they say, *'What do you think I should do?'* don't take the bait. That only gives them an excuse to say, *'I told you it wouldn't work!'*
6. Have them write out the steps that will enable them to achieve their chosen solution. Make sure they include dates and deadlines for accomplishing each step.
7. If they still rant and rave about the same problem in the future, refuse to talk about the topic.

If you're the complainer, try these steps on yourself instead of driving your friends and family to distraction.

Eliminating frustration and anger

Additional steps you can take are:

- Stop what you're doing and tune into your feelings.
- Narrow down what caused your anger
- Try to understand why you got angry (fear etc.)
- Deal with your anger realistically and then communicate those feelings with the person who upset you.
- Take a walk to clear your head. Use your adrenalin effectively by using it towards constructive ends.

The following also might help you get situations out into the open and deal with them.

1. Write down situations that cause you frustration, worry or anger. (Include those from your personal, business and social life).
2. Determine whether:
    (a) You *do* have the power to change the situation or
    (b) You *don't* have the power to change the situation. If you don't have the power to change the situation - put these thoughts and worries out of your mind. Otherwise, you'll be wasting your valuable time and energy on wasted effort. This also applies to all the things you say that start with: 'If only ...' or 'I should have ...'
3. If you do have the power to change the situation, what do you intend to do about it? Or are you just going to whine and complain about it? Set some specific goals to make sure it happens.

The above three steps put into action the Serenity Prayer written by Reinhold Nebhaeur:

'God grant me the serenity to accept the things I cannot change, the courage to change the things I can and the wisdom to know the difference.'

Controlling our moods

Do you suffer from moodiness - up one minute - down the next? We can eliminate some of these mood swings by changing our reactions to negative situations. We can overcome our reactions to an angry, rude, impatient or upset person, if we refuse to accept the negatives they're throwing at us. This takes practice, but it really works. For instance:

- You choose to get angry at the other driver who cut you off in traffic.
- You choose to be irritated by your customer's bad mood.
- You choose to get yourself stressed when an extra batch of work is dumped on your desk.
- You choose to be depressed for no reason, other than it's Monday morning.

Repression of anger

The time we can get into serious trouble is when we repress our anger. Since childhood, men and women are told to hold back and control their negative feelings. This kind of conditioning results in two types of people:

Type 1: For whatever reasons, they've never learned to express their anger. No matter what the provocation, they clench their teeth and hold in their resentment. In some cases, they aren't even aware they're angry.

Type 2: They too haven't learned how to express anger. Instead of showing displeasure over the minor, irritating day-to-day episodes that occur in everyone's life, they say nothing at the time. Then, a co-worker, salesperson or friend makes a chance remark that triggers a red flash of rage and they lash out in violent anger. This fury has unfortunate consequences: The person feels terrible and alienates others.

Both are extremes. Correct ways of dealing with anger means knowing your rights and appropriately expressing your feelings. For instance, when someone tries to interfere with your rights, places an obstacle in your path or violates your dignity, confront them with your feelings (using feedback). Uncontrolled lashing out, is not an effective expression of anger. Instead, after taking everything into consideration, decide how best to express your anger.

Some feel (incorrectly) that anger is a dangerous, powerful emotion. They believe that if they really get angry, they'll lose somebody's love, provoke anger at themselves in return or that people won't like them. In fact, they've got this backwards. It's the repression of anger (not its expression) that's dangerous. Besides, it doesn't matter a bit whether everyone likes you. That's an impossible goal - one that's guaranteed to frustrate you. People won't like you any more if you never get mad - in fact, they may like you less for it. You need to express pent-up anger instead of storing it up.

The ultimate goal is to learn to think in new ways that won't create anger. Such as thinking - *'It's too bad that Bill's in such a bad mood - but I'm not going to let him pass it on to me. I'll simply ignore his bad mood or even better; try to help him out of it, without getting angry myself if he doesn't appreciate my efforts.'*

Occasionally, we work too long and too hard and find after a while that our productivity is slipping. If you find this happening to you - you might save considerable time and effort if you have what I call a 'mental health break.' This is when you stop doing everything. Close your eyes and try some relaxation exercises for five to fifteen minutes. Or get up and move around; do something different if necessary to give yourself a break. You'll go back to work refreshed and able to handle the workload better.

You may have trouble expressing anger because you're a passive person. If you have no trouble at all expressing anger, you must ask yourself if you're using aggressive behaviour and taking advantage of others.

Repression of anger can have the following repercussions:

Depression: This can be anger that they turn against themselves because they feel so helpless about the situation. The resulting depression can become so severe that they think of suicide and some even carry out the thought.

Displacement: Unable to face what they're really anger about, they shift it to another cause. For example something goes wrong at a party. They say nothing, but later blame their spouse for something s/he didn't do.

Long fights: These often don't concern what they're really angry about. They occur because they've shifted their goal from sharing, to one of hurting the other person. They forget where they want to go. Their anger takes over and they can't stop themselves. We see this in couples who 'snipe' at each other (degrade each other either privately or publicly).

Temper tantrums: This is inappropriate, uncontrolled expression of anger that can be triggered by anything, whether some trivial current happening or something that took place long ago that they've stewed about for years. Tantrums are the worst kind of bullying tactics.

Psychosomatic illnesses: Their repression of anger can cause them tension, insomnia and other stress-related illnesses.

Ways of showing anger

There are many ways of expressing anger. Some are positive, but others are negative and can hurt ourselves and others:

- Verbal abuse or swearing
- Physical violence
- Threats to others
- Temper tantrums
- Sarcasm and ridicule
- Silence or withdrawal
- Denial
- Sabotage
- Drugs or alcohol
- Vandalism
- Overeating
- Blaming others

How to handle anger

1. Don't rationalise your reasons for not expressing anger.

Don't pay attention to such things as, *'I'm afraid to say anything because I'll hurt the other person's feelings.'* These are ways of explaining to yourself why you don't do what you've never learned to do. Instead of dwelling on the reasons you don't express anger, concentrate on learning how to do it.

2. Try to correct the behaviour of the person causing the anger; don't attack the person themselves.

For example; a child spills his milk. Scold the child for the behaviour, but don't attack him as a person. Say *'Johnny, I'm upset. You spilled your milk again. Will you try to be more careful next time?'* instead of; *'Johnny, you're so sloppy! Can't you do anything right?'*

3. Target your angry behaviour. Get the pattern of your anger.

(a) Check the way you express anger

- Do you show too little?
- Do you come on too strong, too weak or not at all?
- Do you express anger days, months, even years after the provoking incident?
- Do you concentrate your efforts towards getting revenge for others' past wrongdoings?
- Is your nonverbal communication of anger appropriate?
- Do you fall into the trap of attributing your anger to someone else? *('You make me angry!')*
- Do you mouth angry words, but say them in a whisper that the other person can barely hear? Do you slouch or keep your eyes on the floor as you say them
- Remember you 'own' your responses. When you express anger, you should try to relate your comments to what the other person has done. *'I'm angry because you always leave the newspaper on the floor.'*

(b) The different situations in which you have difficulty.

Is it at work? If so, break it down. Does your anger have to do with co-workers, subordinates, superiors?

In impersonal situations? Some people always get angry with taxi drivers and others who can not express annoyance back to them.

Friends and acquaintances? With some people, the more distant the acquaintance is; the easier is to express anger. With others it's the reverse. The closer the friend, the easier it is to say *'I'm furious.'* There are some people who feel that the only time they're 'being honest' is when they express anger.

Social situations? Can you get angry in a group conversation but not in a one-to-one encounter? Do you feel safer in a group - or the reverse?

In close relationships? Some can express anger only to a spouse. When asked *'Why?'* the answer is often *'S/he's the only one in the world who wouldn't leave me if I show anger.'*

What time of the day do you become angry more often? What day of the week or season of the year?

4. Recognise that you have a right to feel anger and express it.

Anger doesn't have to lead to violence. If you have doubts about your right to be angry, perhaps you've done something you don't like. (You'd like to yell at yourself, but instead take it out on another person).

5. Avoid direct expression of anger.

Perhaps you sit and sulk seething inside, but refuse to say why you're angry. When asked *'What's wrong?'* you reply with a curt, *'Nothing.'* Do you communicate hurt instead of anger, *('You shouldn't have done this to me.'*) Or do you use hurting sarcasm to express your anger, making it difficult for the other person to cope with the situation. Others know something's wrong, but your sarcasm pushes them away so they can't pin down just what's bothering you.

6. Express your anger when you feel it.

In this way, you can frequently avoid unpleasant consequences and the little annoyances will not accumulate. Many lash out at the wrong person, for the wrong reasons.

7. Don't make the mistake of not going far enough in your anger.

Some people make tentative stabs at expression of anger then abort it. Don't just say you're angry find a solution to the problem or situation that caused the anger in the first place.

8. Realise that you have the right to raise your voice.

It's perfectly all right to pound the table, swear, shout and do all the things 'Mother' told you not to do, as long as you're not intimidating or taking advantage of another. Expressing anger doesn't involve just a higher voice level, it's the words you use, body position and movement. Some treat anger with silence or place distance emotionally between themselves and the person who has caused the anger.

9. Practice your new skills in a safe environment by:

- Role Play the negative situation with someone you trust.
- Monitor yourself; your level of anger on a scale on 1 to 10.
- Determine ways you could have handled your anger better than you did at the actual time of the anger.
- If there's someone to whom you feel close, but with whom you have trouble venting anger, write down all the situations from the past that have made you furious with them. Ask him or her to do the same. Then make an appointment to get together and discuss your respective lists. Don't dump on each other. Take one item from each list to work through at each session.
- If your anger brings about tension and begins to interfere with other things you do, get it out of your system with physical exercise. This works when you're not able to express anger.
- For instance, the other person is out of town.
- In your bedroom, hit your pillow for two minutes, curse into the pillow - release that anger.
- Draw the face of the person you're mad at on a ball. Smash the ball into the wall.

10. Decide not to express anger.

Initially, expressing anger may make you feel important. There are times, though when you cannot express your anger. For example, when a frail older person has stimulated anger in you, they can't tolerate your anger health-wise.

11. Remember, your choice is not limited to expressing anger or not expressing it.

Sometimes you can use a supportive approach. For example; your boss yells at you and commands you to do something you consider completely unprofessional. Count to ten, then say, *'Is there something wrong Mr. ....? I know there must be or you would never speak to me that way.'*

Are you a worrier?

Mary could handle her worries about work and financial matters, but her life turned into a tailspin when her cat died. She found that she couldn't sleep. The harder she tried the less sleep she got. After seeing several doctors, including a psychiatrist and neurologist, she finally found help at a sleep disorder clinic. Psychologists say that stress often takes its toll on the body in the form of insomnia.

At bedtime, people lie quietly, without distraction from their day's activities. However, that is also when they have time to think about the cares, woes, problems and stressors they've faced during their day.

Lighten up! Worrying is bad for your health (as if you didn't have enough to worry about). You're not alone if you're a worrier. In a recent survey, more than half the people polled said they worry so much that worry itself is a significant problem. Women worry more than men and college students more than senior citizens.

Why worry about it? Worrying is a useless activity. It takes up your energy and time; time that you could spend solving your problems rather than just worrying about them. Some mental health professionals call worry an 'anticipatory anxiety' - because worriers occupy their time expecting future problems. Worry can cause physiological harm and can shorten a person's life. Worriers not only die younger, but have different attributes from those who don't chronically worry. They're likely more self-conscious, daydream more and interpret events differently.

Chronic worriers can spot negative aspects and even potential danger in almost any situation. People prone to worry will magnify the danger involved. Although worry is a potentially harmful pastime, people continue worrying, because they derive some sense of benefit from it.

Worrying can be a substitute for taking action. Others use worry as a way to avoid being scolded or punished. Children who do something wrong may go to their parents and say they're worried. Instead of punishing the wrongdoing, the parent may comfort the child to soothe the child's anxiety.

Similarly, if an adult spent too much money shopping, s/he may go to the spouse and say: *'I'm worried about our finances.'* This deflects criticism about the shopping spree. Some use worry as a way to get attention or to control the behaviour of others.

Some people worry because they're superstitious and see magic in worrying. Some believe that if they worry about something, it won't happen. Others may worry because if the event does happen, they can say, *'See? I told you that would happen!'*

How can you overcome worry?

1. Accept that what you worry about is a problem.
2. Eliminate whatever is causing you to continue worrying.
3. Accept responsibility for dealing with the problem.
4. Deal with the problem.

As long as you see another person or situation as the cause of the problem - it controls you and can make you feel helpless. By realising you have control over the problem and can deal with it, the helpless feeling disappears. This enables you to act.

What do you do if the problem is serious?

a) Imagine the worst case scenario and come up with the worst that could happen.
b) Reconcile yourself emotionally to the worst outcome and accept it.
c) Spend the rest of your time concentrating on taking steps to prevent this outcome.

Try the *'So what?'* technique. This involves imagining a problem and then saying, *'So what? If that happens I can ...'* and think of a solution.

Worriers need to end the all or nothing thinking that plagues them. They think that if a solution hasn't worked 100 per cent perfectly, it hasn't worked at all. We can chip some worries away a little at a time. Setting a goal of reducing worry by ten per cent a week will give a person significantly less stress.

Schedule a worry time into your day

Many therapists suggest that people schedule a 30 minute worry time into their day - but never within an hour of bedtime. That way, when worry at other times threatens to distract them from the job they're doing, they can remind themselves there's time later to deal with the problem. When the worry time arrives, if they've forgotten some of what they intended to think over, it wasn't very important. If daytime worry is a problem, focused-breathing exercises often are helpful. If insomnia is a problem, relaxation exercises can work as a sedative.

Another coping technique is to build 'robustness' into your personality. Recognise your ability to influence events in your life. For instance, if a manager's company has just merged with another firm, she first should imagine how the situation could be worse (they could have fired her). Or she could imagine ways it could be better (they could have kept more jobs intact). She should think about how she contributed to keeping it from being worse (she negotiated and won job counselling for laid off employees). She regained a sense of control and self-worth and could strive for a better outcome (impress the new higher-ups so she'll eventually get permission to hire back her best workers).

Robustness also teaches individuals to read physical signs of stress and develop strategies to overcome them. Finally, robustness training suggests that when individuals face stressful situations (over which they have no control) they can bolster their self-confidence by meeting new challenges. The new challenge could be taking up a new sport, for instance.

CHAPTER TEN

Sleep and Fatigue

The A to ZZZZZZ of sleep

People are leading increasingly busy lives - so busy that researchers say they're not getting as much sleep as they need or would like. However, finding enough time to sleep is half the story. The other half is being able to fall asleep and stay asleep throughout the night. With 24 per cent of adults reporting problems sleeping, learning how to have a good night's sleep is imperative.

Here are some facts about sleep:

- Average number of hours men spend sleeping: 7.4
- Average number of hours women spend sleeping: 7.3
- Time of day when the greatest number are awake: 6 p.m. on weekdays
- Time when the greatest number are asleep: 5 a.m. on Sundays
- How many take a nap: 10.4%
- Average length of their nap: 12 minutes
- Number of times a night a healthy sleeper changes positions in bed: 40 to 60
- Number of hours a day a one-month-old infant spends sleeping: 15.5
- Six-month-old: 14.4
- One-year-old: 13.8
- Three-year-old: 12
- Five-year-old: 11
- Ten-year-old: 9.7
- 18-year-old: 8.2
- Percentage of children aged 5 - 12 who sleepwalk at least once a week: 6
- Percentage of adults who sleepwalk: 2.5
- Percentage of five-year-olds who wet their beds: 15
- Percentage of ten-year olds who wet their beds: 5
- Percentage of people who suffer regularly from nightmares: 13

Researchers say we're waking up earlier, sprinting through the day with one eye on the clock. This is after a night of what never feels like enough sleep. Excessive daytime sleepiness is increasing because of the number of families in which both parents are working and it's not only working parents who feel dopey. The 21 per cent who work evening and night shifts are also paying a heavy toll. So are single mothers, children of single mothers, the poor, the unemployed, the elderly and people with health problems. These groups have higher rates of sleep problems than the average person. Many of us, though, are just busy and can't (or won't) sleep as much as we'd like.

In the past 100 years, people have cut their sleep by 20 per cent, from more than nine hours a night to seven and a half hours. In the past 20 years, we've added 158 hours (the equivalent of four work weeks) into our annual work and commuting schedules. There's no question about it; we're sleeping less and we cope during the day by drinking coffee.

Sleep deprivation is becoming a major public-health problem. Lack of sleep makes us irritable and reduces our memory, judgement and concentration. Government inquiries relate sleepiness as a factor in many serious disasters. Such as the 1979 Three Mile Island nuclear accident, the 1984 gas leak at a Union Carbide plant in Bhopal, India, the 1986 Chernobyl nuclear accident and the 1989 Exxon Valdez oil spill in Alaska.

Many major disasters are the result of human error in mid-afternoon or the middle of the night. These are the two times of day when our body temperature drops, which helps promote sleep. Our biggest temperature drop is at night, from 2 am to 7 am. The other is from 2 pm to 5 pm. These are also, coincidentally, the peak automobile accident times. With more demands on their time, people are waking earlier. Twenty years ago, the highest-rated time slot on morning radio was 8 to 8:15 am; now it's a full hour earlier.

Nurses who work shifts, sleep one hour a day less on average, than nurses who don't work shifts. However, we don't know what this does to a person over a lifetime, because sleep research is only 15 or 20 years old.

Over the years, we've seen shift workers who think that once they retire, their sleep patterns will return to normal. We're finding out now that they don't.

It used to be so much simpler. In prehistoric times, people worked during the day and lay down to sleep shortly after the sun set. With the discovery of fire, they could stay up later and when they installed oil lamps on many city streets, people began to burn the midnight oil.

When Thomas Edison, a century ago, invented the light bulb, sleep patterns changed even more dramatically. An even bigger change is looming. Russian scientists put a giant mirror into orbit, to see whether it could reflect sunlight onto the dark side of the Earth. It did, but the light was faint. Still, the Russians intend to keep working on the idea.

Life wasn't supposed to be this hectic. In the 1960's futurologists were predicting something called the Leisure Society. By the end of the century they said, we'd all be working three-day weeks, our continued affluence assured by the productivity of computers. So, what happened that changes this prediction? People went into more and more debt and had to work harder to pay for their purchases. City real estate values soared, as the bulk of the baby-boom generation entered their 30s and bid up prices.

In many households, both parents had to work to pay the mortgage, so that they had less free time for the rest of their lives, including their children. Women entered the workforce in droves.

That's just part of it though. Many couples couldn't afford to own a home and have children unless they moved to outlying suburbs, where housing was cheaper. The result: many of these people now routinely spend a large portion of their waking lives driving downtown, which eats into their free time even more. To beat the morning traffic, they wake up earlier and come home later. This puts their evening schedules behind as well.

Adolescents aren't getting anywhere near the sleep they need either. A recent U.S. study suggests that teenagers need about nine and one half hours sleep a night to function well, but are lucky to get even the eight hours doctors recommend for adults. Many more teenagers today have part-time jobs than they did a generation ago. This cuts into their time for homework, friendships, dating and even sleep. Some educators are blaming sleepiness for the chronically low scores adolescents achieve on international exams.

All those predictions about the wonders of industry and innovation, where we'd all have more free time, haven't materialised. Indeed, what we're seeing is the reverse; people are working harder, longer, going to bed later and getting up earlier. They're irritable and run into problems at work.

On the one hand, some people are going to bed earlier, to make up for waking up earlier and are thus giving up free time in the late evening. On the other hand, many aren't willing to make that sacrifice and are staying up as late as they always did. They restrict their sleep in favour of more free waking time.

What we're going to see is an increase in body abuse. However, we're beginning to understand what sleep deprivation is doing to people.

The problem is that, the more we cheat on sleep, the more we're likely to feel the effects of sleep deprivation. We build up a sleep deficit and our patience and concentration wear thin. This could get worse before it gets better. Throughout the recession, companies have been pushing their employees to work harder, longer, make wage concessions and give up vacation time. We're constantly told that we're not competitive enough. This raises two questions: Just who or what are we competing with anyway and how's that going to affect our ability to sleep?

Daily rhythms

Here are some of the highs and lows that are normal in most people. Assuming you go to bed about 11 pm, sleep soundly and wake up around 6 am (varies with each person):

- 7 to 10 am - Female sex hormones are at their peak, triggering an appetite for sex.
- 8 to 10 am - Your tolerance for pain is at its highest. This is the time to schedule your dentist and doctor appointments.

- 1 to 3 pm - Alertness takes a dive. Some have a quick catnap, others exercise to revitalise themselves.
- 4 pm - You work best with your hands in the mid-afternoon. Practise the piano, do woodworking or crafts.
- 5 to 7 pm - Long-term memorisation skills peak, so if you have a speech to give or exam to write, now's the time to study.
- 7 to 9 pm - Your senses are most acute in the early evening. This is when you should indulge your urge to enjoy sensory activities.
- 11 to 1 am - Night owls may experience a creative burst and do their best painting, composing, writing or drawing.
- 1 to 5 am - Watch out! You're at a low ebb mentally and physically. This can be a dangerous time to work with power-driven equipment or to drive a vehicle.

Why do we sleep? Why do we dream?

Why do we sleep? Nobody knows. Why do we dream? There's no consensus. Some say dreams provides clues to our deepest tensions and preoccupations. Others say dreams are no more than random images resulting from the random firing of neurons in the brain. Still others say dreaming is the brain's way of processing information - including the elimination of useless information. All three theories have their supporters.

Why do we dream? Turn that question around and ask, *'Why does every advanced animal, from the birds on upward, including mammals, dream?'*

Most people go through three to five cycles of sleep in a night, each characterised by four stages. First, they fall into what sleep researchers call Stage 1 sleep. This is a transition stage between wakefulness and slumber, lasting 10 to 15 minutes.

After Stage 1, the sleeper falls into Stage 2 sleep. In this stage brain waves get longer and higher - a sign of increasing relaxation. Wave lengths and amplitudes are even bigger in Stage 3 sleep and still bigger in Stage 4 sleep. Stage 4 is the most restful sleep of all.

It takes an average sleeper about an hour to go from Stage 1 to Stage 4. Then, after about 15 minutes in Stage 4, the sleeper moves back up through Stages 3 and 2. Then they move onto the most fascinating stage of all - the rapid-eye movement (REM) stage of sleep. In this stage, our eyes move rapidly behind our closed eyelids and we dream. Now, our brain waves (short period, shallow amplitude) closely resemble our brain waves when we're awake. Clearly the brain is doing work in this stage. This work completes the first cycle of sleep, almost two hours after it started.

Sleepers go through another three or four cycles like this, depending on how long they sleep. With each cycle, the time spent in the REM stage increases, while the time spent in the other stages - particularly Stage 4 - decreases. So the first third of the night provides the deepest sleep.

To sum up, the brain alternates during sleep between episodes of intense activity and episodes of hardly any activity at all. It's like a light that goes on and off by itself, without anyone controlling the switch.

Sleep problems:

Insomnia

While insomnia is common, we shouldn't underestimate the suffering it causes. In the most severe, long-term cases, the bedroom becomes an area of avoidance. As many as one-third of adults occasionally suffer from insomnia.

Insomnia can be triggered by physical problems such as pain or mental disorders, such as depression. Daily habits like consuming too much caffeine or having an irregular sleep schedule also can trigger it. About half of those cases are temporary bouts caused by stress called situational insomnia. It can even be a positive stress like getting married or negative, like war. Insomnia lasting only a few nights is normal. When it goes on for a longer time (one or two weeks and certainly a month) it's clinical insomnia and requires evaluation.

Periodic leg movement is another major sleep-disturber. In this syndrome, leg muscles contract repeatedly, jarring the brain hundreds of times a night. As with sleep apnoea, victims are usually oblivious to their plight. They only know they feel terrible in the morning. One sign is a feeling of restlessness in the legs after lying down but before falling asleep. A warm bath at bedtime can help or our doctor may prescribe calcium tablets or other medication.

Stress and sleep do not mesh. Emotions such as anxiety, anger, fear, sadness, depression, excitement, even a person's job, arouse the body. Heart rate and breathing accelerate and blood vessels constrict. This speeding-up process interferes when the body is supposed to be slowing. When you're under stress, the central nervous system starts up and inhibits the systems in the brain that control aspects of sleep. Usually the worry or anxiety that started the insomnia pattern passes. Nevertheless, some people continue to have trouble falling asleep and may still approach bedtime with trepidation, afraid they won't sleep.

Many people don't know why they're having trouble falling asleep. They're not aware they're thinking of what's keeping them up. Usually sleep researchers say that they can predict what will happen next. The insomniac begins 'trying' to sleep. They say, *'I've got to fall asleep.'* But 'trying' is hard work and effort. When you try to do something, you arouse the system that inhibits sleep.

Insomniacs who don't seek treatment can often make the insomnia worse. Some err by using alcohol to help them sleep. While alcohol can promote sleep, it is shallow, less refreshing sleep. Alcohol is thought to be toxic to the area of the brain that controls sleep.

Insomniacs also should use caution with any self-medication. Instead, the best thing is to do all your worrying during the daytime. A couple of hours before bedtime, clear your head, distract yourself and do something enjoyable until bedtime. Watch a relaxing movie or read a book, but once you hit the sheets, don't try to think, but direct your thoughts to something pleasant.

Keep your bedtime hour as regular as possible. The more you try to catch up by sleeping weekends and taking cat naps, the more the sleeping regimen is undermined. Many people with stress-induced insomnia recover on their own. Their insomnia disappears with their stress. Long-term insomnia is more serious and calls for behavioural changes. (Long-term insomnia is defined as being unable to fall asleep after thirty or forty minutes, several times a week for a month or more. A pattern of waking up several times during the night that lasts for a month or more also requires treatment.

My own special cure for insomnia is:

1. When I find myself mulling over a problem that's keeping me from sleeping, I take the time to write down all the details about the problem and find all the possible solutions I can.
2. Then I hand the problem over to my subconscious brain (as if it was another person) and ask it to work on the problem while I'm sleeping.
3. I read something frivolous or humourous to get my mind off the problem.
4. After turning out the light, I relax my muscles and make myself comfortable.
5. If my mind refuses to give up the problem, I allow it to spend an additional half-hour on the problem, then I go back to step 2.
6. If I still can't sleep, I resign myself to the fact that I'm not likely going to have much sleep that night. I don't get up and do something else. Instead I do some relaxation exercises (tightening and loosening my muscles). Even though I can't turn off my brain, I make sure my body receives the physical rest it requires.

I find that I might not sleep well one night in two or three months. I realise that I can manage quite well the next day, with only three or four hours of sleep. Within the next couple of days I catch up and soon feel rested.

Before I tried the above, I found I was not only mentally tired the next day, but physically tired as well. It's better to have one than to have neither.

Women suffer more sleep problems than men

A single mother figured she hadn't had a good night's sleep in four years. She'd lie in bed worrying about her two children, about money, about the stresses of her job as an auxiliary nurse. The seventeen cups of coffee a day she was drinking didn't help. She was also spending a lot of time during the day and evenings just holed up in her bedroom working and smoking.

She didn't realise how much coffee she was drinking until she visited an insomnia clinic. The clinic gave her a log book to record how long she slept (three to five hours a night) average daily coffee consumption and other habits. After four counselling sessions, she now sleeps 7½ hours a night and eight on her days off.

As a result of the counselling she received, she made three changes in her life.

- She cut her daily coffee consumption from seventeen cups to five and no longer drinks coffee in the evenings.
- She doesn't spend as much waking time in her bedroom working.
- She decided to quit smoking.

Being able to have more sleep can only be a dream for many women. Sleep studies found that 28 percent of females aged 15 and over, reported difficulty getting to sleep or staying asleep, compared with 19 per cent of males. Although people with low incomes, the elderly, the unemployed, single parents, children of single parents and shift workers, all reported higher rates of insomnia than the national average, the rates within each group were higher among females than males.

The incidence rose to 41 per cent for women with low incomes, 38 per cent for elderly women, 37 per cent for unemployed women and 34 per cent for single mothers. It's easy to understand why. Women had more responsibility than men, even among couples who live together.

The reason more women have trouble sleeping, they say, is simply that the factors associated with insomnia - stress, low income, pain and health problems - are more common among women than men. For example, the survey found that 62 percent of females aged 15 - 64 reported at least one health problem, compared with 56 per cent of males.

The difference has to do with the social structure of women of all ages. It's a problem of two identities; work for low pay and work for no pay and sadly those two are the stressors that come with their lives. Either women are more stressed or they're genetically more likely to suffer from insomnia or they're more likely to visit a doctor with a complaint than a man. Women are less likely to deny symptoms than men. Only five percent of people who have sleep problems actually talk to their doctors abut it, statistics suggest.

Many who do are prescribed sleeping pills. Pills though, just mask the symptoms of insomnia, not the actual condition, which is usually the result of psychological, physiological or lifestyle problems. Once one starts taking sleeping pills, it's difficult to stop. Users can develop a strong psychological dependence on medication. Many of those who do quit taking pills without having had any treatment for their insomnia, later experience episodes of 'rebound insomnia.' Instead of toughing it out many just go back on the pills.

I am man, hear me roar

Snoring has noble origins in the murky prehistory of mankind. For snorers, this knowledge probably won't make up for being elbowed, yelled at and kicked out of bed. A recent study suggests that we shouldn't hit the snoring man - because he may be protecting us!

That rafter-shaking din may be the remnant of an ancient protective device that has gone sour with time. Male hormones may be the culprit, for men snore far more than women. Moreover, snoring occurs during the periods of deepest sleep, when the conscious mind is least aware of its surroundings and when a man is most vulnerable.

But why do men snore louder than women? When our human ancestors left the safety of the forests and ventured onto the emerging savannas some five million years ago, sleep proved to be one of man's most vulnerable times of the day. By mimicking the sounds of their most common predators (the carnivorous nocturnal cats and hyenas) early humans could broadcast throughout the night: *'We are carnivores, we are many, we are strong and we are healthy!'*

People who snore usually do so because there is an obstruction to the free flow of air, often caused by excessive tissue in the uvula and soft palate. Laser treatment can eliminate snoring in most patients. The technique burns away tissue in the passages at the back of the mouth and nose, reshaping and reforming the openings and allowing a greater airflow. After three to five 10-minute office visits under local anaesthesia, 85 to 90 per cent of patients given the laser treatment stop snoring.

When you just can't wake up

Does every day start with a confrontation between you and your alarm clock? If so, you're not alone. Research shows that millions of people have serious difficulty waking up in the morning. These 'owls' (as sleep experts call them) are no lazier than anyone else, but they are different. They need more or better quality sleep than they're getting. The most common reason for not being able to get up is that they haven't finished sleeping yet.

The 'night-owl syndrome' is one of the commonest causes of poor morning functioning. Its frustrated victims don't need more sleep than other people, but they need it at times (normally from about 3 am to 11 am) that aren't compatible with the workaday world. For most individuals, body temperature is at its lowest during sleep, begins rising around dawn, peaks in the afternoon, then subsides. By 11 pm or midnight, drowsiness sets in. Night owls, on the other hand, usually don't achieve peak temperature and performance levels until evening; thus, low sleep-inducing body temperatures don't arrive until the wee hours of the morning.

Night-owls can delay bedtime on a progressive schedule where they go to bed three hours later than the previous night for seven successive nights, until they finally work around to midnight. Once they've re-set their internal clock this way, they must stick to it.

Pinpointing the problem can be difficult. For instance, take the following case. We'll call her Jane. For years she'd been waking up exhausted no matter how much sleep she had logged during the night. Her doctor could find nothing wrong, nor did tests at a sleep research centre turn up any clues to her fatigue. Finally, one doctor asked if her husband snored. *'Yes,'* she replied, *'I have to poke him once or twice a night.'*

Here at last was the key. Helen only remembered waking up once or twice, but her brain was aroused from its normal sleep pattern every time her husband snored. She was, in effect, 'waking up' 300 to 400 times a night. She solved her problem with a pair of earplugs.

Many of the factors that leave us unrefreshed after a night's sleep are just that minor. For instance, a hot, stuffy room ensures restlessness, while a cold one makes it hard to emerge from the covers and face the day. The most comfortable bedtime temperature ranges from 18 – 20 0 C. Experts say that sleeping in a room that's too bright can confuse the brain, which wants to sleep yet is given the cue to wake up. Continued night after night, these mixed signals can result in morning exhaustion.

Some sleep researchers believe that sleeping in a room that's too dark also may cause difficulties. Normally, the change from night to daytime brightness acts as nature's alarm clock. That's why it can be so hard to get up on those black winter mornings.

Noise is another culprit and it doesn't have to be very loud. One slow-starting friend of mine used to fall asleep to music. She learned that she was aroused many times during the night by changes in the volume of sound from her radio. Then she began switching off the radio the moment she felt drowsy and within a few days she was hopping out of bed without a backward glance.

Although regular physical activity promotes better sleeping and easier awakening, exercise immediately before bed is a stimulant. The exception to this rule is lovemaking, thought to be the best nightcap of all.

To counteract morning grogginess, here are some additional tactics suggested by sleep experts:

Consume less caffeine. Heavy coffee consumption is one of the commonest causes of slow awakening. People who drink too much coffee may actually suffer withdrawal symptoms. During the night their bodies must go without the accustomed doses of caffeine and in the morning they're sluggish. If you need something to get you going, have chocolate milk or cocoa (chocolate is a mild stimulant).

Don't take sleeping pills for extended periods. Avoid most sleep medications. They can relax the central nervous system to a point where it no longer affectively directs the restorative processes that go on during normal sleep.

Alcohol taken shortly before bedtime has a similar effect.

Keep regular hours. Once you've found a bedtime that allows you to rise and shine in the morning, stick to it. If you're not a regular napper, don't nap - it can encourage late hours. Don't cheat on weekends - get up even when you don't have to.

Early each morning, do something you really enjoy. One man dreaded getting up, until he began taking morning walks in the woods behind his home. *'I treasure that half-hour alone with nature,'* he says. *'I used to think when I woke, of all the problems that would be waiting for me at work. Now my first thoughts are of what I'll see outdoors.'*

Not all wake-up problems are so easily dealt with. Stress of almost any kind, including dieting, may increase sleep requirements. The breakup of a relationship or any circumstance causing grief, anger or depression may cause a greater craving for sleep. If you can sleep in such instances, experts advise trying to get the extra hours but urge patients not to use sleep as a means of ignoring problems.

Sleep apnoea

Far more serious is sleep apnoea. Often, a distinct, rhythmic form of snoring (four or five times in quick succession, then a 20- to 40-second pause, then a new eruption) results from a blockage of air passages. This can be caused when their tongue falls back in the mouth and throat muscles relax. These sufferers lack the ability to sleep and breathe regularly at the same time. Their snores are actually the brain rousing itself so their body can gasp for air.

People with short, receding jaws are prone to this condition. Many sufferers have fat necks that narrow the throat passages further. The first treatment prescribed in those cases is weight loss. There are also medications that promote regular breathing and small nasal masks work with some patients. Put on at bedtime, the mask is connected by a tube to a miniature blower that forces air into the nose to keep breathing passages open.

A simple operation to cut away tissue lining at the back of the throat, remedies most cases. Extreme cases however may require a tracheotomy. (If you snore constantly or snore and feel good in the morning, you probably don't have apnoea.)

Narcolepsy

People who suffer from narcolepsy also have trouble waking up refreshed. The chief symptom is a tendency of dozing off without warning at inappropriate times, such as while driving. Some researchers believe that narcoleptics dream more than the average person and that this activity may wear them out to the point where they're constantly in need of more sleep. A key symptom is muscle weakness in the presence of strong emotion. These people go limp when they laugh hard or get angry. To treat the condition, a specialist may recommend carefully scheduled naps throughout the day or a prescribed stimulant.

Akin to narcolepsy is sleep drunkenness, an inability to come to a state of complete wakefulness. Usually caused by a chemical imbalance in the body, it can be detected only by scanning brain-wave patterns during sleep. Stimulants can be helpful. Medication is usually prescribed.

If you have chronic, serious trouble awaking, you may want to consult your doctor. For minor tribulation, one of the tips described earlier may get you up wide awake and eager to be in motion. Can't sleep? Then perhaps you need to talk with experts at a sleep clinic.

Having a mid-day nap may be natural

Three times a week, Beverly Beatty secretly surrenders to her desire for something that's frowned upon. She takes a nap.

'I don't tell anybody,' says Beatty, 58, a woman who began napping several years ago when she retired from a career in real estate.

'In my upbringing, I was taught that only lazy people lie down and have a nap during the day. I feel like I should be doing housework.'

While other countries (such as most of Latin America and Spain), schedule a siesta into their working day, napping in developed countries is somewhat taboo. This may be slowly changing. The airline industry is starting to bring in nap rooms to help employees fight jet lag. A common pattern is to go without enough sleep during the week and to catch up on the weekend. People in siesta cultures often don't get enough sleep at night and make it up during the day.

The brain is programmed for two sleep periods in twenty-four hours. That's what accounts for sleepiness at night and the groggy feeling after lunch - both are natural sleep zones. The mid-afternoon nap is a natural phenomenon, but most North Americans work right through it fuelled by coffee and willpower. They pay a price for this diligence.

Preliminary evidence identified by a sleep disorder clinic, is that regular napping may help protect against heart attacks, high blood pressure and increase alertness. If there are significant benefits, then obviously it would be better to allow people to sleep for half an hour in the daytime. There could be scientific basis for re-arranging time schedules.

Next to night-time, mid-afternoon has the second highest rate of death of all kinds in industrial countries. It's also a peak time for work-related and automobile accidents. Are we missing something?

Research has shown that a good length of time for a nap is either 20 minutes or 80 minutes. At 50 minutes, people are in the middle of Stage 4 (the deepest level of sleep) and if awakened, will be extremely groggy. While sleep needs vary considerably, the average adult needs about 7 ½ hours in a 24-hour period.

Good or bad tired

Fatigue is one of the most frustrating of complaints. Whether it strikes as a cabin-feverish mid-winter funk or a longer-term plague of exhaustion, fatigue saps the very energy we need to overcome it. Varied causes make chronic, intense fatigue one of the hardest conditions to diagnose. For persistent, serious fatigue, see your doctor. For less serious fatigue, take the following simple steps to eliminate many causes. Be sure you distinguish fatigue from sleepiness. Everybody falls asleep occasionally during a boring lecture, but a sleepy person does it much too often. On the other hand, fatigue doesn't always mean you're sleepy. Many people suffering from fatigue can't fall asleep. Even if deprived of sleep at night, they don't fall asleep during the day.

We all know what it's like to be tired. There's the 'good' tired feeling that comes from playing sports, gardening or a day at the beach. You go to bed, fall asleep quickly and awaken refreshed. Then there's the 'bad' tired, when you wake up, day after day, feeling tired and listless. You lack energy, zest and enthusiasm to face a day's work.

Doctors call to this chronic fatigue and it's a common complaint in people over age thirty. Doctors ran a battery of tests on the patient for diabetes, kidney and heart disease, thyroid and low blood sugar that turned out to be inconclusive. Meanwhile, the patient believes there's nothing physically wrong and that it's 'all in his or her head.'

Why don't the doctors find anything wrong? It's most likely because they're not trained to think in terms of nutrition. Frequently doctors are not familiar with the tests available that will determine nutritional inadequacies. One of these involves the B-complex vitamins. A B-complex deficiency may be a significant contributor to the mental confusion and depression that frequently accompanies chronic fatigue. Cooking and processing destroy most of these vitamins and stress rapidly uses up these water-soluble nutrients. The family of B-complex vitamins are vital to the creation of new blood cells and they aid in the digestion of carbohydrate, fat and protein. In fact, they're crucial to our mental and emotional health and add to our well-being by combating our negative responses to stress.

Vitamin C is important for energy as well as an infection-fighter. Research has shown that it helps in the production of adrenaline.

These two vitamins should be used to complement a well-balanced diet. In addition, exercise and finding healthy ways to deal with the emotional energy drainers (fear, anger, hate and guilt) will help restore balance and bounce to your step.

How to get a good night's sleep

Here are a few tips to help you drift off into dreamland.

1. Keep regular hours. Get up at the same time every morning, regardless of how much you've slept. This keeps you in sync with your biological clock. If you frequently sleep late one morning and get up early the next, you'll develop your own version of jet lag. Don't sleep in too late on weekends - or you'll risk getting 'Sunday-night insomnia' and drag into work on Monday. This is why so many people hate Monday mornings.

2. Exercise regularly. Those who are physically fit, sleep better than people who aren't. Be careful not to exercise too late in the evening. The best time is late afternoon or early evening. This allows you to burn off the stresses of the day and still have time to wind down before going to bed.
3. Cut down on stimulants. This doesn't mean only coffee. It means tea, cola drinks, chocolate, nicotine, harsh red wines, sharp cheeses and diet pills.
4. Don't nap too much during the day. Naps, like cod-liver oil, are best in small doses.
5. Don't smoke. Heavy smokers take longer to fall asleep (since nicotine is a stimulant) and wake up more often during the night (owing to nicotine withdrawal). In one study, two-pack-a-day smokers who quit cigarettes cut the time they lay awake in bed by almost half.
6. Drink moderately. Too much alcohol at dinner makes it harder to get to sleep, while too much before bedtime makes it harder to stay asleep. As alcohol breaks down, rapid eye movement or REM sleep intrudes on the body making you dream more. The more time you spend in REM sleep, the less time you spend in more restful sleep.
7. Go for quality time. Six hours of uninterrupted sleep is better than nine hours of fragmented sleep. Don't try to sleep eight hours a night if you feel refreshed after six. If you need only six hours, it means you're a short sleeper; it doesn't mean you're an insomniac.
8. Don't worry in bed. Worry away from your bed. Instead of lying there thinking about what you should have done during the day or what you should do tomorrow, make a list of your worries and commitments before turning in. Then forget about them.
9. Develop a sleep ritual. Create a pre-sleep ritual that helps put distance between the day that was and the night that will be. Read, take a bath, stretch or listen to quiet music.

CHAPTER ELEVEN

How to relieve stress

There are two truisms about stress. First, most people are under an inordinate amount of stress and second, most individuals lack the stress skills to deal well with even ordinary stress, (much less inordinate stress). As a result, the brain (or the intellect) becomes damaged and so overworked that it becomes sluggish. The heart (our emotions) is under such constant assault that it becomes impervious to daily joys and sorrows and the spirit (or soul) is so overburdened that it becomes leaden.

The irony is that individuals have the power within themselves to change both the amount of stress in their lives and their reaction to it. Some people need only to make a few minor adjustments in their daily lives for stress to become more constructive and manageable. Other people will have to make some radical external or internal changes.

A majority of the people who, with courage and support, undertake such challenges, have only one regret: they didn't do it sooner.

Most people know what relieves their stressors - but for one reason or another, they don't use them effectively or consistently. What are your main stress relievers? Could your stress relievers be walking, taking a bath, listening to music? Take a minute to write down what you do to relieve stress. Now, how often do you use your stress relievers? Shouldn't you be using them as often as you require relief from your stress?

Have a strong personality?

Normally, personalities are made, not born. Several things contribute to a strong will, but two of the most important are self-esteem and a sense of purpose. You're more likely to keep going and finish a task if you have self-esteem. If you think you're a terrible person and hit an obstacle, you're more likely to stop.

Some psychologists say self-esteem goes back to the kind of bond you formed with your parents as a child and there are tactics adults with low self-esteem can use to improve how they feel about themselves. If you think you're not a good person, change the way you think about yourself. Whether you've succeeded or failed at something, give yourself the credit for trying, rather than berating yourself about what you should have done, could have done or should have done better.

Try your hand at activities you're good at. This will boost your self-esteem. To achieve a sense of purpose, set goals that are meaningful to you. Whether it's spending more time with your grandchildren, living to celebrate the year 2050 or learning how to paint, decide what you want and set out to get it.

If having a positive outlook is already part of your makeup, you can use those techniques to deal with stress as well. However, if you view stressful events pessimistically, this technique may not work for you.

When a person carries around a load of stressful feelings, it doesn't take many more stressors to break the camel's back. Individuals are in a good position, when they can sense their stress limits as clearly as they can sense their limits for food. Just as they say, *'I'm full and I can't eat another bite,'* they can say, *'I'm full with my daily allotment of stress. I can't accept another stressor today.'* Although they cannot always ignore stressors (especially at work), ignoring or forestalling even 10 to 30 per cent can be very helpful.

A disease-resistant personality

Studies have shown that many people who are under a great deal of stress have colds, the flu or other illnesses more often than people under less stress. But this doesn't explain why some people seldom get sick despite high stress levels. Can you develop a personality that's robust enough to resist many illnesses? Research suggests that you can. People who stayed healthy perceived and dealt with stressful events differently from others who became sick. The differences focused on three characteristics - commitment, challenge and control (the 'three C's' of the robust personality). Robust people typically have a sense of purpose. They're more likely to regard change (good or bad) as an opportunity for new experience and personal growth rather than a threat to security.

At least one major study has linked chronic stress to reduced longevity. Bad stress leaves you feeling angry and hostile. Chronic stress can compromise your immune system and lead to anxiety disorders or depression, all of which can reduce longevity.

Positive vs. negative thinking

Replace negative energy with positive energy. Adopt a positive attitude. For years, we've read and learned about the power of positive thinking. Positive thinking builds momentum with even a modest start. So, no matter how negative and stressed-out you may feel, start your day with a proclamation such as, *'I love my life, my family, my friends and my job. It's good to be alive!'* The results will amaze you.

When you feel rage or frustration, use the energy towards accomplishing something constructive, rather than destructive. Ask yourself, *'Is there any way I can look at this stressful situation more positively?'* If you feel stressed at work because your manager is unsupportive despite your best efforts, consider the possibility that he habitually communicates gruffly and is not being as negative as you think. Or perhaps you do need to improve your work in some way. Regard this as an opportunity to discuss your concerns with him.

Positive stress can be useful. This happens when you direct nervous energy towards getting crucial assignments completed. Seek worthwhile projects to use your energy, such as setting goals and objectives for your company, division or you. The result can be that you'll feel re-energised.

Don't let others' negative emotions affect you. Possibly staff around you are tense because they have to meet a tight deadline. Before you lunge in and panic, too, consider the realities and decide the significance of the problem. Then plan and manage what you can. Even if a deadline looks impossible, take positive action to work as well as you can. You might get the deadline extended or delegate work so the most important tasks get done in the available time.

Improve your environment by turning around negative group emotions. You'll soon be worn down, if you work for any length of time with a group of stressed-out co-workers. So you'll have to act.

Set positive objectives that challenge and energise people. *('We did such a good job the last time, that our client wants us to do a double order. Let's show them we can meet their deadline. We've done it before with the Miller account. We can do it again with this one too.')*

Experts say that excessive fatigue leads to depression. Yet the reverse is also true; depression causes bone-crushing fatigue. Positive thinking is a prime preventive tactic. Exercise can provide a crucial ego boost by making us look younger. When people start telling you that you look better, you begin thinking, *'I must feel that way too.'*

In contrast, stress saps energy. To control it, try setting self-imposed deadlines for yourself that are earlier than your normal ones. Control your worrying too - another energy drain. Some people reserve times to worry, leaving the rest of their days clear for worry-free activity. The mind, body and the person's lifestyle play a role in determining the level of fatigue a person feels.

Imagining the worst that could happen, may help break down what's bothering you into manageable components. For example a woman facing an impending divorce might imagine herself homeless and without means to support her children. Instead of becoming overwhelmed by the stress, she can then tackle each issue - housing and employment - separately.

Negative stress relievers

Many people relieve their stress negatively. Some use tranquilisers which doctors often over-prescribe. Other negative stress relievers are smoking, alcohol and caffeine. Rather than get into the rut of exchanging one negative situation with another, consider using positive stress-reducers instead.

Smoking: Cut down or stop smoking. Smoking can cause heart attacks, strokes, cancer and impotency in men. It's encouraging that so many people are stopping their smoking habit. Unfortunately, young women are still starting smoking at an alarming rate. This goes against the publicity they hear relating to the harm smoking does, not only to them, but to their future children. Many

Westernised countries are hoping to have a smoke-free society by the year 2020.

Alcohol: Alcoholism in women is increasing and because their bodies can't tolerate as much alcohol in their systems, their bodies are breaking down at a faster rate. Chronic alcoholism can be a cause of strokes, cirrhosis of the liver and again, impotency in men.

Caffeine: Drinking ten cups of coffee a day sends your system into overdrive and distorts your perception of time. Try to limit your intake to two cups (before 7 pm or better yet, drink decaffeinated coffee.

Positive Stress Relievers:

Recognise where your stress comes from. Is it striving to accomplish more, to do more? Try removing the negative feelings (such as worrying about what you haven't done or having to work with difficult co-workers) and concentrate on the good (a wonderful energy that you could turn toward reaching positive goals).

Muscle tension can indicate that you've been sitting too long in one position. Painful spasms often follow if you ignore the initial tenderness. Getting at the root of any stress is the best way to dissipate its physical symptoms, but any form of exercise or relaxation that releases muscular tension is healthful. Studies show that the most popular stress relief techniques are exercise, massages, hot baths, sex and creativity. Researchers are beginning to paint a clearer picture of the relationship between physical symptoms and stress.

Here are some ideas on how you can relieve many of your stress symptoms. They require a conscious effort on your part, but they can soon become as much a part of your conditioned reflexes. Use them instead of such bad (and often unconscious) choices, as reaching for a cigarette or a sleeping pill. The result will be to add years to your life and life to your years. If you master the responses, you can thrive under pressure and learn the true joy of stress. See how many of the following you already use to relieve your stress:

Look after your health

People who live to healthy old ages have several things in common: a good immune system, a balanced lifestyle and a strong personality - in particular, a strong will. Occasionally, stop nurturing others and try to get some nurturing for yourself. Take care of your body. Don't skip meals or disregard your need for sleep.

Whether or not you have a good immune system, is mostly the luck of the draw. If your parents weren't susceptible to infections, if they were healthy most of their lives, chances are good you'll enjoy the same type of robust health.

In the same way, we inherit many diseases related to a defect in the immune system (such as certain types of diabetes). The immune system also changes as we age. Cells in people aged 75 and older take longer to produce the antibodies that fight infection. It takes about seven days for the cells in a young or middle-aged adult to produce the antibodies that fight infection. It takes the cells in elderly people between 14 and 21 days. This probably accounts for why elderly people are more likely to suffer infections and that these infections are more likely to be severe, sometimes requiring hospitalisation.

Make sure you get all your immunisations at the right time, including booster shots. If you travel to a Third World country, remember you have no immunity against some diseases there, like cholera and typhoid. Get shots for them too.

Take good care of yourself when you do become ill. If you have a cold, you're more susceptible to a bacterial infection. When you're sick stay away from large crowds where the likelihood of picking up another infection is greater. Don't worry about sitting in drafts or getting caught in the rain. There's no scientific evidence that running around in the rain or sitting in a draft actually causes colds.

Exercise: Exercise provides one way to help your body return to normal by working off the chemical and physical changes resulting from stress. Exercise helps you relax by lessening the tension placed on muscles and body organs. It provides a physical release for the pent-up rage and hostility that accompanies stress.

However, don't use competitive sports as stress relievers. Competitive sports just add to a person's stress level. Many avid competitive sports people will argue strenuously with me about this. It's not the competition of the game that relieves the person's stress; it's the hot tub or sauna after the game that relaxes them. So, rather than competing, do something just for the fun of it. If you're a jogger, don't always think it's necessary to keep adding to how long or how fast you cover a course. If the joy goes out of the exercise and you feel pressed to do better, you're just defeating the purpose of exercising.

Proper exercise helps increase circulation, giving a sense of overall well-being. It helps develop your self-confidence and gives a sense of accomplishment. You don't have to become a jock to benefit from exercise. Biking, gardening and walking can all help protect you against stress. The key is to be active every day. Get off the bus a few stops away from home. Play badminton with the kids. Walk to the movie theatre.

Vigorous activity is a boon to sound sleep, yes, but much more than that. Physical under-activity is at the root of some fatigue. Exercise, on the other hand, battles fatigue in ways that scientists don't understand. When people start to exercise, they say, *'Hey, I feel better and have more energy.'* It's likely because more blood flows to the brain and muscles. Or they may have greater lung efficiency that makes it easier for them to breathe. Or it could be the release of endorphins (the hormones linked to feelings of well-being).

Aerobic exercise is another option. Aim for three times a week. If you don't have time for a workout, try a brisk walk to work or during your lunch hour. Studies have shown that exercise improves mood and has a calming effect, perhaps by influencing brain chemistry.

Before beginning any exercise plan, check with your doctor who can tell you the exercises that will best benefit you for total fitness.

Getting proper sleep and rest: Sleep helps your body recover from stress, by allowing it time to heal. How much you need, depends on your age. There's also a wide variance between people. You may feel refreshed after four hours, while your partner needs nine. Both are normal.

When Bill started suffering from severe insomnia, he became addicted to sleeping pills, but never saw the relationship between his insomnia and stress. His stress-relief program included learning relaxation techniques and identifying the source of his stress. He developed a plan on how he could reach company goals, hired an outside consultant and enlarged his social circle to break his workaholic lifestyle. Ultimately, he broke his destructive cycle and he could dispense with the sleeping pills and sleep through the night.

Solitude is also important for most people. Schedule 30 minutes or more to relax and be alone to think, read, write, reminisce, plan, meditate or dream. It's also important to have something to look forward to at the end of the day or at least, the week. Looking forward to family, friends, a vacation or recreation can help lubricate a psyche that is beginning to experience too much friction.

See Chapter 10 - Sleep and fatigue for more information on this topic.

Have a well-balanced diet: Eat the proper kinds of foods in the proper amounts. People under stress have greater nutritional needs than people who are not prone to stress. It's critical that you get enough protein, vitamins and minerals to repair damaged tissues that result from stress. Avoid sugary food and other junk food. It's easy to get into the habit of eating junk food. Many do so because they don't have time to prepare proper meals.

Keep your weight down too. Excess weight places extra strain on the same body organs and functions that stress does. It might be the straw that breaks your back.

A good diet for stress is one that's balanced (50 percent carbohydrates, 30 to 35 per cent fats, 15 to 20 per cent protein) high in fibre (50 grams), vitamins and minerals and washed down by eight glasses of water a day. It requires natural foods (with few additives) and should provide the right number of calories to maintain your ideal body weight.

A balanced diet beats any single food or vitamin for stoking energy. The many advertisements for various supplements have no scientific basis for reducing fatigue. The exception is iron. Surveys show that more than half of women have diets providing 60 per cent or less of the recommended dietary allowance for iron. The result is their most common symptom is fatigue.

As we move to a lower-fat (with less meat) diet, the risk of iron deficiency goes up, because these diets have far less iron and include more foods that interfere with iron absorption. Taking a modest iron supplement that is often in typical multiple daily vitamins. Potassium is another essential that can be found in bananas. Most people feel better on a diet where they restrict junk foods.

There are four components to eating well: variety, moderation, lower fat and higher fibre. Don't get into a rut and always eating the same food. To get all the nutrients you require, eat different foods. There are no bad foods - even alcohol, salt and caffeine are okay in moderation. Stick to lower fat foods, including leaner meats and lower fat dairy products. Pick foods that are high in fibre, like cereals, breads and grains. Stay clear of any soy products because of the serious health problems they cause.

Fishing or golfing: These can be very relaxing to some (mostly Type B people) and another stressor to others (Type A people). The Type A people will try to catch more fish every time they fish and will be very competitive when playing golf. These activities should be for enjoyment, relaxation and a chance to be in the outdoors (not another stressor).

Doing nothing: When life closes in on us; sometimes just goofing off is the answer. If you encounter a serious problem escape (at least try) for a brief time. After a short escape, you'll be better prepared to return to your problem and tackle it. Adjust your schedule to fit your personality type. Not everyone would be happy dropping out or moving to Hawaii or the Mediterranean. Most of us are more efficient when we take time off occasionally to refuel. Learn to put situations in perspective.

Doing something! Some people don't have enough to do, which causes them stress. These can be the newly retired or those convalescing from an illness or injury. Not doing enough can be a very big stressor to those forced into this role. Keep busy if you're a retiree. If you're convalescing, you might consider reading books that you've wanted to read or pursuing a more passive activity while you recover. Type As may need to remind themselves that it's all right to do this - they don't have to always be producing.

Create a balance: Some people find that work leaves little time for anything else - spouse, children, friends and, least of all, oneself. Time that you take for yourself is important. Being able mentally to leave the stress of work and relax is necessary for creativity. It's simple: We have to recharge our batteries. Insist on taking vacations. It's not shameful to take one and don't feel guilty about taking time off. The most important change in priorities is creating a balance between your personal and professional lives. If there's a significant imbalance, the chances are that you won't do terribly well in either sector.

No one can or should tell you what to do with your life. Periodically, you must evaluate it. It's only when you take the initiative that you can control your life. It's the essence of being able to leave any plateau.

Making love: This is high on many people's list. The sense of belonging, knowing they're loved and accepted by another intimate person goes far to relieving at least your sexual tensions. It's also known to be a prelude to a good night's sleep.

Getting away from it all: Change your environment. Take a stroll around the office, shop floor or home. Look out the window and watch the birds or go outside and breathe deeply for two minutes. Periodically, get up from your work and stretch. If you can take a break, go outside and get some fresh air, even if it's winter. If you're a city dweller, get out into the country and 'commute with nature.' There are many outdoor sports and activities that you can enjoy whether you're alone or with others. Many like to camp or hike outdoors, but just doing a different activity can help you to unwind.

One alternative way to unwind is to do something else that's also stressful. This activity should require full concentration, but involve different circuits of the brain and body. The tennis pro may get relief from tension by playing the stock market, while the professional financial expert would find whacking a ball on the tennis court is the ideal break in his or her routine.

Music and reading: Use music to help calm yourself. Turn on your favourite music, darken the room, close your eyes and drift. For those who enjoy novels, pick up a favourite and immerse yourself into another world. Many find that reading a chapter of a book before bedtime, acts as a pleasant unwind to a busy day.

Taking time to linger: Enjoy the experience of eating a relaxed meal in calm surroundings. When you take a vacation (and do take one) make sure you're not frantically running from place to place. Settle down in one locale and stay there. At work, don't be afraid to let your mind wander occasionally. People are always more creative when they're not forced to rush activities. Reflection and introspection are good for you. Diminish the intensity in your life by pinpointing those areas or aspects that summon up the most concentrated intensity and try to lessen them.

Pamper yourself: Do you like to sit out in the back yard and read your newspaper? Is that one of your stress relievers? Do you run into interference from others because you want to do this every morning or evening? Explain to them that this is one of your special stress relievers and want their co-operation in allowing it to happen.

Do you look forward to the time when it's possible to run yourself a bath and luxuriate in the swirling water around you? Do all your cares wash away with the bath water? Many women find that a scented bubble bath in a room lit by candlelight and soft music is their best stress-buster. Maybe it's having a half hour of private time so you can gather your thoughts at the end of the day. Whatever it is, do it! If you run into interference from others, explain how important these activities are for your mental health.

Doing things you like: Start with obtaining a job you love: one where you get up vitalised and raring to go. You say there is not a job like that for you? Yes there is. Start with career counselling and find the job that's suited to you and your personality.

Love yourself. Let go of the need to prove yourself to anybody but yourself. Accept that you're a significant person just the way you are. Spend time every day doing something that you enjoy and that you do not feel pressure to succeed at. During that time, forget about the problems that are weighing on you as a result of your job, your family or some situation that concerns you. Really enjoy yourself; let your 'little kid' out.

Get in touch with your needs. Maybe you need to get outside into the sunshine every day. Maybe you need to give service to someone else every day so you'll feel fulfilled. Or maybe you need to develop a closer relationship with someone. Once you've found out what your needs are, set about working on ways to fulfil them.

Don't do something because it's expected or because everyone else is doing it. Don't buy season tickets to the football games if football bores you. Pamper yourself - frequent small rewards are far more effective than one big reward after years of sacrifice.

Evaluate why you do the things you do. Check to see if you're doing them because they should be done or because you feel the need to fulfil the expectations of others. Let go of the myth that success depends on doing more and having more. Let go of the myth that taking care of yourself is self-indulgent. Find ways to integrate relaxation into your day. Take time to connect with yourself. Change your circumstances. If your job, your relationships, a situation or person is dragging you under, try to alter the circumstances or if necessary, leave.

The next time someone cuts you off on the road, don't overreact. She's not doing anything to you. It's not up to you to teach her a lesson. All it means is that she's a bad driver. If you can't manage the stress in your life, think about what effect changing your life would have. Is it time to make a career switch or take a sabbatical?

Set realistic goals: It's important to set clear realistic goals. Proper goal-setting involves knowing yourself. If you like contact with people, you'll obviously not find happiness working in a back room for the rest of your life. Realistic financial goals are equally important to your happiness. Assess where you'd like to be in one, three and five year's time. Set yourself a timetable to attain your goal. This would include thorough preparation for the right job for you. In the right job, you should be at your level of competence and have the necessary skills. Proper preparation will give you greater job satisfaction. This will decrease your stress level. So get career counselling. (See Chapter 5 - The Importance of Goal Setting).

Support group: If you don't have at least two people you can rely on to help you celebrate your successes and help you deal with your failures, you're not likely to bounce back quickly from stressful situations. The reason you need two is that, one might not be available or they too might be having a bad day.

If something's worrying you, talk it over with a trusted friend or family member. Keeping a worry bottled up inside you can only cause you to become depressed. Find a good listener. Choose a patient person - one who won't interrupt or give advice. One of the most devastating results of stress is a feeling of hopelessness and helplessness. Someone else could offer a solution you hadn't thought of.

If you feel upset about the death of a close friend, let yourself grieve. If someone makes you angry, express your anger reasonably. Love people and use things - instead of the other way around. Start with your family and friends: tell them that you love them. Hug someone. Practice giving a minimum of four hugs a day.

Don't expect too much of others: It could be that the stress people experience is not only at work and home, but also within themselves. In fact, at least half the stress that people experience daily is self-induced. Sometimes there's nothing they can to do about external stress, but often they can reduce their internal stress so their overall stress quotient is manageable.

The following are some common social beliefs. People:

- That I help, must help me in return,
- Must treat me fairly,
- Who I like and respect, must like and respect me,
- Must keep promises,
- Must keep confidences,
- Must recognise that I'm special and treat me accordingly,
- Must reward my hard work and sacrifice,
- Must not gossip about me,
- Must tell me the truth,
- Must recognise and appreciate my talents.

The elements that make these attitudes problematic are that they're absolute. For example, the attitude 'people must treat me fairly' will give a much more stress than the more realistic attitude that says, *'It would be nice if people always treated me fairly, but I cannot expect that they always will, any more than they can always expect me to treat them fairly.'*

A second way people manufacture their own stress is to stretch attitudes considered virtuous to the point where they become vices. To use an analogy, eating and drinking are important for physical and psychological health, but overdoing them causes physical and psychological illnesses. People who handle stress well, have learned to recognise the difference between virtue and vice and catch themselves before they fall over the precipice. The following are some common virtue-vice combinations:

- I always want to do a good job.
  Stress Point: I need to do a perfect job and when I don't, I berate myself or others.
- I want to change people and situations for the better.
  Stress point: I expect to change people in ways and to degrees that they can't change and, when I fail, I feel deeply frustrated.
- I genuinely care about people and situations.
  Stress point: I become so emotionally involved with people and situations that my peace and happiness depend upon their doing what I say.
- I'm always trying to better myself.
  Stress point: I always try to be and do better than everyone else. When I don't, I feel like a failure.
- I try to be helpful to others.
  Stress point: I can't say no to people, so I often find myself overtaxed and resentful.
- I dislike it when anything goes wrong.
  Stress point: I hate it when anything goes wrong. I hate myself or others who cause this to happen.
- I'm smart enough to realise that someone will stab me in the back if they get half the chance.
  Stress point: I'm smart enough to know that most, if not all people, will stab you in the back if they get half a chance, so I'm on my guard all the time.

- My work is one of the most important activities in my life. Stress point: My work is the most important activity in my life. Therefore, my whole life goes as my work goes.

Have a good cry

If you've been holding negative feelings in, having a good cry can be the key to releasing it. Some may stimulate this by watching a sad movie that can help the person let go of their emotions. Instead of choking back your tears, let them flow so you can relieve the tension you're feeling.

Humour and laughter

This is high on the list of necessities of a balanced life. If you've lost your sense of humour - go out and find it! If you're feeling down, watch a funny movie or comedy show. Smile, read a joke book or visit someone known for their sense of humour. Allow yourself to have a good laugh.

Research suggests that laughter increases the body's level of endorphins. This can, in fact, ease the pain and help improve resistance to disease. It's now being used on cancer wards to help patients fight their disease. Laughter also enables you to gain new perspectives on your problems - especially if you can laugh at yourself!

Organise your life

Make a list each day of items that you need or want to do (To Do list). Look at the list and decide which items on it are absolutely critical. Then concentrate on the activities that are necessary, that you enjoy and will help you achieve your goals. It's important to feel a sense of accomplishment, so keep your list within the bounds of what you can realistically handle.

Schedule personal activities the same way you do business assignments. When you plan your week, block out time for the activities that are the most important to you. This could be helping your children with their homework, spending time with a sick friend or writing a thank-you letter for a thoughtful gesture. This is as important as your work commitments because when you do nothing but work, even your work suffers.

Learn to delegate at work and at home. Try to identify the tasks that you could delegate to someone else or that you could forget altogether. Rank the items that are important in your life and make sure that your behaviour matches those priorities.

Distinguish between minor crises and major ones. You'll find, to your surprise, that most problems and crises in life are minor. Drop unnecessary activities from your life. Don't cut out the activities that give you relaxation and enjoyment.

Pinpoint the situations that cause you stress and eliminate them as much as you can. If the telephone is a constant bother while you're trying to concentrate, temporarily unplug it or have someone else take over. If your appointment book is a source of stress, don't overbook yourself.

If faced with a workload that seems unbearable, divide it into a series of smaller tasks. Then tackle the tasks, one by one, until you finish the larger job. Hurrying is a learned behaviour that can be changed. Plan far enough ahead so you aren't always in a rush. Get up 15 minutes earlier. Prepare for each morning the night before. Make duplicates of all keys. Take advantage of office hours for banking, shopping and anything else that usually brings lines to your brow. Don't put up with anything that doesn't work properly. Un-clutter your life - get rid of stuff you never use.

Perfectionism

Don't try to be perfect in everything you do. Certainly, set high standards, but free yourself from the need to be 'perfect' at everything and spend your time on quality personal relationships.

Learn to relax

When you feel yourself getting rushed or panicked, stop. Simply sitting at your desk for a few minutes with your eyes closed and your hands flat on the desk can help. Don't resume your activities until you feel you've regained control, instead of senselessly rushing to get everything done.

Can you relax under pressure? If not, learn how to take a power nap. Most people can relax on a two-week vacation, many can relax on a weekend and some can relax every evening after work. But how many can count to ten, suddenly be at complete rest for a few moments and then wake up refreshed? Taking a power nap slows your pulse and breathing rate and reverses many of the natural stress responses in your body.

Try guided imagery for relaxation that is a form of mental relaxation or meditation. Begin by 'turning off' your life. Find a place where you won't be disturbed for 5 or 10 minutes. Sit comfortably, loosen your clothing and close your eyes. Take a few deep breaths. Each time you breathe in say to yourself, 'I am' Each time you breathe out, say 'relaxed.' Then in your mind's eye paint a picture of one of your favourite places. Remind yourself to let yourself go and put anything you wish into this picture - it's yours. Move yourself into the mental picture you've just created. 'Feel' the many textures and details of the scene. Spend five minutes or so in your chosen spot, then slowly open your eyes to the real world about you. You will feel refreshed and relaxed. (See Chapter 14 for more information on relaxation, biofeedback, meditation, breathing, massage and self-massage.)

Less Competitiveness

Learn to control your competitive nature. The highway is a good place to practice this. When you see a car trying to edge in from a side road, pause long enough to let it into the stream of traffic instead of hitting the accelerator.

Face your problems

Learn to live day by day instead of living in the future. Learn to appreciate the beauty and enjoyment available to you now, instead of constantly driving yourself for some intangible pleasure you can enjoy in the future. Live in the present - not the past. If you're constantly saying, 'If only or I should have,' you're living in the past - and don't do it. Concentrate your efforts on the future - you can't change the past.

Stop stonewalling your progress. Ignore all those comforting but uncontrollable excuses. Often people in difficulty, place the blame for their problems and stresses on something they can't change. But if you train yourself to look behind that stone wall, you'll find the true cause of your problems - which you can likely control.

Worry only about those situations you can control. Uncontrollable causes of stress such as natural disasters and genuine bad luck are fortunately rare. Don't look to the future with a fatalistic shrug. Be justifiably optimistic. Take an active role in your life; don't be a passive tourist through your life.

Change the situation

If you don't like your life the way it is; decide how you can change it so it suits your liking. For instance, a realtor of expensive homes changed her situation. Having sold a craft shop to join a real-estate firm, she experienced such gastrointestinal distress that her diet became bananas and bread. The competitiveness among the firm's realtors and the uncertainty of income, left her questioning why she ever gave up her safe, if unexciting, former business.

When she discussed with colleagues the cutthroat atmosphere of her new company, she found that they felt the same way. The stress was affecting their health too. They decided it was time to spend their hard-earned commissions on vacations instead of on doctor bills. They set down some ground rules that encouraged co-operation, instead of competition with one another. For example, if one worked with a potential buyer for weeks and then went on vacation, one of the colleagues would take up the slack and they would share the commission. This alone changed the atmosphere in the office.

Change your response

Negotiations, deadlines, sales campaigns, speeches - all can and should be exhilarating. They should be the short-term good stresses that enable us to prepare for the important highlights of our careers and consistently perform at our best. It's when we don't resolve these stressors that they become manifested in physical symptoms.

Sometimes it's difficult to see how best to resolve such stresses. Not everyone can follow such a simple course of action. It might be necessary to change one's response to the situation. Look back at some of your past negative situations. Did you respond correctly or could you have taken a more successful approach to your problem?

Controlling stress is power

A key to surviving and thriving on stress is having control of situations. One interesting research project involved two groups of workers exposed to distracting background noises; machinery, street noises and people speaking in foreign languages. One group had a button placed on a desk, so they could shut off the noise whenever they wished. The other group had no button.

The productivity of the group with the control button was as expected; consistently higher than that of those without control. The interesting point is that no one actually pushed the control button. Just knowing it was there appeared to be enough. The lesson here is important; it's essential to have some personal 'control buttons.' They help you live satisfactorily with the stresses that surround you. Learn to ignore what you can't control and to control what you can. The critical fact is that most of the events in your life are within your control.

It's well-known that people's lives would be a lot happier and longer if they identified and reacted to stress in more effective ways. A superficial understanding of stress is a good place to start, but a poor place to finish. Stress, especially in today's world, is a complex affair. The more we understand about the basic intricacies of stress, the better position we'll be in to survive the experience of stress and to use it as an instrument for growth.

Do you need psychotherapy?

Jobs with high demands but low control leave women more stressed than men, because they're more inclined than men, to find ways to deal with stress. The woman with the highest risk of heart disease is a clerical worker with an insensitive boss, three children and a blue-collar husband.

If you're like most people, you probably have your ups and downs. You may even have wondered if you need psychotherapy or mental-health help. But how do you decide? What is the difference between normal ups and downs and the kind of emotional problems that call for therapy?

Psychiatrists and psychologists say it's time to get help when you feel so poorly that you can't function - when your problems start interfering with your daily life, your job or your marriage. Then the crucial question is, how long has it been going on? A week? A couple of months? If the answer is a couple of months or so, you probably could use some help - unless of course something has happened that would upset anyone. Don't think you have a problem just because you occasionally feel or act upset.

Emotional problems may start when people can't get back on their feet after a crisis - a death, a divorce or loss of a job. Sometimes, though, a person begins to show signs of emotional stress for no apparent reason.

Perhaps you react to small problems with excessive rage, experience increasing difficulty in getting along with others or are suspicious of others, (especially those who may try to help you). You may not be able to stop thinking about problems or to change unsatisfactory or destructive behaviour. There may be physical symptoms (dizziness, fatigue, chest pains) loss of appetite or erratic sleep patterns, that have no medical basis. There may be fear of certain situations for people that increases feelings of inadequacy and self-doubt and feelings of hopelessness about yourself or the future.

If you find that you're having problems dealing with the stress of life, by all means, get help. Start with a visit to your family doctor to see if there is a physical problem. You may be referred to a specialist or a mental health clinic. Please go. Life is too short to spend it unhappily.

CHAPTER TWELVE

Handling stress at work

We all suffer from stress at work - the stress of handling more work than we feel we can handle, supervising employees who don't fit in or get along and dealing with unreasonable upper managers in the company or organisation. Most of it is good stress - but some obviously, is bad.

The next time you're about to call yourself a 'stressed-out person,' stop and analyse how you're really feeling. You'll likely find you're using the term incorrectly to identify a set of emotional states, not just one. You may be using this term when you're simply tired or just nervous, rather than stressed-out. Occasionally, you may use the term even when you're excited about some workplace difficulty - even though you're uncertain about the conclusion.

Put workplace predicaments in perspective. Few workplace problems are do-or-die situations. Even losing your job (which could be your worst nightmare) may only be a momentary setback - not a life-threatening one. Start by putting business stress in its place. When mulling over some problem such as an insensitive manager or the sudden important deadline, gain perspective by appraising it against something in your life that is authentically meaningful. Use this philosophy to react correctly.

Facing deadlines, personality clashes and the rush, rush, rush of daily work life, we may want to yell, *'Stop. Give me a break!'* If you're facing problem after problem, consider using the following process:

First determine if you can solve the problem and, if so, solve it. For instance, if you face a series of deadlines at a particular time each month and know you can't sprinkle the deadlines throughout the month, prepare for the crunch as well as you can ahead of time. Fretting endlessly over the four reports that are always due within a few days of each other rather than working to meet the situation head-on will only make the problem appear worse than it actually is.

Or the situation might be unsolvable - say, a boss you simply can't get along with. Then your choice is tougher. Do you quit or hang in there? When you can do something about the situation, all the advice (and common sense) weighs in on the side of solving the problem.

Second, the best approach may be to avoid the situation entirely. If it upsets you to see people you don't need to see, don't go where you know they'll be or duck out if they head your way. Avoiding or at least not dwelling on the person or issue, can be the right ploy for a few intractable problems. However, when it becomes the overall pattern of response to all difficulties, it can lead to a feeling of dependency and powerlessness, which in turn can bring on depression.

Third, an appraisal - an optimistic one - of the situation may provide a psychological escape route from an apparently hopeless situation. When you blow it at a meeting, for instance, you can tell yourself that you can recover your status at next week's meeting and a week in the doghouse is survivable. When reviewing a tight budget or a poor sales report, you can tell yourself the figures aren't as bad as you thought or that your figures aren't much worse than the industry's average. Or perhaps you can make certain changes today, to brighten the picture for tomorrow.

Fourth, confrontation can help reduce stress for some individuals. The effect usually is short-term and may not endear you to fellow workers. The best use of confrontation is to trigger changes for the better, not to vent feelings. Use feedback to explain to them what their actions do to upset you and try to obtain their co-operation in changing the situation.

Replace the idea of 'stress' with 'stressing.' You'll be stressing quality workmanship that results in your doing an outstanding job on projects. This approach is more than just playing word games - it builds a fresh outlook that defuses anxiety and channels new energy and direction to your life.

The trick is to have the entire repertoire of stress-busters on hand and to know when to apply which one. Integrate proven stress-defeaters into your daily plans. Use your break time for fun. Work a crossword puzzle or play a game. This will bring renewed energy and concentration to the job.

The most popular cures for reducing stress are taking frequent work breaks, doing deep breathing exercises, taking a short walk and doing neck and muscle movements to untie knots in shoulders, neck, back and legs. A change of physical atmosphere can help resuscitate an individual. In addition, this can be a good time to combine physical exercise and solitude. Keeping one's emotional slate clean gives the individual a resistance s/he would not ordinarily have.

Try visualising - seeing yourself at your favourite vacation spot, watching a sunset or on a beach - to see if it works for you. A five-minute mental-health break can do wonders.

Physical surroundings play a large role in either advancing or reducing stress. Little trials like jumping out of your shoes every time your too-loud phone rings, having to always make a fresh pot of coffee every time you want one or frequently having to un-jam the photocopier, can add up to a stressed employee. So can office clutter, so take time to organise and rearrange your work area.

Reducing stress for co-workers

How can you reduce the anxieties and stresses of your peers within your organisation? Why should you invest your valuable time and energy doing so? If you do, your workplace will be healthier and your co-workers will be more productive. Employees who make the jobs of their peers easier, are the people sought after when interesting challenges arise or when innovative teams are chosen.

Be a source of support to your staff. Use your insights to lighten the workloads of those around you. Consider the job functions of your peers and any immediate problems they may face. Don't commit too many of your resources, but try to find ways you can help. This could be by choosing an article you read or a person you met, who could provide the information a peer needs to make his or her work easier or less stressful.

Recognise squabbling and petty politics for the stress-builders they are. You have too much work to do, to waste time and mental energy battling with peers. You should be cooperating, so when petty conflicts surface, you can send your energy toward solving problems. Even when stress makes emotions boil over, keep centred on the project you're completing. Focus on organisational goals and objectives and on the role you should be playing to make it happen.

It's not surprising that competitiveness has increased among peers over the past few years. The weight falls squarely on employees to do better and better as organisations are pressed to do more with fewer and fewer resources. Because there are fewer positions available, the competition gets higher between potential corporate climbers.

Managers are forced to push their staff to do more; budget restraints have tightened, to accomplish more with less. No wonder stress rises! Still, an effort at co-operation and a willingness to set aside interpersonal problems are key factors in reducing stress in the workplace. Your ability to stand above the fray and remain focused on important issues marks you not only as a co-operative colleague, but as a leader as well.

Today, the workplace is anything but a calm place to work. There are often too many challenges from competitors, pressure from upper management and problems particular to job tasks, such as production quotas, the need for updating equipment and downsizing. Thankfully, we can build an energised, positive work environment instead of one that's negatively stressful. We achieve this kind of work atmosphere through consistency, thought, fairness, a positive attitude and above all, good leadership from top management.

Have the self-discipline to keep focused, even if you're the object of the negative anger or verbal assault. When others direct hostility at you, adopt an open attitude. Ask what you've done incorrectly and how you can make it right. Often, you'll learn that some reason, unknown to you, caused the flare up. Perhaps you made a comment at a meeting that your peer misinterpreted. Clear the air. In the process, you'll redirect energy positively and end conflict before it germinates and spreads to other issues.

Don't stay angry for too long. In highly competitive and political organisations, you can't immediately replace negative energy with positive. When tempers flare or you've handled negotiations poorly, strive to put conflict aside and approach people openly and cooperatively. Concentrate your efforts on the work you're doing -

not on competition - and you'll soon reduce both your stress and that of the people around you.

Reducing stress of your staff

If you're a supervisor or manager, distribute work fairly. Everyone should pull his or her weight and get an equal share of assignments (especially those that involve imagination and excitement). Stress is higher in departments where workers observe others getting too little work or that the 'prestigious assignments' go to a favoured few.

If you observe that a member of your staff is showing signs of excess stress, step in. Refer him to the employee-assistance program or give him the name of an outside counsellor.

Keep in mind that stress doesn't always result from pressures at work; it's usually a combination of personal and work-related stress. Your employee may be trying to juggle too many professional and personal demands at once and may need a specialist's help in sorting them out.

How to improve working conditions

Studies prove that working conditions have a direct bearing on employees' productivity. Anything that companies can do to make working conditions better for their staff, increases not only productivity, but the morale of their staff. Consider the following situations:

Employees who stand all day or work behind a counter: In a grocery chain, employees at the check-out counter could not work for more than four hours without suffering from muscle spasms in their legs and backs. Employers thought the cause was because of the body movements made by putting food through a scanner and packing heavy bags of groceries. However, this problem stopped as soon as the employees were given half-inch thick rubber matting to stand on.

Noisy working environment: Listening to constant noise can increase one's stress level. The more stress the person is under, the more acute his/her hearing becomes. The fight or flight response enhances the person's hearing (so s/he can hear the dinosaur coming through the trees). Providing ear protection is not only much better for the employees, but it's a requirement of most work safety laws.

Offices can minimise noise, by installing carpets, acoustic tiles, matted wallpaper and fabric-covered dividers to absorb the noise. Bells and buzzers on telephones can be turned down.

Bright lighting: When a person is under stress, their vision is also enhanced (to see that dinosaur coming through the trees). When bombarded with overly bright lights, many employees find that they're squinting or have a headache before the day is over. Most office working environments provide fluorescent lighting. This is fine, except that most are far too bright. If you have a four-bar fluorescent light fixture in your office, have every second light replaced with a burned-out one (leaving only two bars of light). If possible, replace the white fluorescent lights with orange coloured lights that are easier on the eyes.

If you were out in a boat on a sunny day, you'd likely wear sun glasses for protection from the glare. This might be necessary in an office (whether or not you wear glasses). When fluorescent lights reflect off paper (normally white) it hits your eyes at the same level as reflection off water. Try tinted glasses if you find yourself squinting or have headaches at the end of your day or consider an alternative lighting system.

Working with a computer: Make sure your eye level is even with the top of your monitor screen. Is your chair at the right height? Do not place your computer with a window behind it or behind you. If you do, your eyes will continually have to determine whether they're to adjust to the window light or the computer screen.

Do colours make a difference? One warehouse staff found the staff morale and productivity improved when the floors and walls of their building were painted. It improved even more when the shelving was painted in different bright colours that allowed for easy identification of their stock. It also brightened their psyches by providing a more pleasant working atmosphere.

When sitting: Good posture when sitting or standing keeps everyone's body fit. Try to keep your back straight, not rounded or hunched. When working at a desk, sit tall and bend at the neck slightly, instead of leaning forward. Avoid a 'poking chin' - keep your chin tucked in, eyes level and shoulders relaxed. Keep feet flat on the floor or on a small stool.

Sit with hips and knees at 90 degrees. Knees should be slightly higher than hips. Change positions often to rest and move your muscles and joints. Chairs should have a firm seat and fairly straight back. The work surface should be just below elbow level. Rest forearms on the work surface or armrest.

Choosing a chair: Most executive chairs were designed for men, but everyone needs a chair to fit his or her frame. It's ironic that so many support staff sit on chairs that give little back support. Many of these employees sit in substandard chairs for a large portion of their day. Many of the newest secretarial chairs do not have high enough backs to support the worker's back properly. Even if some were high enough, when the person leaned back in her chair to make use of the back support, the chair would likely tip over backwards. Most of these chairs do not have arms, which means that the person must support his or her arms all day while working at his/her computer. No wonder s/he has an achy back, shoulders, wrists and hands by the end of the day!

If you have to use this type of chair, ask your boss to change chairs with you for a couple of days. You'll soon have yourself a chair that's better suited to your needs. Four rules should be considered when buying an office chair:

1. The seat back should be at shoulder height, wider than the torso and have slightly curved sides for lateral support and a firm pad in the small of the back. (You can upgrade any chair by adding a pad made for this purpose.)
2. The seat should be shallow enough so you have a few inches between your knee and the seat edge.
3. Armrests are a good idea. They decrease stress on the back by allowing weight to shift to your arms and support arms while working with a computer.
4. The chair should swivel easily and be covered in non-stick fabric.

When people are under stress, they sit on the edge of their chairs. Check often throughout your day and slide back, to take advantage of the back support.

Reducing stress for your supervisor or manager

As stress builds at work, it's a natural response to view your superior as an adversary. After all, s/he's the one who makes the demands, hands out the work, reviews your decisions and ideas. But viewing your superior as an enemy, only builds stress and turns emotions negative. Instead, keep perspective on the roles the both of you play within the organisational structure. Instead of dwelling on emotions that are negative or competitive, find ways to elevate your relationship to the level of collaboration instead of competition.

Both you and your boss are stressed, yet you can put a strategic plan in place that concurrently reduces your manager's anxiety level and yours. There's a simple principle behind this. When you anticipate your manager's needs and meet them ahead of time, s/he feels less stressed. Remember that your main function as an employee is to make your boss look good.

Because there's less need for your manager to interfere in your activities, you enjoy more autonomy. As a result, you become less stressed too. Here are some concrete steps you can take immediately to encourage this relationship.

Present solutions, rather than problems. When you face a challenge, resist the temptation to ask your manager for a solution. This builds your manager's stress level and undermines your image as a decisive professional. Instead, present the problem and identify several solutions you have considered. Then identify the solution you feel, is best under the circumstances. This way, the supervisor does not have to waste his or her time finding possible solutions and can spend his or her time rating the worth of your solutions. Communicate often, but without taking up too much time. Don't expect your manager to read time-draining, lengthy memos, when a brief summary will do.

When opening a discussion about some problem or challenge, be sure to have available the supporting materials you need to save time. This approach takes discipline, because it's natural to want to talk problems through before acting. See it from your manager's perspective otherwise s/he may see your actions as indecisive. Psychologically, your manager needs to see that you have everything under control.

Don't overlook the important details. Small things do count in increasing your manager's confidence in what you can do. Prepare thoroughly for your manager's meetings and run yours with well-prepared agendas. Make sure that anything you write for your manager or any written work that comes out of your area, is letter-perfect, neat and well organised. Detail-orientation convinces your manager that you have everything under control.

Do a little better than you're asked to do. Whenever possible, make it a practice to beat deadlines, to provide a little more information than was necessary, to produce polished results when they requested only a rough draft. Even a little extra effort on your part defuses your manager's stress and increases your value to your company or organisation. Pretend that you own the company. What could you do within your department to make it run more smoothly?

Job stress - How to cope during the tough times

Are you so overworked that you have to drag yourself to the office? Do rumours of layoffs keep you awake nights? If so, you've got plenty of company. Mergers, cutbacks and mass terminations have created an epidemic of job-related stress, according to a recent study. Of 600 workers interviewed, almost half described their job as highly stressful, compared to just 20 percent in a similar study done six years ago. One-third said they seriously considered quitting their job last year because they couldn't take the pressure. And one-third said they expected to burn out soon.

Work is literally making people sick. About 70 percent of the survey respondents reported frequent health problems, such as headaches, exhaustion, insomnia and digestive upsets. A similar number admitted to lowered productivity because of stress and 17 percent to higher absenteeism.

Longer hours and vanishing job security is not what pushes employees to the breaking point. The number one culprit identified in the survey is a sense of powerlessness. People want respect for their ability to make decisions, but managers have a hard time trusting them. Managers are more reluctant to share decision-making power in tough economic times.

Foreign-management policies and practices may change the corporate culture to one that is unfamiliar and quite possibly hostile to employees. So the corporation no longer is the family it once was to employees. Workers feel more and more like numbers filling a slot, rather than like members of a cohesive group. These factors add up to a level of job-related stress the likes of which we've never seen before.

To change the atmosphere, corporations should make sure that lines of communication to the top are accessible to everyone, (even those at the bottom). Senior managers need to know how their employees are doing and what they require to do their jobs better. Accurate, up-to-date job descriptions are a must. Flexibility about how and when the job gets done (especially in this day of the two-career-couple) gives a feeling of corporate caring as no other business practice can. Positive feedback in front of peers, even if it's a simple, *'Thanks, you did a wonderful job!'* further boosts morale and makes the corporation 'user friendly.'

However, all too often, none of this happens. A corporation eventually will recognise that its employees are stressed to the breaking point - or they're quitting in droves - so will call in an expert to 'fix' the problem. The first priority is to find out what the problem is and if it's to have any effect, the company has to be willing to change. Consultants normally suggest that companies implement stress-management programs.

Ideally, a stress-management program begins with a stress inventory that goes to everyone in the corporate pyramid to flush out problems that the usual routines hide. However, to save money, some corporations choose to concentrate on only one group of managers, such as human resources, because that group can transfer what it learns to other departments. This can work extremely well.

At weekly discussions in one company, group members identified their collective source of stress; failure to meet the needs of the corporation and a feeling that if they compared the corporation to a family, they were often the picked-on child. By airing their feelings and then learning stress-reduction mechanisms, they could move on and create a ground-breaking support system for their company.

In today's tight job market, you can't count on beating stress by finding another job with a more supportive manager. Nevertheless, that doesn't mean that you have to grin and bear it.

If you're afraid of losing your job, try to rechannel the energy that worrying wastes. Focus instead on analysing your options while you still have a job. Can you make yourself indispensable in your current position? Whom can you call for leads on openings in your field?

Take care of yourself. Don't let fatigue and poor eating habits erode what's left of your stamina. If you can't relax enough for a good night's sleep or an enjoyable meal, take a course in progressive relaxation. Your doctor can likely recommend one. It will teach you to reverse the physical manifestations of stress. When your body relaxes, your mind will follow.

Make time for leisure. If you're emotionally battered at work, you can boost your self-esteem by pursuing a favourite hobby or lunching with a friend who makes you smile. Treats for yourself belong in your appointment book alongside obligations to your boss and family.

Give yourself credit where it's due. Don't expect to meet last year's standards on this year's shoestring budget. Instead of kicking yourself for not working miracles, remind yourself what you have accomplished and be proud.

CHAPTER THIRTEEN

Stress relievers

There are many things a person can do to relieve their stress. I discussed some of them in earlier chapters. Here we're going to concentrate on relaxation exercises, transcendental meditation, biofeedback, massage and self-massage.

Relaxation exercises

It's only 2 o'clock, but you feel as if you've already put in a full day. Work is piling up on your desk and the phone is constantly ringing. Your mind and body can be stuck in first gear. Your back is killing you and you feel a tension headache coming on. To revive yourself, you have another cup of coffee, but it's a losing battle. You feel exhausted.

You're not really exhausted, but your inability to deal with stress has made you feel that way. You've fallen prey to 'stress exhaustion.'

You can, however, transform such stress or fatigue into renewed zest and vigour through a series of easy, sweat-free energisers drawn from yoga, Tai Chi and other martial arts. The exercises take one minute each, which encourage deep breathing that will stimulate circulation and pump oxygen into your body. Stretching will ease tension, isometrics will strengthen muscles and relaxation exercises will promote better concentration.

Taking a mental health break instead of a coffee break will help you feel, look and work better. If you don't have ten minutes to spare, do as many energisers as you can, picking those designed to overcome what's troubling you.

When it was time to put the following information into my computer, I realised that I was showing signs of stress exhaustion myself. My sign is that a muscle begins to twitch near my left shoulder. I had been ignoring it (I know, I should practice what I preach) but after I put the information into my computer, I did each exercise. I'm very careful not to put my chin up too far, because it's one of the positions that can put my back and neck out of whack.

Although many of the exercises had me tilt my chin, they were gentle and didn't over-extend my neck too much.

After completing all the exercises, I felt wonderfully refreshed, my muscle ache was gone and I could carry on with my task. Even if you're sceptical, try the following. I'm sure you will be as delighted with the results as I was.

Begin these energisers sitting up straight, with both feet flat on the floor about 15 centimetres apart, palms resting comfortably on your knees, elbows slightly bent. Keep your spine upright, but not stiff. (Imagine that a puppet string atop your head is gently lifting you until your spine is straight). Breathe easily; a relaxed approach is vital. Now you can start the exercises.

1. Bow-and-arrow - helps posture, perks up circulation and melts away strain in arms and shoulders. Raise your arms in front of you to shoulder height, palms facing each other. Keep shoulders relaxed and elbows slightly bent. Gently clench your fists. Take a deep breath as you tense your right arm and slowly bring it back - elbow bent close to the body and shoulders relaxed - as far as you comfortably can. Hold counting slowly to three. Imagine an archer pulling a bow, then releasing the arrow. Slowly exhale as you return right arm to starting position. Repeat using left arm. Do ten times.

2. The bird-hug - eases aching neck, back and shoulder muscles, revitalising the mind as well as the sagging spine. Take a deep breath as you slowly arch your back and extend your arms to the side, palms up. Imagine an eagle spreading its wings. Lift your chin until you're gazing at the ceiling. Count to three. Exhale slowly as you round your back and bring arms forward to form a wide circle. Imagine you're a bear hugging a tree. Drop your chin to your chest. Repeat five times.

3. Chin tuck - stretches the back of the neck and helps to correct posture. Stand or sit up straight with knees slightly bent, head level and looking straight forward. Put your index finger on your nose. Then draw your head back gently from your finger. Keep looking forward as your head moves backward. You'll feel the back of your neck lengthen and straighten. Repeat three times.

4. Head-roll - puts that stiff 'telephone neck' on hold, relaxes aching shoulder muscles and relieves tension headaches. Take a deep breath. Place right hand on left shoulder, left hand on right shoulder. Keep shoulders relaxed, elbows close to body. Maintain this arm position throughout. Slowly exhale, firmly pressing fingers into shoulder muscles. Relax. Take another deep breath as you slowly roll your head to the right, then back with your gaze on the ceiling. Pause. Begin to exhale as you roll head to the left and down, your eyes leading the way. Complete the roll with your chin on chest. Repeat head roll three times to the right, three to the left.

5. Head tilt - revitalises arm, shoulder and neck muscles and helps relieve headaches. Relax shoulders; let arms hang loosely at your sides. Take a deep breath as you lift your shoulders toward your ears. Hold for a count of five. Exhale and drop your shoulders, imagining heavy weights falling from your hands. Roll shoulders in a slow circular motion; five rolls forward, five backward.

6. Shoulder roll - relieves tension in shoulders and upper back. Stand with feet parallel, two foot widths apart and knees unlocked. With your right hand, clasp your left wrist behind your back. Inhale, smoothly rotating your shoulders forward - up, down and around - in two and a half full rotations. Finish with shoulders up. Now exhale quickly and let shoulders fall forward. Repeat six times.

7. Picking apples - aligns the spine, stretches the neck, torso and shoulder muscles and soothes lower-back tension. Lift chin and gaze at the ceiling as you raise both arms over your head. Keep shoulders relaxed, elbows slightly bent. Take a deep breath as you reach up as high as you can with your right hand. Open fingers wide as if you were plucking an apple. Exhale slowly as you close your right hand in a fist. Relax your right arm. Repeat with left arm. Alternate arms for ten stretches.

8. The cat - boosts circulation, eases lower-back strain and loosens a crimped neck. Inhale as you slowly arch your back and lift your chin until you're gazing at the ceiling. Count to three. Exhale slowly as you round your back and drop your chin to your chest until you're looking at the floor. Keep shoulders relaxed. Imagine a cat taking a luxuriant stretch. Repeat five times.

9. The pretzel - is an invigorating toner for your waist, to counter lazy stomach muscles that come with a desk job. It also relieves lower back tension and improves flexibility. Cross right leg over left leg. Bend forward slightly and place straightened arm against the inside of right leg, elbow even with knee. Reach left arm behind you and stretch it across your back as far as it will comfortably go. Take a deep breath while twisting torso to the left and turning your head left. Press right arm firmly against right leg. Count to four, then exhale as you return to the neutral position. Reverse leg and arm positions and repeat to the right. Increase holding count to ten as you progress.

10. Over-the-shoulder reach (moves the shoulders and elbows through full range of movement). Stand up with slightly bent knees. Holding a piece of elasticised fabric (1 metre long) behind your back. Reach up and over your shoulder with your right hand. With the other hand, reach behind your back and grasp the band. Now, as if you were towel-drying your back, straighten your right arm slowly, resisting the pull with your left hand. Hold for a few seconds. Lower your right arm slowly to starting position and straighten your left arm. This time resist with your right hand. Repeat the entire movement three times. Change sides.

11. Body fling - Loosens up entire upper body and hips. Stand with feet parallel, three foot widths apart, knees bent slightly. Extend your arms forward – shoulders level, palms down. Inhale flinging your arms to the left as far as possible. Let your hips and torso swing with your arms. Your head follows the motion - imagine you're throwing something behind you. Feel the stretch in your spinal column and trunk muscles. Don't move your feet or let your arms drop below shoulder level. Exhale swinging arms forward to the centre. Exhale bringing arms to the centre. Do six complete motions.

12. Tummy tuck - This exercise is particularly effective if you're vulnerable to 'nervous stomach.' It's vigorous, so check with your doctor if you've had surgery recently or have other medical problems. Stand with feet parallel, three foot widths apart. Bend your knees. Place hands on your thighs just above the knees, fingers pointing inward. Keep your neck and spine straight, your shoulders, arms and hands relaxed. Exhale, pushing your stomach out (you may find this hard at first). Push all the air out of your lungs. Before you take another breath, pull your stomach muscles in as deeply as possible and then release them. Still holding your breath, repeat this motion as often as you can. Aim for ten contractions.

13. Front runner - boosts tired blood and dissolves tension in aching arms and shoulder muscles. Hold arms at sides, elbows bent and fists loosely clenched. Keep elbows close to body as you pump your arms with an easy, swinging motion - right arm forward, left arm back; left arm forward, right arm back. Breathe deeply and rhythmically as you gradually increase the speed of your swinging arms. Imagine you're running through the countryside on a beautiful morning. Lower your chin and close your eyes. See yourself winning a race. Swing your arms back and forth 25 times. For even more productive 'run,' tighten arm and chest muscles as you swing your arms.

14. Shoulder blade pinch - strengthens the middle and upper back and stretches the chest muscles. Sit or stand with your shoulders relaxed. Raise your arms out to the sides with elbows bent. Pinch your shoulder blades together by moving your elbows as far back as you can. Hold briefly. Relax. Repeat three times.

15. Wrist extension - maintains wrist flexibility and increases gripping strength. Press your hands together in front as if praying. Keep your elbows away from your body and your hands at right angles to your forearms. Push just a little. Hold for a few seconds. Change your hand position by pressing the back of your hands together slightly in an upside-down praying position. Repeat three times.

16. Finger tuck - keeps the fingers flexible and stretches the tendons in the hands. Hold one hand up, fingers and knuckles straight and pointing toward the ceiling. Bend your fingers and tuck the tips down. Keep knuckles straight and make sure they don't move. Stretch fingers back up. Repeat three times.

17. Side bend - stretches your sides. Stand with feet shoulder width apart, knees relaxed and tummy tucked in. Reach the right arm up and over the head to the left side. (Can also be done sitting in a straight chair.) The left arm reaches down toward the left knee. Let the body lean into the stretch. (If there's any pain, you're reaching too far). Hold. Return to starting position. Repeat three times. Change arms.

18. Leg raise - keeps hip muscles strong. Lie on your side (using a pillow to cradle your head) with legs straight and in line with your spine. Keep your balance by placing your hand on the floor and bend your bottom knee. Lift the top leg straight up, keeping it in line with your body as high as you can without straining. Lower the leg slowly. Repeat three times. Change sides.

19. Leg-ups - are leg stretches that put bounce back in your step and circulation back into aching thigh and calf muscles. They also tone up sagging abdominal muscles. Straighten and lift right leg in front of you. Point and flex toes five times. The higher and straighter your leg, the better the stretch. Return to neutral position. Then do a series with your left leg, keeping your back straight throughout.

20. Knee exerciser - keeps knees strong. Tie the ends of your elastic resistance band together. Sitting in a chair with a firm supportive back and so your legs are supported behind the knees by the edge of the chair, slip the band around your feet. Keep your back straight while you straighten your right leg as far as you can against the resistance of the band. You'll feel the muscles working in the front of your leg. Hold for a few seconds. Repeat three times. Change legs.

21. Knee-ups - ideal exercise when you've been sitting too long at a desk or on an airplane. With both hands clasped around your right knee, bring it slowly towards your chest until it almost touches your forehead. Repeat with left leg. Do five repetitions.

22. Heel-and-toe - are foot stretches that get the kinks out. Press your right heel into the floor as you raise the toes on your right foot and stretch them toward you. Press toes of right foot into the floor and lift right heel. Repeat toe-heel stretch five times.

23. Towel grabber - maintains feet flexibility and strength. Spread a towel out in front of your chair. Place your feet on the towel, with your heels on the edge closest to you. Keep your heels down. Keep the toes straight and draw the towel toward your heel by raising the arch of your foot. Repeat three times.

24. Ankle stretch - maintains ankle flexibility and strength. Stand up and hold onto a chair or table for support. Raise yourself onto the balls of your feet. Slowly lower yourself back onto your heels. Keeping your weight on your heels, raise your toes up in the air. Slowly lower them. (If this hurts your toes, try doing the exercise while sitting down - make it an ankle action and don't put any pressure on your toes.) Repeat three times.

25. Finger-walk - a great pick-me-up for flexibility, circulation and energy. It eases leg and lower-back muscles. Sitting on the edge of your chair, straighten right leg in front of you while pressing your right heel into the floor and pointing your toes up. Lift your chin as you take a deep breath. Slowly bend forward and walk fingers of your right hand down your right leg from knee to ankle (or as far as you can go) while exhaling. Let chin drop to chest and count to five. Take another deep breath as you slowly walk fingers back up your right leg to your knee. Exhale as you return to neutral position. Repeat finger walk with left leg. Now straighten both legs in front of you and slowly walk fingers down and back each leg at the same time.

26. Modified sit-ups - strengthens stomach muscles (for good back support) and improves posture. Lie on the floor with your knees bent and feet flat on the floor. Use a support pillow under your neck. With your hands flat against your thighs, tighten your stomach and pull one knee up toward your chest. Push against the knee with your hand at the same time. Hold for a few seconds. Change sides. Repeat three times.

27. Bounce! This too, is vigorous. If you have back, neck or leg problems, get your doctor's permission. The idea here is to shake all the tension out of your body. It's fun. To start, shake your left hand, then your left arm. Simultaneously, begin to shake your right hand and right arm. Now start shaking both legs. Bounce up and down, still shaking your whole body.

28. Sleep inducer. This is very effective if you're having problems relaxing after a busy day. It's a wonderful sleep-inducer too. Lie down on your bed. Beginning with your toes and working up to the top of your head, tense then release all of your body parts.

Meditation

Meditation is an anti-stress tactic that is not difficult or dangerous to conduct. A quiet place and a mantra (word or syllable that's repeated) are the basic requirements. Practised fifteen to twenty minutes a day meditation enables an individual to slip below the tension-loaded level of daily consciousness.

Transcendental meditation: This relaxation tactic is the opposite of the 'fight or flight' reaction to stress. Relaxation response is a state of profound peace, deeper than sleep, in which oxygen consumption drops by 10 to 20 per cent within minutes. Heart output decreases by 30 per cent and secretion of the stress-related product, blood lactate, almost disappears. Through this technique, a person can 'close down' in fifteen to twenty minutes, moving from progressive relaxation to passive concentration.

Transcendental meditation (TM) can cause dramatic physiological changes including decreased heart rate, lower blood pressure and reduced oxygen consumption. Practised 10 to 20 minutes once or twice a day, it produces a lasting reduction in blood pressure and other stress-related symptoms. It's a natural antidote to tension.

TM encourages a relaxation response. Follow these four simple steps:

- Assume a comfortable position,
- Close your eyes,
- Concentrate on a single word, sound or phrase,
- Cast off all other thoughts.

As long as you can become passively unaware of the outside world, the method (listening to music, repeating a mantra, picturing a peaceful scene) doesn't matter. Techniques like muscle relaxation, biofeedback, self-hypnosis, rhythmic breathing and exercise can also elicit the relaxation response.

Biofeedback

Biofeedback is one technique that amplifies chosen biological signals to bring a particular function to the subject's awareness. It's often used by people suffering from migraine headaches, bad backs or ulcers to control their pain. Through training, a connection is established between thought and function, so that eventually, a relaxing thought triggers a relaxing function. With practice, individuals can control their relaxation skills. They can become more productive, alert and able to cope under pressure. This technique is best learned through a qualified instructor or physician.

The severity and frequency of migraines in 80 per cent of sufferers can often be relieved (at least in part) by biofeedback. The patient is connected by sensor wires to a machine with a small screen that feeds back information. This information includes such physiological indexes of stress as blood pressure, tension in the facial muscles or, most frequently, the temperature of one's fingers, which get colder when tense. By loosening their muscles, breathing deeply or letting their thoughts drift, patients learn that they can control their stress response. They can make their blood pressure drop or the temperature in their hands rise by as much as twelve to 14 degrees. After six to ten sessions, patients are weaned from the machines and can elicit the relaxation response at home without mechanical prompting.

Biofeedback makes you more aware of what's going on in your body. You can exercise a significant amount of voluntary control over so-called involuntary responses, as the yogis have shown for centuries.

As biofeedback and other techniques gain acceptance, doctors are testing them against all sorts of ills. Biofeedback and progressive muscle-relaxation exercises can help diabetics maintain steadier glucose levels.

Massage and self-massage

I know very few people who won't welcome a soothing massage after a busy day. Everyone should take a course on how to massage away others' pain and achy muscles. This way, there would be always someone available to give the pleasurable and relaxing plus of having a personal masseuse. I believe that one of the requirements a couple should have is the ability to give a good relaxing massage to each other.

When others aren't available, use self-massage (a definite second-best to having another person do it for you). On days when your nerves are frazzled, your muscles tense and your head aching, you need a way to unwind, to relax in a healthful way. Self-massage can be the answer. You use it often already. For instance, when you have a headache, you rub it. When your neck is stiff, you rub it to ease the stiffness.

When doing self-massage, it's important to relax, breathe deeply and take your time to loosen up shoulders and neck. Relaxing helps you bring oxygen-rich blood to all parts of your body. Try to limit sessions to ten minutes. Here are some self-massaging things you can do to relieve knotted muscles and tension:

Gently rub using fingers or whole hand. Try back-and forth motion then circular motion. This is often the best method of releasing tension around the forehead and eyes and does not stretch the tender skin of the face. Closing your eyes, putting on some relaxing music and soaking in a tub can make this a relaxing interlude after a busy day.

Harder rubbing that causes friction to the deeper muscles. Done in a circular motion you're less likely to stretch or bruise muscles. Use fingers to do smaller circles and the whole hand to make larger, harder circles.

Deep massage uses the outer ridge of one or both of your hands to strike the skin with rapid rhythmic motions. The pressure should be firm, but never painful.

Pinch gently (to avoid bruising) to stimulate circulation.

Now use knuckles (again gently to avoid bruising). It is best for deep muscle massage in fleshy parts of the body.

Massage Devices: A helpful household item is a rolling-pin which can be gently rolled over the surface of tension. It's best to roll it in the direction of your heart with light even rolling motions. The pressure should be firm, but never painful. You can purchase another device at the Body Shop. It's called a 'Twin Ball Massage Roller' that comes in several sizes. It's used to roll out the kinks in muscles. I found this one especially helpful for those shoulder muscles that tighten up after several hours at my computer.

Massage techniques: Start at the top and work downward on your body for a complete body massage. Gently massage your ears then place the fingertips of both hands in the centre of your forehead. Apply moderate to deep pressure with the balls of your fingers, moving back and forth across the forehead, down the sides of your face and along the cheekbones.

With both hands and your fingers flat, pat vigorously across the entire face for 15 to 20 seconds. Keep wrists loose and be careful not to pat too hard around your eyes.

To help lessen tension in your neck, with elbows point outward, put fingers at the top of your spinal column. Keep your fingers straight and apply pressure by rubbing gently with the balls of your fingers. Arms and shoulders relaxed let your head slant slightly backward and stroke down the back of the neck and the upper border of your shoulder blades.

With your head slightly back (keeping back and neck muscles relaxed) pick up the muscle at the back of the neck near the hairline. This can be accomplished most comfortably by crossing one hand across the chest to the opposite shoulder. Pinch the muscle lightly as you gently pull it away from the bone. Release gradually. Continue this pinching motion down the back of the neck and along the shoulder muscle. One minute on each side should be sufficient. Use your fingers to push one side, then the other toward the spine. Repeat this motion rhythmically along the spine as far down the back as you can reach comfortably.

For your upper and lower back, reach behind you and up the spine as far as you can. Place your hand on the stroke downward along the sides of the spinal column to the tailbone. Use heavier pressure with your thumb. Place your hand one half inch further from the spine each time you make a pass down your spine. Return to the centre of the back and stroke outward, repeating the motion as you work your way by half-inches down your back. Alternate sides if your hands become tired.

Deep breathing and stretching

Take eight long, deep breaths. Breathe in through your nose, out through your mouth, releasing the air slowly and steadily. Stand up, stretch and raise your arms above your head. Stretch to the right and hold for a count of five. Stretch to the left and hold. Repeat several times.

Stress quickens your breathing rate. This exercise will slow it down.

Take your breath deep into your abdomen, filling your lungs from the bottom up. Stand with feet parallel - two foot widths apart, shoulders relaxed, knees unlocked and slightly bent. Clasp your hands gently in front of you. Now inhale very slowly and evenly while gradually raising your arms above your head. Imagine that your breath is lifting your arms. Continue to inhale while you let your forearms and clasped hands drop behind your neck. Now exhale slowly and evenly, bringing your hands and forearms over your head and back down in front of you. If you feel light-headed, you've taken in more oxygen than you're accustomed to - shake your hands or bounce. Repeat this motion three times in succession.

Take a full deep breath and hold it for a count of ten. When you exhale, let it all out at once, letting your body go completely loose and limp.

For sore hips: For stiffness in hips, lie on one side and with the opposite knee bent toward your chest, make a fist and place your knuckles on the edge of your hipbone. Apply firm pressure with your knuckles diagonally across the buttock toward the tailbone. Continue down and across the underside of your buttocks. Release your fist and stroke back up with the palm of your hand. Repeat ten times and then reverse sides.

Aching feet: To relieve aching feet, try gentle toe stretches. Sit with one leg crossed over the opposite thigh. Keep foot relaxed. Curl your fingers over the toes (with the palm of your hand on the top of the foot and your fingers at the base of the toes). Move your hand forward stretching the toes so they curl under and hold for ten seconds. Then reverse the motion and gently point toes toward your face and hold for ten seconds. Repeat five times on each foot.

Make circles with your ankles, five times to the right and five times to the left.

Taking a warm bath after these exercises will keep the muscles relaxed for an even longer time. If you're short of time, use a massaging showerhead with water comfortably hot to plummet your muscles. So you don't bruise or scald yourself, place a towel over the area you're massaging. This is especially helpful when you've overtaxed your neck and back muscles and they ache.

No single approach to relaxation is right for everyone. Meditation may be good for somebody with hypertension and bad for someone with a peptic ulcer. One person may need psychotherapy to get to the roots of his or her behaviour, while another needs nothing more than regular exercise and vacations. As responses to stress vary widely according to age, sex, temperament and other factors so do the requirements for treatment to offset it.

Treatment programs, however, don't attempt to eliminate stress entirely. Nor should they try to. A certain amount of stress is a positive and pleasurable occurrence. It leads to productivity in the human race.

CHAPTER FOURTEEN

Workaholism and burnout

Workaholism can manifest itself in children, teenagers and those in their early adult years, but it usually occurs more in those in their forties and fifties. Work addiction usually happens to middle-class people who are not driven to overwork by economic need. Some workaholics gradually becomes emotionally crippled and addicted to control and power in a compulsive drive to gain approval and success. The excuse that they're 'doing it for their family' just doesn't hold water.

When people spend too much time on leisure activities, society does raise an eyebrow, but cheer on those who spend weekends in the office rather than at the lake. The current trend toward lifestyle management and balance will help, but an entire overhaul will have to take place for this mindset to happen.

Like any other addiction, workaholism can harm not only one's health and family, but can cause severe anxiety and depression. We all want acceptance and respect for the work we do. However, a compulsive drive towards success and approval is what many people find themselves quickly caught up in. Many don't even realise this, until a major crisis like a divorce or heart attack occurs in their lives.

Workaholics can also come from dysfunctional families, whose patterns of behaviour and interactions are not healthy. Perhaps some form of addiction (alcohol, drugs, food and perfectionism) has distorted the way the family functions. As adults, they pride themselves on being free of any addiction with which they grew up. *'This is never going to happen to me!'* is a familiar statement. The families of workaholics can become co-dependents. Many fall into the trap of supporting the addiction, when they try to 'keep the peace.'

What is a workaholic

We all know the negative kind of workaholics:

- They work late, often bringing work home in the evening and on the weekend.
- Their social and family life suffer,
- They suffer nervous disorders (caused by excessive stress),
- They don't eat or exercise right (still use competitive sports to 'relax'),
- They never seem to be away from work because of illness, but they're often the ones who pass on the 'flu' to the rest of the office because they do come in when they shouldn't.

Another school of thought takes a different view that workaholics aren't slaves to their work - they're doing exactly what they want to do. They're happy. Surprisingly, this seems to be true for some people. They're doing exactly what they love - work - and they can't get enough of it. If the circumstances are right (that is, if their jobs fit and their families are accommodating) then workaholics can be astonishingly productive.

The bad news is that workaholics are hellish to work and live with. At work these addicts are often demanding and sometimes not very effective. At home - well, you'll seldom find workaholics at home (unless they work there).

Work defines our character and consumes about 50 - 60% of most adult's lives. The first most common question asked when people meet is, *'What do you do?'* It's a social nicety or acceptable protocol, but this simple question has led society into a state where there's little hope for quick recovery from workaholism.

When asked, *'Are you a workaholic?'* most people's first impulse would probably be, *'Me? Of course not!'* Society has taught us that we can never work too hard. To admit that you're a workaholic seems like a black mark on your character. However, it's never weak to realise that your life is out of balance and that perhaps your priorities need re-adjustment.

Is the company at fault?

Ironically, the employees that companies care most about keeping on board are the ones they're likely to lose to burnout. Employees who work the longest hours and put the most into their jobs, are the most vulnerable.

Because early signs of burnout usually are subtle, managers preoccupied with the demands of their own jobs may miss them. High-achievers may hide their problems. Even when signs are more blatant, a manager may refuse to acknowledge that the person they hired is having difficulties. Managers may see it as a reflection on themselves. So the tendency is to look the other way.

Avoiding the problem is the worst action they should take. When an employee is showing signs of burnout, wise managers stop the process by giving their staff a mental health day or two away from work. This is especially recommended for dedicated employees who are seldom away from work and feel guilty if they are away from work. Used wisely and when necessary, mental health days allow employees to stay home and recoup their resources. This way, they'll raise their productivity level when they return to work. If they stay at work without a break, their productivity will inevitably go down.

The very structure of a corporation, with its pyramid pointing to the top, encourages the workaholic climate, because it pits one employee against another as they vie for too few positions. This is another factor that gets the stress juices flowing. The global economic environment in which corporations operate today also gets the stress juices flowing. Takeovers and mergers mean that the job the workers thought was so secure only yesterday; may be uncertain tomorrow.

Are you a workaholic?

If you've ever wondered if you're a workaholic - the following questionnaire will help you in finding out for sure. Answer *'Yes'* or *'No'* to each of the following questions.

1. Do you communicate better with your co-workers than with your spouse (or best friend)?
2. Are you always punctual for appointments?
3. Are you better able to relax Saturdays than Sunday afternoons?
4. Are you more comfortable when you're productive than idle?
5. Do you feel uneasy or guilty if there's nothing to do?
6. Do you carefully organise your hobbies?

7. Are you usually terribly annoyed when your spouse (or friend) keeps you waiting?
8. When you participate in recreational activities, is it mainly with work associates?
9. Does your spouse (or friends) think of you as a work-driven person?
10. In competitive sports, do you sometimes see your boss's face on the ball?
11. Is work sometimes a way of avoiding close relationships?
12. Even under pressure, do you usually take the extra time to make sure you have all the facts before deciding?
13. Do you usually plan every step of the itinerary of a trip in advance and become uncomfortable if plans go awry?
14. Do you hate small talk at a reception or cocktail party?
15. Are most of your friends in the same line of work?
16. Do you read work-related material when you eat alone?
17. Do you take work to bed with you when you're home sick?
18. Is most of your reading - work related?
19. Do you work late more frequently than your peers?
20. Do you talk 'shop' over coffee or cocktails on social occasions?
21. Do you wake up in the night worrying about business or family problems?
22. Do your dreams centre on work or family - related conflicts?
23. Do you play as hard as you work?
24. Do you become restless on vacation?
25. Do you find it harder and harder to take long vacations?
26. Are you afraid of failing?
27. Is it important that you're always 'right?'
28. Do you suffer periodic bouts of extreme fatigue?
29. Find it difficult to do nothing?
30. Do you forget or minimise family occasions or celebrations?
31. Do you try to avoid conflict instead of dealing with it?
32. Do you concentrate on future events instead of enjoying the present?
33. Do you like volunteering for job assignments that others would consider impossible?
34. Do you hate delegating authority?
35. Do you rarely phone friends, simply to chat?

36. Insist on taking all phone calls, even if you're in a meeting or busy with colleagues in your office?
37. Find your work all-encompassing - more important to you than your spouse children, hobbies social life?
38. If you're home sick, do you insist that you work while recovering?

How many answers are *'Yes?'* The more you said *'Yes'* the more a workaholic you are! Some people thrive on this hussle-bustle while others become distressed. Different strokes for different folks!

If you find you're having negative physical or mental signs, it's time to do something. With a little self-analysis and honesty, you can take positive steps towards breaking out of this destructive path. You might also answer these questions for your loved ones or encourage them to do so themselves.

Others set themselves up to fail by how they look at their jobs. For instance:

Stop competing with yourself:

Do you compete with yourself? Work addicts are usually highly competitive perfectionists. They can be merciless in the demands they impose on themselves and others for peak performance. Because of their impossibly high standards, they're perpetually frustrated. The all-or-nothing sales manager feels that achieving 95 per cent or better of his goal for monthly sales is acceptable - 94 per cent or below is the equivalent of total failure.

Is your job your only hobby?

Does your work consume your private life too? Let up a little and diversify your life. Try something new that's different entirely from your paid work.

Do you have to excel at everything you do?

Be content with being very good at one thing - don't insist that you excel at everything.

Do you find vacations hard to take?

When work addicts take a holiday, it's not the natives, but the tourists who get restless. These people characteristically hate taking vacations, unless they can combine holiday and business. Just sitting on a beach doing nothing makes them nervous. They keep wondering why the phone doesn't ring. They often take a cellular telephone and their answering machine with them on vacation, *'So they won't miss any messages.'*

Choose a vacation that differs widely from what you do. If you're dealing with people every day, choose a deserted beach or island and commute with nature. Give yourself permission to take time off and indulge yourself in sheer idleness. Go with the flow. If you really try, you can enjoy a walk in the woods without having to learn the names of trees, flowers and insects.

Do you equate your worth with work?

Do you log 16 hours a day at work and spend the rest of the time living, breathing and thinking about work? Are you totally committed to your career? Do you bore others by constantly talking about your work?

Are you a business bigamist?

If you choose work for a lover, you'll have trouble with your spouse (especially if you're a woman). Many workaholics are unaware until it's too late that they've short-changed their families - and themselves of warm family affection. The maddening thing for many spouses is that even when their workaholic mates do come home, they're either working or thinking about work. In the middle of a conversation, addicts are apt to pull out a pocket tape recorder and start dictating a 'to do list' or produce a notepad to jot down notes. Their compulsion is almost extreme if they happen to have a glamourous job.

Only the threat of divorce will induce some work addicts to consult a marriage counsellor and finally face the crisis. The advice of many counsellors: If you're a workaholic, marry another workaholic who understands your obsessiveness.

According to social scientists, workaholics must strive for a balanced perspective. If you're a frenzied treadmill-runner, you may miss many of the simple pleasures of life.

Take control. Once you've learned to value yourself as a person, you'll find it easy to protect yourself from the ravage of diseases caused by needless stress. Often, a time management course or quietly sitting down to determine our priorities or asking such questions of ourselves as:

- What am I doing?
- Why am I doing it? and,
- Is this what's important to me?

If we see this problem in others, we should make every effort to point out to them the problems they are heading for (or at least make them aware of the symptoms).

Have you identified yourself as a workaholic? Are you a workaholic through choice or are you forced to be a workaholic because of home and work pressures? If this kind of behaviour keeps up and you feel this distress, you're likely on your way towards burnout. This can completely disable you. You must be wary of these symptoms and deal with them quickly.

How can we tell we're under too much pressure?

Most people do better with a little bit of pressure, but if that pressure increases, the person's performance drops off. If you go home exhausted with a terrible headache from work, your company isn't going to care. You pay the price for overreacting to stressful situations.

When you suffer from burnout, you feel too tired to get out of bed. Even if you could muster the motivation, you're so cynical about your work that you wonder what it's all for. When you do get out of bed, fatigue becomes worse. You find yourself getting angry and judgemental. You walk and talk faster, but forget what you said and take twice as long to get your work done. Stomach aches, headaches, sore muscles and fatigue become part of your daily experience.

Behaviours and attitudes such as these often signal the approach of burnout - a battering form of depression that can cost you your job and ruin your health. Pretending you can cope will only carry you so far. Instead of elevating your blood pressure, change your behaviour. Use your head, social skills and business experience to cope with irritating experiences. Examine your behaviour to see if you're making your day harder on yourself.

Get enough sleep and tackle uncomfortable tasks early in your day. Set priorities for your daily activities and avoid dwelling on the list of activities you have left to do. Perpetual worrying will make you physically tired.

Take a break from pressure and make sure you take time out before making any major decision. When you go to bed, tell yourself it was a wonderful day and then when you wake up, tell yourself that you feel rested and alert and have enough energy to get through the day.

What is burnout?

The description 'burnout' is good, because it graphically conveys what happens when human organisms operate too fast and too long without proper fuel and lubrication. Sooner or later, the friction builds to such a degree, that parts begin to erode, crack or explode.

In the early stages of burnout, star performers may become irritable, procrastinate, miss deadlines, balk at routine assignments or accept challenging ones without properly preparing to handle them. They might come to work late, take longer lunches or call in sick more often. In the later stages, these symptoms become more severe and could lead to serious depression.

Women are especially susceptible to burnout. In an attempt to overcome sexual stereotyping, they may try to do too much while bottling up their feelings. Both men and women often have a strong sense of responsibility to their job and many are in the grip of a 'be perfect' dictum learned early in life.

Denying how bad you feel, in hopes that the problem will disappear, won't solve job burnout. Sometimes, the only way out is getting another job, perhaps in the same field but with a different employer.

A career change may be their best choice. If they have difficulty overcoming burnout, they should consider seeking professional help.

Some people change careers, some take sabbaticals, some slide into immobilising depression and others even contemplate or follow-through with suicide. When dealing with burnout, the rule of thumb is when your head says 'go' and your body says 'no,' you should listen to your body. Often, all these burned out individuals need is an extended break from routine. Recovered employees can charge back to work with their abilities unimpeded (preferably with a newly recognised ability to pace themselves and achieve balance in their lives). Some learn transcendental meditation or yoga, others start taking frequent short vacations.

Watch for signs of burnout

Some burnt-out cases tough it out and resign themselves to miserable lives, stoically accepting hypertension, ulcers, alcoholism, irritable bowels and other physical awfulness associated with joyless overwork. It's the price they pay for 'success' or at least for maintaining their existing condition. Left untreated, burnout can be incapacitating.

You may be headed for burnout if you:

- Need more hours to do less work,
- Suffer chronic fatigue,
- Can't sleep,
- Are too busy to do routine things like sending out Christmas cards,
- Start forgetting appointments and lose personal possessions, such as house keys,
- Feel you have no control over your life and your future seems as bleak as the present,
- Drink more alcohol and use more drugs, prescription and otherwise,
- Feel more and more irritable, cynical or disenchanted,
- Feel no real joy in anything, not even your job,
- Work is your life,
- Feel down or depressed all the time,

- Feel tired all the time,
- Have trouble eating and sleeping properly,
- Have the feeling you've failed, no matter how much you try,
- See no hope for improvement,
- Are constantly complaining,
- Feel that no one cares,
- Withdraw from society,
- Feel upset, frustrated, angry most of the time,
- Feel intense job pressures,
- Are highly competitive in everything you do,
- Feel that no matter what you do - it won't be enough,
- Fear that you're going under any day now.

The tensions implicit in this unbalanced lifestyle can cause very real problems. The problems can result in a business or marriage crack-up - emotional and physical burnout and even early death. It's all a matter of degree.

The danger arises, if they let their work compulsion become an insatiable need, so that they become unglued without it. To a workaholic, loss of a job is tragedy. They lose the sole prop for their self-esteem, the only validation that they're love-worthy.

The final extreme can be suicide. Observers of burnt-out people should be alert for signs of pending suicide attempts. In adults, one of the signs is that they get their life 'in order.' They make sure their insurance is paid up, that their bills are paid and their affairs are in order. Troubled children and teenagers may begin to give away their prized possessions to friends and relatives.

Misconceptions about burnout

Because there are some misconceptions about burnout that can have adverse results, it's important to recognise and understand the true nature of burnout. These misconceptions are:

#1. Burnout is a new-fangled notion that gets lazy people out of work while they receive a disability pension.

In fact, although burnout is a rather new term, the behaviour is as old as the human race. It used to be called nervous exhaustion, tired blood, battle fatigue, neurasthenia, mental breakdown, premature aging and plain laziness. History is full of writers, artists and scientists who gradually or suddenly stopped producing, sometimes in the midst of their most active years.

Unfortunately, it's true that burnout and stress-related illness are claimed by some individuals who are simply malingering. However, just because some people avoid work by presenting themselves as burned-out, doesn't mean this is true for everyone.

#2. As long as people really enjoy their work, they can work as long and hard as they want and never experience burnout.

This is comparable to stating that as long as people really enjoy eating and drinking, they can eat and drink forever without becoming ill. Any work that includes significant and continuing amounts of frustration, conflict and pressure without proper psychological refuelling can cause burnout. For example, medical interns and residents typically enjoy their work immensely, but after only a couple of years of intense work, a significant percentage of them experience burnout. Some even leave medicine frustrated, disillusioned and embittered.

#3. Individuals know when they're burning out and when they do, all they need to do is to take a few days or weeks and then they'll be as good as new.

It's rare for people to realise that they're burning out - even in the final stages. They either ignore the signs or underestimate their importance. If caught in the early stages, some attitudinal or life adjustments can remedy burn-out. However, it's possible for a person to suffer third-degree burnout and never function again on a level that even approximates his or her previous capacity.

#4. Individuals who are physically and psychologically strong are unlikely to experience burnout.

Not correct - the opposite is more true. Keeping in good physical shape is an important antidote to stress overload, but it's not the cure. Physically strong individuals may be able to work twice as hard as less strong people, but, without proper stress skills, the inordinate amount of work can cause serious damage. Similarly, if an individual can hold prodigious amounts of alcohol, this does not mean that the alcohol is not seriously damaging his or her body or psyche.

Psychologically strong people can suffer the same fate. They can experience a vicious circle where the stronger and more competent they are, the more they're given extra work. This leaves them with less time and energy for refuelling mentally and physically.

#5. Job burnout is always job related.

It's rare for burnout to relate only to a person's job. Individuals have three lives - work, family and social. Each stressor can be carried from one life to another. The worst situation is when they have an inordinate number of stressors in each life. For example, they're overwhelmed by projects at work, have marital or parenting conflicts at home and may feel dissatisfied with their social life. When they burn out, their disorder will likely be viewed as job-related, when, in fact, it's life-related. In some cases, burnout may be least of all related to their job. It may come from home pressures, lack of a social support network or from problems with leisure time.

Who is more prone to burnout in the workplace?

Burnout is the product of years of near-constant stress. It can occur as workers claw their way up the slippery slope that leads to success as defined by popular culture; big houses, big bank accounts, power, prestige and plenty of toys.

Actually reaching the crest of the corporate hill can bring scant relief. The novelty wears off; the pressure continues for ever-higher profits in an ever-shifting economy. The road to happiness had been clearly marked - so where, when you've arrived - is happiness? Burnout strikes those in their mid-thirties or later. While those on the executive track are prime targets, it also hits dogged, mid-level workers, who never manage to muscle their way into the corporate boardroom. They find their careers stalled, their territory invaded by cocky, newly minted MBAs, their idealism dissolved into a pool of cynicism bred of reality.

Some feel mired in a workaday limbo. If they work hard, it doesn't get rewarded. If they goof off, it doesn't get punished. Up to a point, stress keeps the creative juices flowing and adds a spark and crackle to the drudgery of daily life. However, heap on too much stress and everything deteriorates. Morale goes down, productivity plummets, mistakes get made, motivation dies and a sense of futility creeps in.

Job burnout

Are you an extremist where work is the be-all and end-all? Here are some case histories of people who have suffered from burnout:

Phil was a disciple of the ethic that you can neither work too hard nor work too long. One workaholic week chased another, although he did set aside time to indulge an old passion for downhill skiing. Then a pattern began to emerge. Three years in a row he broke a bone in his arm or leg. This was Phil's way of buying time off from work. He had to resort to busting up his body to get some time off. The annual broken bones had been a desperate, pathetic way of coping with burnout, the widespread malady of the '90s. At the turn of the century, Phil realised what he had been doing and made changes in his life.

Job burnout can use up the fires that energise you. After a period of sustained effort, your enthusiasm and driving power can burn out like a light bulb. Fortunately, you can be re-energised.

Consider the case of Barbara - one of two women managers in a fast-growing company. Barbara likes the pressure of her job, has worked hard in the past year to meet the challenging goals set by her demanding boss. She's studied at night for her Master of Business Administration degree. Unfortunately, when her work is over, there's no one with whom she can share the joys and frustrations of her job. The other woman manager rushes home at night to a young family and Barbara is too tired to seek friends' company. Although an extra martini at night helps her relax and fall asleep, she wakes up at 5 am and can't get back to sleep. A lingering cold has left her feeling blah and she's starting to find her life unsatisfying.

Barbara is in the early stages of job burnout. The problem most often hits people who have an excess of external pressure on top of internal pressure they impose on themselves. Those prone to burnout are usually perfectionist take-charge types. Members of the helping professions - teachers, nurses and therapists - are particularly vulnerable. Nevertheless, burnout can be as prevalent among other employees who plan too many perfect projects. Others burn out because of the frustrations of supplier delays, pressure from their superiors or lack of recognition for good work.

Burnout in the helping professions

Karen, a 28 year-old social worker, tries to convince one of her teen-aged clients to go back to high school. She's spent the last few years fighting battles like this, trying to instil delinquent girls with values their parents never taught them. She used to love her work, but lately, it all looks futile. As her conversation with the girl goes on, she feels a deep sense of fatigue and helplessness. She starts thinking that there's no point in continuing, that nothing she does is going to make any difference.

Jack (a 40-year-old police officer) comes home from work. He deals with the pressures of his job by putting up a barrier of toughness and cynicism. He used to take it off when his shift ended, but now he feels he needs a few drinks before he can relax. Every time he takes a drink, his wife complains about his drinking.

A patient asked Catherine, a 34 year-old nurse, to get him a glass of juice. A few months ago, she would have treated that request as the simple chore it is, but she works on a cancer ward and has seen too many people fight losing battles with illness. Most of her patients are between 20 and 40 years of age. She gets close to them and identifies with them. When they die, it's very stressful. Now, getting the juice demands an act of will.

These individuals have two things in common. They work in the helping professions and they suffer from burnout. In some, the problem expresses itself as a sense of exhaustion and helplessness; in others, as callousness. In both, it may look like simple physical fatigue - but it's more than that. It's a sense that one has given everything there is to give, that there's nothing in reserve any more. Their gas is all gone; they come to a halt.

A decade ago, the predicament didn't even have a name. In the last few years, helping professionals have not only identified the burnout dilemma, they've also developed ideas about what they can do to prevent the syndrome and deal with it when it strikes. These remedies go far beyond cutting back on work. That can help sometimes, but contrary to what many believe, burnout is not simply a matter of individuals working themselves to exhaustion. If that was the case, workaholics would be highly vulnerable. It's not the dynamic, energetic workaholic types who are burning out at all. Dealing with burnout requires that one focus on the stresses in the environment and see how people are coping with them.

One area to start is to have a place to leave the job behind and recharge the batteries. For instance, Kate, a 32 year-old Paediatrician says, *'In medicine, you don't have much control over your time when your work depends more on what other people's needs are, than on what you want. After working three 12-hour days in a row, you just feel, 'leave me alone.''*

Kate's solution to that dilemma is one identified by many people who've examined the burnout phenomenon - she creates time for herself. *'I try to withdraw,'* she says. *'I might go out or read or sleep. I just make sure I don't have continual demands from others.'*

Taking time for yourself can take many forms. Frequent vacations may not be possible, but one can get a good deal of benefit out of a break of even a few minutes.

Of course, many burnout victims aren't in any shape to use their free time in a satisfying way. Wanda, a 38 year-old nurse says, *'You get demands from doctors, patients and other staff members. You feel caught in the middle, powerless and overwhelmed. I get very angry and irritable so at the end of the day, I feel like saying 'To heck with this. Why am I beating my head against the wall?''*

Fortunately, Wanda overcame that feeling. One of the activities that helped pull her out of it was taking up jogging regularly. There's a strong relationship between physical and psychic fitness.

Of course, changing one's lifestyle will only have a limited impact, if the situation is intolerable at work. It's hard for outsiders to appreciate the pressures that many helping professionals face, but they clearly exist.

Take Jack the police officer who found himself needing a few drinks to relax after getting off work. What upset him wasn't the criminals he had to deal with or the courts he felt weren't supporting him. It was what he called, *'The indifference of the Silent Majority - the 'it-*

isn't my-problem types.' You respond to a call and find a person beat up in a lane. Twelve people witness the beating, but none stepped in to help. You can only see so many of those and you say *'Who needs this? Nobody really cares anyway.''*

To a certain extent of course, those impossible situations are unavoidable in any profession. Life, after all, is unfair. It's extremely important to distinguish between situations over which you have some control and those over which you have none.

How to relieve burnout

There are ways to help individuals deal with those tough situations. One is to provide a place where people can get their feelings off their chests such as in regular staff meetings. Another is by providing a place to talk problems over more intimately. Some organisations already offer this. One hospital has staffers meet regularly with a psychotherapist, even if everything looks okay. Often, this isn't practical, because therapists are not available or people are reluctant to go to them.

Among police officers, there's a sense that they'd rather die than go see a psychiatrist. There's a real stigma, a sense that they've failed. So what some police departments offer instead are peer counselling units. They have two police officers, trained as counsellors, who are available anonymously to other officers at any time, in a place away from the station. One of the ironies of burnout is that it's often the most caring and empathetic, helping professionals who are the most susceptible.

Police officers pay a price when they let their guards down. For instance, crime victim officers find it hardest to deal with the very young and the very old. When police officers observe the victimisation of these people they often see their own parents or children. It's very hard not to react. They can be much colder and unemotional when dealing with young adults and adults.

While some burnout victims have to become less emotionally involved with the people they're treating, others should develop closer relationships. It's the absence of these relationships that plagues many helping professionals.

Dentists often get very little challenge in their work. How much excitement can you get from doing fillings after you've been doing it for several years? They often resolve this dilemma by telling themselves that since the work is not rewarding, (and might never be) they'll concentrate on making as much money as they can. Then they'll get out of the profession as soon as possible. The result is that they spend less time with more patients, the opposite of what they should do, to become less prone to burnout. The problems dentists treat don't change - only the people. So if they spend more time talking to their patients and really getting to know them it'll make their work more interesting.

A nurse on a children's cancer ward can do something similar. Of course, it's not easy to watch children suffer and die, but a way to lessen the pain is to change the routine. Do something crazy on the ward. Put on silly costumes, put on a musical show for the children or just talk with the parents about some pleasant topics.

People battling burnout also might consider changing their shift. That was enough for Julie, a 26 year-old nurse. *'I was working nights,'* she recalls. *'And it seemed that all I was doing was work. I felt a general frustration with the demands of the patients and doctors and the skeleton staff. So I changed to more normal hours and that helped a lot. I felt I could get more done and have more time for myself.'*

If that fails to do the trick, consider a change in job. A nurse treating children with cancer might move to a maternity ward. Sometimes, the only way to deal with burnout is to cut back on one's hours or quit entirely for a while. The latter option though, is not a recommended course of action, especially in a tight job market.

The final area where helping professionals can battle burnout is by strengthening their social support networks. The lack of support affected Catherine, the cancer ward nurse who was having trouble performing the simplest of tasks. One of the reasons she was having such difficulty, was that it was a time in her life when she had no outside activities to turn to. If people are happy with themselves, they usually do better at work. If they aren't getting positive support at work from the doctors and the rest of the staff and don't have anybody at home to talk to, they may feel abandoned.

Catherine's isolation is not unique. The lone-wolf syndrome is very conducive to burnout. The lone-wolf syndrome does more than play a role in the creation of burnout. It also makes it harder to acknowledge that the condition exists. It's obviously easier to pretend that something isn't happening if there's no one around to tell you that it is. Fortunately lone wolves need not look very hard to find a warm lair. Dentists, stuck in an office all day, can still find the support from professional organisations. Getting together with their colleagues can lessen some of the pressure.

Conventions are particularly important. They do two things - they provide a person with intellectual stimulation, as well as a chance to share problems with colleagues and get a different prospective. It's often a relief to find that colleagues have the same stressors as you.

So burnout is not untreatable. For all its capacity to create unhappiness, it does have the redeeming trait of providing warning signs. If you can recognise burnout in time, you'll still have the energy to make changes.

CONCLUSION

You now have the tools that will enable you to deal with time and stress problems. These essential skills will help you to handle all types of time and stress pressures. Learn these skills and you can't help but improve your ability to pack more activities into your busy day. It will allow you to have some time for yourself to do what you've decided is important to you.

Now it's time to sit down and do some critical planning. Analyse ways you can use your time better and establish concrete, written, realistic goals for yourself. Identify what is causing you stress right now and how you'll overcome those stressors in the future. You can identify your personal signs that you're under stress and step in before they become serious health problems or lead to burnout.

You will now know how to:

- Accomplish what you want in life,
- Live a longer, fuller life,
- Set priorities (yours) and follow them,
- Stop procrastinating,
- Overcome the fear of failure or success,
- Say 'no' when someone tries to force you to do something you don't want to do,
- To prevent interruptions and crisis,
- To use proven business practices at home as well as at work,
- Set concrete, written, realistic goals for yourself - both career and personal,
- Identify your stressors,
- Recognise how vulnerable you are to stress,
- Deal with type A or B personalities,
- Eliminate serious health problems caused by too much stress,
- Deal with your own and other's anger,
- Stop senseless worrying and do something to correct the problem,
- Get a good night's sleep,
- Use positive vs. negative stress relievers,

- Handle stress at work,
- Do relaxation exercises.

Learn the techniques and practise them daily. They do work! Like any new skill, however, you need to use them consistently until they're automatic. When you've mastered them, you can look forward to being able to control how you deal with time and react to the stresses and strains of our busy world.

No longer will you allow yourself to become stressed out. The more you can control your stress, the more energetic and enthusiastic you'll feel. If you use these skills, you'll need to be prepared for success, because success will inevitably follow!

BIBLIOGRAPHY

Allen, David, *Getting things done – the Art of stress-free productivity*, Penguin Books, 2002

Berglas, Steven, *Reclaim the fire: How successful people Overcome burnout*, Random House, 2001

Burns, Dr. David, *Feeling Good – the New Mood Therapy*, Avon, 1999.

Cava, Roberta, *Dealing with Difficult People: How to deal with nasty customers, demanding bosses and un-cooperative colleagues*, 22 publishers – in 16 languages and *Dealing with Difficult Situations – at Work and at Home*; Pan Macmillan 2003 and Ankh Hermes 2004And *Dealing with Difficult Spouses and children*, Cava Consulting, 1995 and *Dealing with Difficult Relatives & In-Laws*; Cava Consulting, 2002.

Covey, Stephen R., *The 7 Habits of highly successful people*, Simon & Schuster.

Elkin, Allen, Ph.D. *Stres Management for Dummies*, 2011.

Fasel, Diane, *Working ourselves to Death - The High Cost of Workaholism and the Rewards of Recovery*, Backinprint, 2000.

Killinger, Barbara, *Workaholics – the respectable addicts*, Firefly Books, 2004.

Lakein, Alan, *How to get control of your time and your life*, New American Library, 1996.

McGugan, Peter, *Beating Burnout, The Survival Guide for the 90's*, Potential Press, 1992.

McKenzie, R. Alex, *The Time Trap, The Classic Book on Time Management*, AMACOM, 2009.

McRae, Bradley C., *Practical Time Management; How to get more things done in less time*, Self Counsel Press, 1993.

Walters, Lynne, Webster, Kathleen M. *Kindtouch massage; Self-massage for health and well-being*, Sterling, 2002.

Zeller, Dirk, *Successful Time Management for Dummies*, John Wiley & Sons, 2008.

www.ingramcontent.com/pod-product-compliance
Lightning Source LLC
Chambersburg PA
CBHW070141100426
42743CB00013B/2784